BANKER TO THE POOR

Muhammad Yunus was born in 1940 in Chittagong, now in Bangladesh. He was educated in Chittagong, was awarded a Fulbright Scholarship and received his PhD from Vanderbilt University, Tennessee. In 1997 Professor Yunus led the world's first Micro-Credit Summit in Washington, DC.

Alan Jolis is an American journalist and writer whose books include *Love and Terror*, *Speak Sunlight* and several novels for children.

D1622324

MUHAMMAD YUNUS

BANKER TO THE POOR

The autobiography of Muhammad Yunus,
founder of the Grameen Bank

WITH ALAN JOLIS

AURUM PRESS

First published in Great Britain
1998 by Aurum Press Ltd
7 Greenland Street, London NW1 0ND

Published in paperback 1999

Re-issued in paperback 2003

A catalogue record for this book is available from the British Library.

ISBN-13: 978 1 84510 924 8

7 9 10 8
2009 2011 2010 2008

Design by James Campus
Printed in the UK by CPI Bookmarque, Croydon, CR0 4TD

This is dedicated to all my co-workers
who made the Grameen story possible.

ACKNOWLEDGEMENTS

The publishers would like to thank the following for their kind permission to use photographs reproduced in this book:
Grameen Bank
Grameen Foundation USA
Alan Jolis
The Office of the First Lady, The White House

CONTENTS

CONTENTS

All that is needed for evil to triumph
is for good men to do nothing.

Edmund Burke

I first met Muhammad Yunus in February 1997, during a short visit to Dhaka. I had heard a little about him and his ideas from friends in Britain and was most curious to meet him.

I found a remarkable man. He not only spoke the greatest good sense but had, against huge odds and in the face of dreadful cynicism on the part of the so-called experts, followed his ideas through and made them work. I also found an inspiring, entertaining and confident interlocutor who sent me away with a new and invigorating sense of what can be achieved with energy and determination.

I have since done all I can to encourage a wider consideration and appreciation of micro-credit. It is an essential part of any sensible mix of development policies – as Muhammad Yunus has demonstrated beyond all doubt in Bangladesh. It has a use, too, in the developed world – whether in remote rural Norway or run-down suburbs of British cities. It is remarkably cost-effective. It has a proven track record, described in a full and entertaining way in the pages which follow. Best of all, it allows poor and disadvantaged people to take control of their own lives, make something of themselves and improve the lot of their own families.

I hope that this book will bring the benefits of micro-credit to an even wider audience. I know that it will fascinate and entertain. Perhaps it will also serve as a reminder to those who think they have grand and global solutions to the challenges of the world that it is often through the grass roots, by listening to those whose lives they seek to change, that true and sustainable solutions, in tune with the land and the human spirit, will be found. I commend it to you.

AUTHOR'S PREFACE

My experience working in the Grameen Bank has given me faith; an unshakeable faith in the creativity of human beings. It leads me to believe that humans are not born to suffer the misery of hunger and poverty. They suffer now as they did in the past because we turn our heads away from this issue.

I have come to believe, deeply and firmly, that we can create a poverty-free world, if we want to. I came to this conclusion not as a product of a pious dream, but as a concrete result of experience gained in the work of the Grameen Bank.

It is not micro-credit alone which will end poverty. Credit is one door through which people can escape from poverty. Many more doors and windows can be created to facilitate an easy exit. It involves conceptualizing about people differently, it involves designing a new institutional framework consistent with this new conceptualization.

Grameen has taught me two things: first, our knowledge base about people and their interactions is still very inadequate; second, each individual person is very important. Each person has tremendous potential. She or he alone can influence the lives of others within the communities, nations, within and beyond her or his own time.

Each of us has much more hidden inside us than we have had a chance to explore. Unless we create an environment that enables us to discover the limits of our potential, we will never know what we have inside of us.

But it is solely up to us to decide where we want to go. We are the navigators and pilots of this planet. If we take our role seriously, we can reach the destination we seek.

I want to tell this story because I want you to figure out what it means to you. If you find the Grameen story credible and appealing, I would like to invite you to join those who believe in the possibility of creating a poverty-free world and have decided to work for it. You may be a revolutionary, a liberal or a conservative, you may be young, or you may be old, but we can all work together on this one issue.

Think about it.

Muhammad Yunus

PART I: BEGINNINGS

1940–76

From my village bank to the World Bank

1

Jobra Village:
From Textbook to Reality

The year 1974 was the year which shook me to the core of my being. Bangladesh fell into the grips of a famine.

Newspapers were reporting horrible stories of death and starvation in remote villages and district towns in the north. The university where I taught and served as head of the economics department was located in the south-eastern extremity of the country, and at first we did not pay too much attention to it. But skeleton-like people started showing up in the railway stations and bus stations of Dhaka. Soon a few dead bodies were reported in these places. What began as a trickle became a flood of hungry people moving to Dhaka.

They were everywhere. You couldn't be sure who was alive and who was dead. They all looked alike: men, women, children. You couldn't guess their age. Old people looked like children, and children looked like old people.

The government opened gruel kitchens to bring people to specified places in town. But every new gruel kitchen turned out to have much less capacity than was needed.

Newspaper reporters were trying to warn the nation of what was going on. Research institutions tried to collect information about where all the starving people were coming from. Would they ever go back, if they survived? And what was the chance of their surviving?

Religious organizations were trying to pick up the dead bodies to bury them with proper religious last rites. But soon the simple act of picking up the dead became a manifestly bigger task than they were equipped to handle.

One could not miss these starving people even if one wanted to. They were everywhere, lying very quiet.

They did not chant any slogans. They did not demand anything from us. They did not condemn us for having delicious food in our homes while they lay down quietly on our doorsteps.

There are many ways for people to die, but somehow dying of starvation is the most unacceptable of all. What a terrible way to die. It happens in slow motion. Second by second, the distance between life and death becomes smaller and smaller.

At one point, life and death are in such close proximity one can hardly see the difference, and one literally doesn't know if the mother and child prostrate on the ground are of this world or the next. Death happens so quietly, so inexorably, you don't even hear it.

And all this happens because a person does not have a handful of food to eat at each meal. In this world of plenty, a single human being does not have the right to a precious handful. Everybody else all around is eating, but he or she is not. The tiny baby, who does not yet understand the mystery of the world, cries and cries, and finally falls asleep, without the milk it needs so badly. The next day maybe it won't even have the strength to cry.

* * *

I used to get excited teaching my students how economics theories provided answers to economic problems of all types. I got carried away by the beauty and elegance of these theories. Now all of a sudden I started having an empty feeling. What good were all these elegant theories when people died of starvation on pavements and on doorsteps?

My classroom now seemed to me like a cinema where you could relax because you knew that the good guy in the film would ultimately win. In the classroom I knew, right from the beginning, that each economic problem would have an elegant ending. But when I came out of the classroom I was faced with the real world. Here, good guys were mercilessly beaten and trampled. I saw daily life getting worse, and the poor getting ever poorer. For them death through starvation looked to be their only destiny.

Where was the economic theory which reflected their real life? How could I go on telling my students make-believe stories in the name of economics?

I wanted to run away from these theories, from my textbooks. I felt I had to escape from academic life. I wanted to understand the reality around a poor person's existence and discover the real-life economics that were played out every day in the neighbouring village – Jobra.

I was lucky that Jobra was close to the campus. Field Marshal Ayub Khan, the then President of Pakistan, had taken power in a military *coup* in 1958 and ruled until 1969 as a military dictator; because of his strong distaste for students, whom he considered troublemakers, he decided that all universities founded during his rule had to be located away from urban areas so that students would not be able to disrupt the centres of population with their political agitation.

Chittagong University was one of the universities founded during his regime. The site chosen was in a hilly section of Chittagong District, next to Jobra village.

* * *

I decided I would become a student all over again, and Jobra would be my university. The people of Jobra would be my teachers.

I promised myself to try and learn everything about the village. I thought I would be fortunate if I could understand the life of one single poor person. This would be a big departure from traditional book learning. By attempting to equip the students with a bird's eye view, traditional universities had created an enormous distance between students and the reality of life. When you can hold the world in your palm and see it from a bird's eye view, you tend to become arrogant – you do not realize that when looking from such a great distance, everything becomes blurred, and that you end up imagining rather than really seeing things.

I opted for what I called the 'worm's eye view'. I thought I should rather look at things at close range and I would see them sharply. If I found some barrier along the way, like a worm, I would go around it, and that way I would certainly achieve my aim and accomplish something.

I started to feel useless in the face of so many starving people pouring into Dhaka. Social organizations set up feeding centres in various parts of the city. Neighbourhoods made special efforts to find food for the hungry. But how many can one feed every day? Famine was spreading before our eyes in all its ugliness.

I tried to overcome the feeling of uselessness by redefining my role. I explained to myself that I might not be able to help many people, but I certainly could make myself useful for a day, or just a few hours, to one other human being. That would be a great accomplishment for me. This idea of providing small-scale yet real help, not just theory, to at least one living person gave me enormous strength. I felt alive again. When I started visiting the poor households in Jobra, I knew very clearly what I was looking for, and why. My motivation had never been clearer.

* * *

I began visiting the poor households in Jobra to see if I could help them directly in any way. My colleague, Professor Latifee, usually accompanied me. He knew most of the families and had a natural gift for making village people feel at ease.

There were three parts to the village: a Muslim, a Hindu and a Buddhist section. When we visited the Buddhist section we used to take our student, Dipal Chandra Barua, with us. He came from a poor Buddhist family in Jobra and was always ready to volunteer for any assignment.

One day, as Latifee and I were making our rounds in Jobra, we stopped at a completely run-down house. We saw a woman working with bamboo making a stool. We did not have to strain our imaginations to guess that her family found it extremely difficult to survive.

'I want to talk to her,' I told Latifee.

He led the way through scavenging chickens and vegetable plants. 'Anybody home?' Latifee asked in a friendly voice.

She was squatting on the dirt floor of her verandah under the low rotten thatched roof of her house, totally absorbed in her work. She was holding the half-finished stool between her knees while plaiting the strands of bamboo cane.

On hearing Latifee's voice, she immediately abandoned her work, sprang to her feet and disappeared inside the house.

'Don't be frightened,' said Latifee. 'We are not strangers. We both teach up at the university. We are neighbours. We want to ask a few questions, that is all.'

Reassured by Latifee's manner and warmth, she said in a low voice, 'There is nobody home.'

She meant there was no male at home. In Bangladesh, women are not supposed to talk to men who are not close relatives.

Children were running around naked in the yard. Neighbours appeared and watched us, wondering what we were doing there.

In the Muslim sections of the village, we often had to talk through a bamboo wall separating us from the women we interviewed. The Muslim custom of *purdah* (literally 'curtain' or 'veil'), whereby married women stay in a state of virtual seclusion from the outside world, was strictly observed in Chittagong District. That is why I sometimes used a female intermediary, a student or a local schoolgirl, to run back and forth with messages.

Since I am a native Chittagonian and speak the local dialect, it was easier for me to gain their confidence than it would have been for an outsider. But, still, it was difficult.

I love children, and complimenting a mother on her baby was always a natural way for me to put her at her ease. My mother had fourteen children (nine of whom survived), and as I was the third eldest I grew up feeding and changing the nappies of my brothers and sister. Whenever I had a free moment at home I would pick a baby up in my arms and cuddle it. This experience has been invaluable to me in my fieldwork.

I now picked up a small naked baby, but he started crying and rushed over to his mother. She let him climb into her arms.

'How many children do you have?' said Latifee.

'Three.'

'He is very beautiful, this one,' I said.

Feeling reassured, the mother appeared in the doorway holding her baby.

She was in her early twenties, thin, with dark skin, black eyes. She wore a red sari and could have been any one of a million women who labour every day from morning to night in utter destitution.

'What is your name?'

'Sufia Begum.'

'How old are you?'

'Twenty-one.'

I did not use a pen and note-pad for that would have scared her off – I let my students do that on return visits.

'Do you own this bamboo?' I asked her.

'Yes.'

'How do you get it?'

'I buy it.'

'How much does the bamboo cost you?'

'Five *taka*.' That was 22 US cents.

'Do you have 5 *taka*?'

'No, I borrow it from the *paikars*.'

'The middlemen? What is your arrangement with them?'

'I must sell my bamboo stools back to them at the end of the day, so as to repay my loan. That way what is left over to me is my profit.'

'How much do you sell it for?'

'Five *taka* and 50 *paisa*.'

'So you make 50 *paisa* profit?'

She nodded. That came to a profit of just 2 US cents.

'And could you borrow the cash and buy your own raw material?'

'Yes, but the money-lender would demand a lot. And people who start with them only get poorer.'

'How much do the money-lenders charge?'

'It depends. Sometimes they charge 10 per cent per week. I even have a neighbour who is paying 10 per cent per day!'

'And that is all you earn from making these beautiful bamboo tools, 50 *paisa*?'

'Yes.'

Usurious rates have become so standardized and socially acceptable in all third world countries that not even the borrower notices how oppressive the contract is. In rural Bangladesh, a weight of unhusked rice (a maund of paddy) borrowed at the beginning of the planting season has to be repaid with two and a half weights (2.5 maunds) at harvest time.

There are many alternatives. If land is used as security, it is placed at the disposal of the creditor who enjoys ownership rights over it until the total amount is repaid. In many cases, the formal documents (such as *Bawnanama*) are made to establish the right of the creditor. To make repayment of the loan difficult, the creditor refuses to accept any part-repayment. After the expiry of a certain period, the creditor has a right to 'buy' the land at a predetermined 'price'. Another form of security is the obligatory supply of labour on the creditor's land.

Under the *dadan* system, traders advance loans against standing crops for the compulsory sale of the crops at a predetermined price which is obviously lower than the market rate. (Sufia Begum was producing her bamboo stools under a *dadan* arrangement with a *paikar*.)

Sometimes the loan is taken out for social or investment purposes (to marry off a daughter, to bribe some official, to fight a court case, for a social occasion), but sometimes for physical survival (the purchase of food or medication, or to meet some emergency situation).

But in all cases it is extremely difficult for the borrower to extricate him- or herself from the burden of the loan. Usually the borrower will have to borrow again just to repay the prior loan, and ultimately the only way out is death.

There are usurers in every society. Unless the poor can be liberated from the bondage of the money-lender, no economic programme can arrest the steady process of alienation of the poor.

Sufia Begum set to work again because she did not want to lose any time talking with us. I watched her small brown hands plaiting the strands of bamboo as they had every day for months and years on end. This was her livelihood. She squatted barefoot on the hard mud. Her fingers were callused, her nails black with grime.

How would her children break the cycle of poverty and aspire to a better life? It seemed hopeless to imagine that her babies would one day escape this misery. How could they go to school when the income she earned was barely enough to feed her, let alone shelter her family and clothe them properly?

'That is what you earn from a whole day's work, 50 *paisa*? Eight *anna*?'

'Yes, on a good day.'

She earned the equivalent of 2 US cents a day and it was this knowledge which paralysed me. In my university courses, I dealt in millions and billions of dollars, but here before my eyes, the problems of life and death were posed in terms of pennies. Something was wrong. Why did the university course I taught not mirror the reality of her life? I was angry at myself, angry at the world which was so uncaring. There was no glimmer of hope anywhere, not even a hint of a possible solution.

Sufia Begum was illiterate but she was not without useful skills. The very fact that she was alive, squatting in front of me, working, breathing, struggling on in her quiet way despite such adverse conditions proved beyond a doubt that she was endowed with a useful skill – the skill of survival.

Poverty is as old as the world itself. There was no chance of Sufia improving her economic base. But why? I didn't know why. We grow up with poor people all around us, and we never question why are they poor. It seemed to me that the existing economic system made it absolutely certain that her income would be kept perpetually at such a low level that she could never save a penny and could never invest in expanding her economic base. So her children were condemned to live a life of penury, of hand-to-mouth survival, just as she lived it before them, and as her parents did before her.

I had never heard of anyone suffering for the lack of 22 US cents. It seemed impossible to me, preposterous. Should I reach into my pocket and hand Sufia the pittance she needed for capital? That would be so simple, so easy.

Why had not my university, my economics department, all the economics departments in the world for that matter, and the thousands of intelligent economics professors, why had they not tried to understand the poor and to help those who needed help the most?

I resisted the urge to give Sufia the money she needed. She was not asking for charity. Also, it would not have solved the problem on any permanent basis.

* * *

All around, men were working, some in the fields, others fixing their rickshaws, others hammering metal. The work here in rural Bangladesh is endless. I am always overwhelmed by the physical agility and strength of my fellow Bangladeshis.

Latifee and I drove back up the hill to my house. We walked slowly around my garden in the last heat of the day.

Walking up and down this hill is good for me. I grew up with flat feet and was never a sportsman, never physically strong. I learned to swim early on, but that was for fun. I never do enough exercise, the doctor says. So I try to walk everywhere. My friends always urge me to take better care of myself, but the truth is I do not have time or interest to waste on my health.

I thought of what a huge gap there was between the high-falutin words of governments and the realities on the ground. The Universal Declaration of Human Rights states that:

Everyone has the right to a standard of living adequate for the health and well-being of himself and his family, including food, clothing, housing and medical care, and necessary social services, and the right to security in the event of unemployment, sickness, disability, widowhood, old age, or other lack of livelihood in circumstances beyond his control.

The Declaration also demands that member nations secure the 'recognition and observance' of these rights.

It seemed to me that poverty created a social condition which negates all human rights, not just a select few. A poor person has no rights at all, no matter what his or her government signs on paper or what officials put in their big books.

I was trying to see the problem from Sufia's point of view. I imagined I was a worm and had to overcome the obstacle facing me: how does one get around the cost of the bamboo? Do I go around? Climb the wall? Do I find a crack and go through?

I had no solution to Sufia's problem. I simply tried to understand why she suffered: she suffered because the cost of the bamboo was 5 *taka* and she didn't have the necessary cash. Her life was miserable because she could survive only in that tight cycle – borrowing from the trader and selling back to him. She could not break free of that circle. Put in those terms it was simple. All I had to do was lend her 5 *taka*.

Right now her labour was almost free. It was a form of bonded labour, or slavery. The trader always made certain that he paid Sufia a price that only covered the cost of the materials and just enough so that she would not die, but would need to keep on borrowing from him.

It seemed to me that Sufia's status as virtually a bonded slave was never going to change if she could not find that 5 *taka* to start with. Credit could bring her that money. She could then sell her products in a free market and could get a much better spread between the cost of her materials and her sale price.

* * *

The next day I called in Maimuna, a university student who collected data for me, and I asked her to assist me in making a list of how many in Jobra, like Sufia, were borrowing from traders and missing out on what they should have been earning from the fruits of their labours.

Within a week, we had prepared a list. It named forty-two people who in total had borrowed 856 *taka*, a total of less than $27.

'My God, my God, all this misery in all these forty-two families all because of the lack of $27!' I exclaimed.

Maimuna stood there without saying a word. We were both astounded, shocked, but also sickened by the pathos of it all.

* * *

My mind wouldn't let this problem lie. I wanted to be of help to these forty-two able-bodied, hard-working people. I kept going around and around the problem, like a dog worrying his bone. If I lent them $27, they could sell their products to anyone; they could then get the highest possible return for their labour, and would not be limited to the usurious practices of the traders and money-lenders.

I would lend them $27, and they would repay me whenever they could afford to.

Sufia needed credit because she had no cushion to tide her over the adverse conditions which too often arose in meeting her family obligations, in carrying on her bamboo weaving and for mere survival in times of total disaster.

Unfortunately, no formal financial institution was available to cater for the credit needs of the poor. This credit market, by default of the formal institutions, had been taken over by local money-lenders. It was an efficient vehicle, creating a heavy rush of one-way traffic on the road to poverty.

People were not poor because they were stupid or lazy. They worked all day long, doing complex physical tasks. They were poor because the financial structures which could help them widen their economic base simply did not exist in their country. It was a structural problem, not a personal problem.

I handed Maimuna the $27 and told her, 'Here, lend this money out to the forty-two on our list. They can repay the traders what they owe them and sell their products wherever they get a good price.'

'When should they repay you?'

'Whenever they can,' I said. 'Whenever it is advantageous for them to sell their products. They don't have to pay any interest. I am not in the money business.'

Maimuna left, puzzled by this turn of events.

* * *

Usually when my head touches the pillow, I fall asleep within seconds, but that night I lay in bed feeling ashamed that I was part of a society which could not provide \$27 to forty-two able-bodied, hard-working skilled persons to make a living for themselves.

Over the next week, it struck me that what I had done was not sufficient because it was only a personal and emotional solution. I had simply lent \$27, but what I had to do was to provide an institutional solution. If anyone else needed capital, they would have to be able to find an easier source of money than chasing down the head of the economics department of the University. My thinking up until then had been *ad hoc* and emotional. I needed to create an institutional response on which they could rely.

A poor person cannot walk up the hill and seek out some department head. For one thing, the campus police would not let the poor through the front gates; they would think they were coming on campus to steal.

Something had to be done. But what?

I decided to approach the local bank manager and request that his bank lend to the poor. What was required was an institution that would lend to those who had nothing. It seemed so simple, so straightforward.

* * *

That was the beginning of it all. I was not trying to become a money-lender, I had no intention of lending money to anyone; all I really wanted was to solve an immediate problem. Even to this day I still view myself, my work and that of my colleagues in Grameen, as devoted to solving the same immediate problem: the problem of poverty which humiliates and denigrates everything that a human being stands for.

2

The World Bank, Washington, DC, November 1993

We have come a long way: from $27 lent to forty-two people in 1976 to $2.3 billion lent to 2.3 million families by 1998. A Micro-credit Summit was held in 1997 to launch a worldwide campaign to reach 100 million families by the year 2005, and Grameen programmes stretch all over the world, from Equador to Eritrea, from the Norwegian polar circle to Papua New Guinea, from Chicago's inner-city ghettos to remote mountain communities in Nepal – by 1998 fifty-eight countries have Grameen clones.

* * *

November 1993 was an extremely important date for Grameen because for the first time our ideas finally reached deep into the inner sanctum of the international donor countries. Louis Preston, president of the World Bank, invited me to address the World Hunger Conference at the Washington DC headquarters of the World Bank.

As I stood up to speak at the conference, pictures of struggling women flashed through my mind. I paused and looked out over my audience. Who would have imagined that from my office overlooking the Monipur slum in Dhaka's Mirpur area, I would be here, at the heart of the world's financial world, giving a speech on our achievements and challenging the World Bank?

* * *

The World Bank and Grameen have been through so many fights and disagreements over the years that some commentators have called us 'sparring partners'. There have always been a few individuals in the World Bank who understand what micro-credit is all about, but our styles are so radically different that for many years we have spent more time and energy fighting each other than helping each other.

As I looked over my audience, I could not help but remember the World Food Day teleconference of 1986. Patricia Young, national co-ordinator of the US World Food Day Committee, invited me to be a panellist along with World Bank then-president Barber Conable in a teleconference which would be broadcast by satellite in thirty countries. I had no idea what a teleconference was, but I accepted the invitation as an opportunity to explain why I felt credit should be accepted as a human right, and how credit could play a strategic role in removing hunger from the world.

In that teleconference, I gave my pitch. I had not intended to go into battle with the World Bank president. But he pushed me into it by stating that the World Bank provided financial support to the Grameen Bank in Bangladesh. I thought I should correct this piece of wrong information, and I corrected it by politely saying that the World Bank did no such thing. But he paid no attention and a few seconds later reiterated that World Bank funds helped Grameen. This time I firmly contradicted him. For some reason, Mr Conable ignored this protest, and repeated for a third time that the World Bank provided financial support to the Grameen Bank. I thought I should make it clear to satellite TV viewers, otherwise I would look like a liar. We at the Grameen Bank have never wanted or accepted World Bank money because we do not like the way they conduct business. Any project which they finance, their experts and consultants end up virtually taking over. They do not rest until they mould it their way. We do not want anybody to come and meddle with the system we have built or dictate to us and make us conform to their views.

Indeed, that year we actually rejected an offer of a $200 million low-interest loan from the World Bank. I also told Conable, who was bragging about employing the best minds in the world, that 'hiring smart economists does not necessarily translate into policies and programmes that are of any benefit to the poor'.

I find multilateral donors' style of doing business with the poor very discomforting. I can cite one example of my experience in the island of Negros Occidental in the Philippines. Because hunger was so bad there, one of our replicators started Project Dunganon back in 1988. More than half the island's children were malnourished, and so in 1993 Dr Cecile del Castillo, the replicator, still innocent about the nature and work habits of international consultants, asked the International Fund for Agricultural Development (IFAD), a Rome-based UN agency created to assist the rural poor, for money to expand her successful programme quickly. IFAD responded by sending four missions to investigate her proposal, spending thousands of dollars in airline tickets, per diems and professional fees. But the project never received a single penny.

However, this led to a process which resulted in an agreement signed in 1996 between the government of the Philippines, the Asian Development Bank (ADB) and IFAD. Under that agreement, the ADB and IFAD were to lend $37 million to the Philippines to support micro-credit programmes there. Because of bureaucratic complications, that money has still not, as of today, July 1998, been made available to the Grameen replicators on Negros Occidental. In other words, after five years of specialists reviewing the problem and spending hundreds of thousands of dollars, the poor of Negros still do not enjoy the increase in micro-credit loans that their dire situation requires.

I cannot help but think that, had the Negros project simply received an amount equal to the cost of a single IFAD mission, it would have been able to assist several hundred poor families with micro-credit.

I think the growth of the consultancy business has seriously misled international donor agencies. The assumption is that the recipient country needs to be guided at every stage of the process – during project identification, preparation and implementation. Donors and the consultants they employ tend to become arrogant in their attitude towards the recipient countries.

Furthermore, consultants have a paralysing effect on the thinking and the initiatives of the recipient countries. Officials and academics in these recipient countries now swear by the figures mentioned in the donors' documents even if they personally know those figures are incorrect.

I know that donor agencies are under great pressure to use the targeted amount for specific countries within each fiscal year; and expensive consultants have the unique quality of getting the job done with an appearance of professionalism. Until the agreements are signed, recipient countries are happy to leave the details to the consultants for they are interested only in the ultimate amount they will receive.

* * *

In 1984, when Grameen made it clear to the World Bank that we would not let them dictate to us how to run our business, they gave up on us and decided to try to form their own micro-credit organization in Bangladesh, combining what we had done with credit with the non-credit activities of successful non-profit organizations. I thought the idea was wholly unrealistic; I said, 'If you take the speed of a horse, the majesty of a lion, the courage of a tiger and the elegance of a deer, in theory you might have a super animal, but in practice it might never get off the ground.'

I shall not go into all the details of why the Bangladesh government took our advice and resisted the World Bank initiative, but what is interesting is that the bureaucracy within the World Bank did not learn anything from this debate. On the contrary, it turned around, removed the name 'Bangladesh' from the rejected project document and gave it to the Sri Lankan government instead.

* * *

Multi-lateral aid institutions have a lot of money to disburse. Officials have their target amounts for each country. The more money one can give out, the better grade one receives as a lending officer.

If you are a young, ambitious officer of a donor agency hoping to move up quickly, you choose the project which carries the biggest price tag. In one go, you move a lot of money, and your name moves up the promotion ladder.

In my work Bangladesh, I have seen the desperation of donor agency officials to give away ever-larger sums of money. They will do almost anything to achieve this, 'bribing' government officials and politicians directly or indirectly. A common practice is to rent newly built, expensive houses owned by government officials for use as project offices. Arranging foreign trips by organizing workshops and conferences in cities which the official concerned wants to visit is another common practice. No one needs a conference or workshop in the first place, but just to please the government official, the donor picks up the bill for the trip and entertainment.

In one particular case, a frustrated official from a multi-lateral financial donor institution who could not get his project any further up the approval chain in the Bangladeshi bureaucracy confided to me that he even accepted a project proposal of $5 million to finance a meaningless project in the home area of the government official who was reluctant to approve the £100 million project. (Even this bigger project, which he was so eager to get approved by the Bangladesh government, I considered useless.)

I was shocked when I heard the details of the $5 million project which he had agreed to finance. I screamed: 'You know very well that money will simply go into the pockets of the government official's cronies.'

The donor agency official said, 'Don't you think I know that? But this is the price I am ready to pay for his approval of my project.'

'You mean you are bribing him?' I said, disgusted.

'Well, I don't think so. This is a legitimate project which goes through all the screening mechanisms. I know I can push it through.'

In this case it was an international institution's own money that was given as the 'bribe'. Worse still, it was the people of Bangladesh who would have to pay back the money with interest.

In other cases, consultants, suppliers and potential contractors facilitate the bribing mechanism. After all, they are the major beneficiaries of projects funded by donors. One research institution estimates that, of the more than $30 billion in foreign donor assistance received in the last twenty-six years, 75 per cent never actually reached Bangladesh in the form of cash. Instead, it came as equipment, commodities, supplies, and the cost of consultants, contractors, advisers and experts. Some rich nations use their foreign aid budget to employ their own people and to sell their own goods. The remaining 25 per cent which actually reached Bangladesh in the form of cash went into the hands of a tiny elite of local suppliers, contractors, consultants and experts. Much of this money is used to buy foreign-made consumer goods, which is of no help to our country's economy or workforce. And there is a general belief that a good chunk of donor money ends up as kickbacks to officials and politicians as grease-money in making purchase decisions and signing contracts.

The problem is the same around the world. The actual level of international aid is $50–$55 billion a year. And everywhere these projects create huge bureaucracies which become corrupt and inefficient and quickly incur huge losses. The aid is designed with the assumption that the money should go to governments. In a world which trumpets the superiority of the market economy and free enterprise, aid money still goes to expand government spending, often acting against the interests of the market economy.

I have often argued that money wasted on huge bureaucracies would be much better spent if given outright to our most needy. For instance, just $100 put in the hands of each of the poorest ten million families in Bangladesh would amount to $1 billion that would then either be invested in capital income-earning goods, or, at worst, spent locally on goods and services.

If foreign aid does reach Bangladesh at all, it usually goes to build roads, bridges and so forth which are supposed to help the poor 'in the long run'. But in the long run you are dead. And nothing trickles down to the poor.

I am not opposed to building roads and bridges. But these become meaningful only when the poor are enabled to take advantage of their existence. That enabling action is completely missing.

The only people benefiting directly and indirectly from this aid are those who are already wealthy, though they do so in the name of the poor. Foreign aid becomes a kind of charity for the powerful, while the poor get poorer.

If foreign aid is to have some impact on the lives of the poor, it must be redirected so that it reaches the poor households directly, particularly their womenfolk. I believe that a new aid methodology has to be designed with new objectives.

The direct elimination of poverty should be the objective of all development aid. Development should be looked at as a human rights issue, not as a question of GNP growth where it is assumed that if a national economy picks up, it will benefit the poor.

Development should be redefined: it should mean positive change in the economic status of the bottom 50 per cent of the population of any given society. If aid fails to improve the economic condition of that bottom half of the population, then it is not development aid. In other words, economic development should be judged and measured by the per capita real income of the bottom 50 per cent of the population.

* * *

An American journalist approached me. I could see he was irritated at my apparently endless carping against the World Bank which he saw as a benevolent and enlightened organization charged with doing a thankless task but doing the best it could.

He raised the microphone of a cassette recorder up in the air between us and said in a challenging voice:

'Instead of criticizing all the time, what concrete steps would you take if you became president of the World Bank?'

In his eyes I could see his wanting to overpower me, as if to say, let us see what you have to say for yourself now!

'I have never thought of what I would do if I were president of the World Bank,' I said, giving myself time to consider the question. 'But I suppose the first thing I would do is move the headquarters to Dhaka.'

'Why on earth would you do that?'

'Well, if, as Louis Preston [then president of the World Bank] says, "The overarching objective of the World Bank is to combat world poverty", then it seems to me the Bank should move to a location where poverty is rampant. In Dhaka, the World Bank would be surrounded by human suffering and destitution. By living in close proximity with the problem, I believe the Bank would solve the problem much faster and more realistically.'

He nodded, less aggressive than he was when he started the interview.

'Also, if the headquarters were moved to Dhaka many of the Bank's five thousand employees would simply refuse to come. Dhaka is not a choice spot for a World banker to raise his children, or to have an exciting social life, so many would voluntarily retire or change jobs. This would help achieve two things: on the one hand, it would allow me to ease out those who are not completely dedicated to fighting poverty and in their stead I could hire people who are committed and who understand the problem.

'The other thing it would do is that it would reduce costs by allowing me to hire people whose lifestyle does not require high salaries. Dhaka is a less expensive place than Washington, DC anyway.'

* * *

The foreign aid machinery was designed years ago when people assumed that a magic quantum of investment would generate enough economic activity to somehow eliminate hunger and poverty. So neither the donors nor the recipients actually bothered about how the poor live. Donor assistance was aimed at eye-catching physical structures – bridges, giant prestige factories, dams – not at institution-building, replacing obsolete institutions, organizing people to solve their own problems. Self-help projects were dismissed as 'boyscout projects'.

This is starting to change slowly now as we move into the third millennium, but what continues to make headlines and please everyone is still the US dollar quantum of assistance. On both sides, bigger is better!

No real attention is paid to the quality of the aid given. The crucial two words in the aid community have been for decades, and unfortunately continue to be, 'How much?'

* * *

In 1990, we allowed the World Bank to commission an in-depth evaluation of Grameen. Within our organization many thought this was like letting the fox into the chicken coop, and that nothing positive would come of it. I argued that if we did not let the World Bank undertake even a biased evaluation project, they could easily tell the world that we had something to hide. In fact, we had nothing at all to hide. So why should we not let them bring their high-powered evaluation team to make an assessment of our work?

When the draft report of the evaluation came to our attention in the spring of 1993, it showed that Grameen would always be financially sick or would soon go bankrupt, and all my colleagues within Grameen who had said the World Bank was biased against us and would never study us with any objectivity felt vindicated.

Checking the Bank's methodology, we discovered that they had based their conclusion on the years 1991 and 1992 when Grameen suffered its first losses due to huge increases in the size and salaries of our staff. But when we asked them to redo their study, using figures for the first half of 1993 which were more typical of our operations, a different conclusion emerged.

This about-face could never have happened if I had not demanded the right to include our response to their study in the final publication, if we had disagreed. (We agreed with their final report, so there was no need to invoke this right.)

Another evolution in our long relationship is the fact that, although we have been on opposite sides in countless issues, many individuals inside the World Bank have become close personal friends and enthusiastic supporters of Grameen and are willing to listen to us, even if this was not, at first, the case.

* * *

In late 1995, we again rejected a soft loan from the World Bank. This time the offer was for $175 million to Bangladesh, with $100 million going to Grameen.

How I refused is almost as interesting as the fact that I refused at all. A fact-finding mission, one of dozens that come every year to Bangladesh, came to see what projects they could invest in. A Bangladeshi official called me and asked me to receive them. I told the official we did not need any funds from the World Bank, that we were raising enough from the commercial market through the sale of bonds and from our own banking business, that we had weaned ourselves off aid money and would soon be able to get off all soft loans and become entirely commercial. The government official insisted that I see them 'because the World Bank wants to see you'. So I agreed.

When the consultant arrived in my office in Dhaka and asked me what Grameen wanted from the World Bank, I told him there must have been some mistake, there was nothing we needed from the World Bank.

A few months later, the World Bank and Bangladesh were about to enter into an agreement whereby the Bank would lend $175 million in soft loans to the government to help in establishing Grameen-like micro-loan programmes.

When the draft documentation was prepared, the finance ministry sent us a copy and a letter requesting our comments. When I saw that a condition of the soft loan was that Grameen take a portion of the loan, I immediately wrote back explaining once again that we did not want or need any part of this loan.

This put the officials in the ministry in a difficult position because the agreement on which they had worked so hard was about to come undone. I was invited by the finance secretary to have a discussion. The man was a respected long-time acquaintance of mine, and I knew that I was going to lose a friend and a supporter. As expected, he tried his best to convince me to agree to the loan:

'Professor Yunus, you don't even need to draw down a single *taka*, all you have to do is say that you are willing to consider this line of credit available to you in the future and that is enough.'

I tried to explain: 'Even if over the next twenty years Grameen does not draw down a single *taka*, for ever in the documents and papers of the World Bank we will be identified as a recipient of their money. They will forever see us as a client.'

'Well, our country does need the money.'

'We at Grameen do not.'

'But think of the millions who are not Grameen borrowers. Think of the poor.'

'I am thinking of the poor. It is exactly for them that I am taking this seemingly inconsistent position. The entire meaning of what Grameen has preached is that the poor are bankable. That one can lend to them on a commercial basis and make a profit. That banks can and should serve the disinherited of this earth, not only out of altruism but out of self-interest. Treating the poor as untouchables and outcasts is immoral and indefensible, but also financially stupid for them. Now after nineteen years of struggle, hard work and endless privations on the part of my colleagues and co-workers, we are about to break completely free of any aid support. You should applaud us for achieving this, rather than asking us to accept this World Bank line of credit.'

The finance secretary looked at me. He was clearly distraught and wanted to convince me, but he said,

'I understand what you are going through.'

'I don't think you do,' I said. 'When I came here today I was worried that I would lose a friend I respect because I would put you in an impossible situation. And I was incredibly agitated and anxious, but I cannot go against my conscience. I cannot repudiate everything Grameen has struggled for. If I accept this loan, all my colleagues will shout, 'What have we been working so hard for all these years? What?''

He stood up and shook my hand, 'I understand,' he said, 'we will not pressure you anymore.'

What a relief – I felt like my death sentence had just been lifted!

* * *

Grameen breaking free of donors' money brings me to the whole problem of charity itself.

Anyone who drives in a car in the city of Dhaka is assailed on all sides by professional beggars to give them a hand-out.

Why not give? For just a few pennies we can alleviate our conscience. When a person approaches who has leprosy and his fingers and hands are eaten away, we are so shocked, we immediately and quite naturally reach into our pockets and hand over a bill that is a pittance for us but a fortune for the recipient. But is this useful? No, most of the time it is actually harmful.

On the donor's side, you have the feeling that you have done something. But in fact you have done nothing.

Handing out money is a way of shielding ourselves from addressing the real issue. Handing out a pittance is a way of making ourselves think we have done something and of feeling good for having shared our good fortune with the poor. But in fact we are leaving the problem alone. We have merely thrown money at it and walked away. But for how long?

Giving alms to a beggar is not a long-term or even a short-term solution. The beggar will only go to the next car, the next tourist and do the same. And eventually he will come back to the donor who gave him money and on whom he now depends. If we honestly want to solve the problem, we have to get involved and start a process. If the donor opened the door of the car and asked the beggar what the problem was, what his name was, how old he was, whether he had sought medical assistance, what training he had, then the donor might be of help. But handing the beggar money is only a way of telling him to buzz off and to leave the donor alone.

I do not question the moral duty to help, nor the instinct to want to help the needy, only the form that help takes.

On the recipient's side, charity can have devastating effects. It robs the recipient of dignity, and it removes the incentive of having to generate income. It makes the recipient passive and satisfied with thinking 'all I have to do is sit here with my hand out and I will earn a living'.

This is one reason that for too long Bangladesh and other third-world countries have had a deliberate policy of playing up their natural disasters. For the last decade, we have given the international image-makers the idea that we are in an incurable situation. While it is true that we have many natural disasters, we are not helpless nor hopeless.

When I see a child begging, I resist the natural impulse to give. But the fact is I do give hand-outs sometimes, I do it when the human misery is so terrible – some disease, some mother with her dying child – that I cannot stop my hand from reaching to my pocket and giving her something. But I fight against this urge as much as possible.

* * *

This example of the individual's experience illustrates what happens with aid on an international level.

Dependence on aid creates an environment which sustains governments that are good at negotiating for more aid.

Promoters of hard work, austerity and self-reliance are ridiculed. Food aid encourages the perpetuation of food shortages: grain importers and exporters, shippers and officials involved in foreign procurement and distribution of grain all have something to lose with the prospect of self-reliance in food.

So aid distorts the economy and the political climate in favour of petitioners, of politicians who are good at pleasing the donors and of contractors and corrupt officials, instead of securing local solutions.

* * *

I got up and stood at the lectern. Now that Grameen was reaching out to 12 million people or one-tenth of the population of Bangladesh, and now that independent studies have shown that within ten years Grameen has managed to push one-third of its borrowers out of poverty, and to push one-third of its borrowers up close to the poverty line, my message is always the same: poverty can be eradicated in our lifetime. We only need the political will.

This is a statement that needs to be repeated over and over again, for we can only build what we are able to imagine. Only if we conceptualize a world without poverty can we start to build it. And my message, that a poverty-free world is within our grasp if we want it, took on a new significance when spoken there in the World Bank.

I looked out over the faces of experts, colleagues I have known for decades. Many there had truly helped us. Others continued to doubt Grameen's viability. They thought this was a dream, a nightmare.

I know that part of the reason the doubters and nay-sayers were listening to me that day was because Grameen had demonstrated the good sense of what we said could be done.

* * *

The banks told me that the poor were not creditworthy. My first reaction was, 'How do you know, you have never lent to them? Perhaps it is the banks which are not people-worthy?'

'They don't have collateral,' they answered.

That is true, but the poor have their self-respect and the peer pressure of their fellow borrowers. We have worked with the poorest people in one of the poorest countries on earth, Bangladeshi village women who have no land and have never touched money in their lives, women who cannot read and write, who have to relieve themselves only at night so as not to be seen, who do not dare stand in front of a man, who must cover their faces when strangers appear. Working with these people we maintained a recovery record of over 98 per cent.

Again and again, the specialists explained that what the Grameen Bank was attempting to do was impossible.

'OK', I said, 'we are mad, but we don't care, we will persevere.'

We were told that even if we were successful in lending to a handful of indigents and getting the money back, this could not be scaled up to reach any significant number of villages. Yet today we work with 36,000 villages, over half of all the villages of Bangladesh, and we operate with a staff of 12,000 in over 1079 branches.

We were told that we should lend to the head of the household, typically a male. Instead we targeted destitute women, and these turned out to be our most determined weapon against poverty. Today out of 2.1 million borrowers, 94 per cent are women.

We were told that the minuscule loans we made (averaging about $150 per borrower) would not create enough income to alter the poverty status of a family; that poverty was too entrenched to be affected by such loans. But independent studies show that our borrowers are steadily improving their lives: within a decade half of them rise above the poverty line, and another quarter comes close to crossing it.

Independent studies show that our borrowers are better off than other families with regards to nutrition, child mortality, use of contraceptives, sanitation and availability of safe drinking water. Our housing loans have provided homes for 350,000 families, while another 150,000 have built houses with incomes from their Grameen-funded enterprises.

We were told that Grameen would always be a sick institution dependent on the subsidies of donors, yet we have been able to make our branch-level operations profitable. In fact, Grameen now deals solely on the commercial market issuing its own bonds and borrowing from commercial banks. Grameen is the soundest financial institution in Bangladesh today.

After the 1993 World Bank study that concluded that the Grameen Bank was viable and worthwhile, relations between our organizations improved, and in December 1993 when I addressed the World Hunger Conference in Washington, DC the World Bank announced a $2 million grant to our sister organization, the Grameen Trust, which is responsible for replicating our experience worldwide, and which has already established sixty-three programmes in twenty-seven countries around the world.

The contribution to the Grameen Trust was a pittance, a fraction of what the World Bank lends daily, but we at Grameen have always considered it an extremely important gesture.

This was the beginning of the Bank's recognition of micro-credit as a legitimate economic tool in the fight against poverty. Soon the World Bank took the lead in co-ordinating micro-credit programmes and bringing together donors, and to that end created the Consultative Group to Assist the Poorest (CGAP). Practitioners of micro-credit were invited to constitute the Policy Advisory Group (PAG), which I was then asked to chair.

* * *

I am eager to put past tensions behind us and to start with a new slate. The stakes are high. And there is reason to hope that we are finally succeeding in beginning to effect changes in the approach of the World Bank.

In 1996, James D. Wolfensohn, president of the World Bank, acknowledged: 'Micro-credit programmes have brought the vibrancy of the market economy to the poorest villages and people of the world. This business approach to the alleviation of poverty has allowed millions of individuals to work their way out of poverty with dignity.'

* * *

Whenever he visits a country, and he visits many quite regularly, Jim Wolfensohn makes a point of spending more time in the villages and on distant bank-financed projects, than in the capital city with the movers and shakers of the country. In October 1997, he came to Bangladesh, and, along with his wife, he visited a Grameen branch, met with Grameen borrowers, visited their homes and had involved discussions with them.

During his stay in Bangladesh he made it clear to me that he was very unhappy with the negative comments about the World Bank which I had made to the press during my trip to Paris for the launch that same month of the French edition of this book. He challenged me to visit Washington, DC to examine the 'new' World Bank he was in the process of creating, which did not deserve the harsh comments I made about the mistakes the Bank had made in the past. So I spent four days in January 1998 with him in Washington, DC, meeting all the important people in the World Bank.

Two things impressed me right away. First, Jim Wolfensohn means what he says, and second, he says it in very clear, crisp words. He officially declared that the mission of the World Bank was to create a world free from poverty. I was thrilled to hear this from none other than the president of the World Bank. But he went further than merely stating a general wish; he defined his task and gave it a completion date. The World Bank's immediate task, he said, was to reduce the number of people in abject poverty (earning less than a dollar a day of income) by half by the year 2015.

I immediately felt I had a very powerful ally here, and that we could build an important and fruitful partnership with the World Bank.

But this excitement started waning as I sat down with key people inside the Bank. The excitement that I had felt in Jim Wolfensohn, and that he had generated in me, was not mirrored in the faces or words of key members of his team. To some, the new mission statement was only a reformulation of the old mission statement. They did not read anything extra in it; to them it was simply business as usual. Others were puzzled, slightly unsettled, and still trying to figure out what these statements meant in concrete terms and how they would change their responsibilities, or how they would carry out the new mission.

If I were to ask Jim Wolfensohn, can you really create a new bank with old bankers, I know what his answer would be: of course not, don't you see how many changes I have made in high positions. But how much can he change the ways of the old World Bank? I don't know, but I have no illusions about how difficult his task is.

After four days, I came back feeling that the new captain of the ship had announced a new and difficult destination. His crew has no experience in plying the turbulent waters of poverty eradication. And the captain has no well-defined route map either. Will the ship reach its new destination? I believe that if the captain is honest and determined, in spite of all the difficulties, he will bring the ship around.

In the meantime, I pray that the captain will remain true to his words and remain determined to reach his destination. History will judge him for his accomplishments, not for his brilliant speeches.

3

20 Boxirhat Road, Chittagong

Chittagong is a commercial city of three million people, the largest port in Bangladesh. I grew up on Boxirhat Road in the heart of the old business district of Chittagong. This was an extremely busy one-way lane just wide enough for one truck to pass. Boxirhat was (and still is) the main axis from the river port of Chaktai to the central produce market.

Our part of the road was in Sonapotti, the jewellers' section. We lived at number 20 (the numbers have since changed), on the upper floor of a small two-storey house. The ground floor served as my father's jewellery shop in the front and workshop behind. Our world was always full of noise, gasoline fumes and the screams of passing street vendors, jugglers, beggars and just plain madmen. Trucks and carts were forever blocking our road. All day long we heard drivers arguing, yelling, blaring their horns. It was a sort of permanent carnival atmosphere. When, towards midnight, the noise of the street finally died down, the sound of low-bit hammering, filing and polishing in Father's gold workshop took over. Noise was the constant background and rhythm to our life.

On the upper floor we lived in just four rooms and a kitchen. We children called these Mother's room, Radio room, Big room, and a room which remained nameless where the mat was spread three times a day for us to sit down to our meals, and where my father presided. The Big room was the communal sleeping and living-room for the children.

Our playground was the flat roof above, with railings on all sides. And when we got bored, we often idled away our time downstairs watching the customers, or the gold artisans at work in the back room, or we would just look out at the endlessly changing, endlessly repeated street scenes.

* * *

20 Boxirhat Road was my father's second business location in Chittagong. The first was abandoned when it was damaged by a Japanese bomb in 1943.

The Japanese had invaded neighbouring Burma and were at the doorstep of Chittagong, threatening all of India. The air battles over our heads were never intensive. Japanese planes mostly dropped leaflets, and as children we loved watching them from the roof. But after a bombing raid destroyed a wall of our house, my father promptly shifted us to the safety of his family village, Bathua, where I had been born at the beginning of the war.

Bathua is some seven miles from Chittagong. My grandfather was a small businessman who had acquired land and a farm there, but he gravitated towards the jewellery trade.

Dula Mia, his eldest son, dropped out before finishing high school, and went into his father's small jewellery business. Goldsmithing is traditionally run by Hindus. But he soon made a name for himself as the foremost local manufacturer and seller of jewellery ornaments for Muslim customers.

Dula Mia, or Father as we called him, was a soft-hearted person. He rarely punished us, but he was strict about our need to study.

I can still hear it today, the central iron drawer of Father's safe. He had three 4ft-high iron safes built into the wall at the back of the store. The safes ran the length of the wall behind the counter. When the store was open for business, he left the safes open. The insides of the heavy doors had mirrors and display racks so that to the customers they did not appear to be safes at all, but simply part of the decor.

We knew exactly the sound that preceded his coming upstairs to see if we were studying. Before the fifth prayer of the day, at closing time, Father pushed the drawers shut, and we recognized these ungreased squeals. Three locks in each door, six locks for each safe. It gave us time, my elder brother Salam and me upstairs – whatever we were doing – to leap back to our books. Usually they were not the books which our father imagined. But he never stopped to look over our shoulder, never examined exactly what we were reading.

As long as he saw us seated in front of a book and heard words cascading from our lips, he was happy: 'Good children, good boys,' he would say, then he would make his way to the mosque for prayer-time.

My father was a devout Muslim all his life, and made three pilgrimages to Mecca. His square tortoise-shell glasses and his white beard made him look like an intellectual, but he was never a bookworm. With his large family and his successful business, he had no time or much inclination to look over our lessons. He usually dressed all in white, white slippers, white *paijama* pants, a white tunic and a white prayer cap. He divided his time between his work, his prayers and his family life.

* * *

My mother, Sofia Khatun, was a strong and decisive woman. She was the disciplinarian of the family, and once she bit her lower lip and decided something, we knew that nothing would budge her. She wanted us all to be as methodical as her.

She was full of compassion and kindness, and probably the strongest influence on me. She always had money put away for any poor relations who visited us from distant villages. It was she, through her concern for the poor and the disadvantaged, who helped me discover my destiny, and she who most shaped my personality.

Her family were also petty merchants, traders who bought and sold goods from Burma. Her father lived as a landowner, leasing out his farmland and spending most of his time reading, writing chronicles and indulging in good food. It was this last trait which most endeared him to his grandchildren.

In these early years, I remember my mother often wearing a bright sari with a gold band around the hem. Her deep black hair was always combed into a thick bun and parted in the front on the right. I loved her deeply. I was certainly the one who most often pulled at her sari and demanded the most attention.

I don't know how she did it; there could be a cyclone, a tidal wave, a drought, and to me she always looked beautiful. She could not make herself unbeautiful even if she tried. Above all through her story-telling and songs, she was the source of our musings and wonderings about the world.

I recall her narrating the tragedy of the Karbala in an emotionally choked voice. And every year, during Moharram – when we Muslims commemorate the tragedy of the Karbala – I remember asking my mother:

'Mother, why is the sky red on this side of the house and blue on the other side?'

'Oh, the blue is for Hassan and the red is for Hussain.'

'Who are Hassan and Hussain?'

'They were the grandsons of our prophet (peace be upon him), the gems of his two holy eyes.'

And when she finished the story of their murder, she would point to the dusk and explain that the blue on one side of the house was for the poison that killed Hassan and the red on the other side was the blood of Hussain. To me as a child, her depiction of this was no less moving than the version I heard much later from our great Bengali epic *Bishad Shindhu* ('The Sea of Sorrow').

Mother dominated my early years. Whenever she would start making her superb *pitha* cakes and crispy fried snacks in the kitchen, we would crowd around her, watch and scramble for a taste. As soon as she slipped her first *pitha* off the frying pan and blew on it to cool it down, I snatched it from her for I had the family distinction of being her chief taster.

But Mother did something else which fascinated me. She worked on some of the jewellery to be sold in our shop. She often gave a final touch to earrings and necklaces by adding a bit of velvet or woollen pompoms to the end of the ribbon, or by attaching braided coloured strands. Amazed, I watched her long thin hands work and make truly beautiful ornaments. It was this money she earned on the side that she gave away to the neediest relatives, friends or neighbours who came to her for help.

She had fourteen children, of whom five died young. Growing up in such a large family taught me early on the central importance of babies (sometimes I took care of two at a time), the importance of family loyalty, peer pressure and peer support, but also the value of compromise when living in a large group.

My sister, Mumtaz, eight years older than me, married when she was still a teenager. Her new home at the edge of town was not far, and we often visited her and ate her lavish meals. Mumtaz inherited three things from Mother, her excellent cooking, a divine pleasure in feeding her loved ones and a gift for telling endless stories.

Salam, three years older than me, was my constant companion. The Japanese war was over, but Salam's and mine was not. We mimicked the machine-gun sounds we had heard. And in the sky we replaced the Japanese planes with colourful kites – usually a diamond-shaped paper kite with a skeleton made of one straight and one arched bamboo stick. To our great excitement, Father bought a few defused Japanese shells in the market and Mother used them as plant-pots on the roof, standing them on their fins, wide end up.

* * *

I attended nearby Lamar Bazar Free Primary School, along with all the boys of our working-class neighbourhood. All of us there, even the teachers, spoke in the Chittagonian dialect.

The general education of a child in my country is limited to those who can afford to go to school. In each classroom, we had about forty pupils, and primary and secondary school were not co-educational.

If you happened to be a good student, then you won a scholarship, and you were asked to compete in nationwide exams which brought the school much prestige. But most of my fellow schoolmates soon dropped out.

Our schools inculcated good values into our children: not simply scholastic achievement, but also civic pride, the importance of spiritual beliefs, respect for the arts, admiration for the music and poetry of our greatest poets (Rabindranath Tagore and Kazi Nazrul Islam), and of course respect for authority and discipline.

Salam and I devoured all the books and magazines we could get our hands on. Detective thrillers were my favourite. I even wrote one, a complete whodunnit at the age of twelve.

It was not easy to maintain a constant supply of reading material on our own. To meet our needs, we had to improvise, buy, borrow and steal. For instance, in our favourite children's magazine *Shuktara* published in Calcutta, there was a contest, and the winners of the contest could receive a free subscription. The magazine listed their names. I picked one of the winners at random and wrote to the editor:

Dear Sir,
I am so-and-so, a contest winner,
and we have moved addresses. From now on,
please mail my free subscription to Boxirhat
Road number —.

I didn't give our exact address, only our next door neighbour's, so that my father would not see the magazine. But every month, we kept our eye out for our free copy. And it worked like a dream.

In spite of our comparative neglect of textbooks, this freelance reading stood us well over the years. Through primary and secondary school, I came top of my class almost all the time.

We also loved to keep up to date on current affairs. In order to do this, Salam and I spent some time every day in the waiting-room of our family physician, Dr Banik – just around the corner – reading the various newspapers he subscribed to.

* * *

The Indian subcontinent, ruled by the British for nearly two centuries, was about to achieve its independence, and this would happen at midnight on 14 August 1947.

At that time the 'Pakistan movement' – demanding that those areas of India which had a Muslim majority should become an independent Muslim state – had reached its peak. We knew that Chittagong was sure to be included in Pakistan, for Muslims were clearly the majority in eastern Bengal. But what other areas of Muslim Bengal would be included and where the exact boundaries would be was not yet decided.

Friends and relatives at 20 Boxirhat Road argued endlessly about if and when an independent Pakistan would be created. We all realized it would be a most curious country, with its western and eastern halves separated by more than a thousand miles of Indian territory.

The eastern part (then eastern Bengal) would be about 55,000 square miles and six times smaller than the western part of Pakistan. It is made up mostly of low flat plains intersected by numerous rivers, canals, lakes, swamps and marshes. It is so flat that even 100 miles from the sea the land is less than 30ft above sea level.

* * *

In our house, my father, a devout Muslim, had many Hindu friends and close colleagues (Uncle Nishi, Uncle Nibaran, Uncle Profulla), but even as a child I knew there were many grievances and much mistrust felt by the minority of Muslims in India. We read in the newspapers and heard on the radio about the violent communal riots between Hindus and Muslims, but mercifully there was little of this in Chittagong.

Our political leanings were never in any doubt. We were all deeply committed to partition from the rest of India. When my brother Ibrahim, five years my junior, started to utter his first words, he called the white sugar he liked 'Jinnah sugar', and the brown sugar which he did not like 'Gandhi sugar'. (Jinnah was the leader of the partition movement, and Gandhi of course wanted to keep India whole.)

Even Mother mixed Jinnah, Gandhi and Lord Mountbatten into our evening stories and her amusing morals and country fables, so that we felt they were almost an active part of our lives.

My brother Salam, though only ten, was already behaving like a political analyst and information source – which he has remained ever since. I envied the bigger boys in the neighbourhood carrying the green flag with the white crescent and star and chanting *Pakistan Zindabad!* ('Long live Pakistan!').

* * *

I recall as if it were yesterday, the night when all these dreams and hopes finally came true.

I see our home decorated with flags and green and white festoons. Our whole street was decorated, and so was the city. Outside we could hear the blaring of some political speech, interrupted every so often by the chant *Pakistan Zindabad!* It was almost midnight, but our street was full of people, it felt like a huge living-room. We set off fireworks from our roof-top and watched others do the same. All around us we could see the silhouettes of our neighbours staring up as the firework explosions filled the night sky. The whole town was throbbing with excitement, and the sky was alive with bright colours.

As midnight approached, Father led us down into Boxirhat Road. He was anything but a political activist, but as a gesture of solidarity he joined the Muslim League National Guard, and that night he proudly wore his Guard uniform, complete with the characteristic 'Jinnah cap'. Even my younger siblings, two-year-old Ibrahim and little baby Tunu, were with us. At midnight on the dot, the electricity was switched off, and the entire city was plunged into darkness. The next moment, when the lights came back on, we were a new country.

The roaring slogan resounded again and again, from every part of Chittagong – *Pakistan Zindabad!*

At the age of seven, this was the first shot of pride and intoxicating enthusiasm for our people I had felt in my veins.

Many more were to come.

4

Through the Viewfinder: Boyhood Passions

After Mumtaz, Salam, myself, Ibrahim and Tunu, my mother gave birth to four more boys, Ayub, Azam, Jahangir and Moinu.

But when I was nine, my beloved mother started becoming irritable for no reason. Her behaviour became more and more abnormal. These were the first signs of her mental affliction which would become the dominant factor of our family life.

It grew steadily worse every year. In her calmer periods she talked disjointed nonsense to herself. For hours on end she would sit in prayer, read the same page of a book or recite a poem over and over again without stopping. At first, we children did not know what to make of her trance-like state.

In her more disturbed periods she started insulting people in a loud voice and often in bad language. Sometimes she would hurl abuse at a neighbour, a friend or a family member, but it could be a politician, or even some long-dead figure. She would insult imaginary enemies, and then without much warning she would become violent.

This was a nightmare for all of us, as she attacked adults and children alike. Usually Father bore the brunt of it. At night while we slept, we were never sure whether it would be an undisturbed and peaceful night, or whether she would erupt in shouts and physical attacks. When she became violent, I had to help Father restrain her, and I also had to protect my younger siblings from the blows and missiles she would throw. After such crises, she would be nice and soft, giving us as much love as she could, taking care of the younger ones.

As her condition worsened, she gradually lost track of our schooling and studies, and what we were doing.

The ordeal she had to suffer when we physically restrained her and when we tried to find a cure for what ailed her was another source of anguish. My father tried everything. He paid for the most advanced medical tests available in the country. Her own mother and two sisters had suffered the same mental illness, so we thought it must be congenital, but no doctor was ever able to diagnose it, and gratefully none of her children had inherited it.

In despair, my father turned to unorthodox solutions, incantations, mumbo-jumbo, superstitions, even hypnosis. Mother never co-operated with any of these treatments, and none of them bore fruit. Some were downright cruel.

But some we children found interesting. After watching a renowned psychologist apply post-hypnotic suggestions to Mother, we performed our own hypnotic experiments on one another. In the course of trying to find anything that would help her, one doctor prescribed too much sedative, and she became addicted to opium.

Gradually we children came to terms with the situation. We learned to live without Mother's help. Her younger sister, 'Auntie', and Mumtaz became substitute mothers for us. And we eventually accepted these difficulties with a certain humour which made the pain easier to bear.

'What is the weather forecast?' we asked one another, meaning what did we expect Mother's mood to be in the next few hours. Whenever she grew quiet, we knew a storm was coming, sometimes a tidal wave. In order not to utter someone's name which would provoke a fresh bout of abuse from Mother, we gave code names to various persons in the household: number 2, number 4, and so on. The code names stuck, and adults as well as children used them even when it was not necessary. My brother Ibrahim wrote a hilarious skit at the age of ten, in which he called our home a radio station, with Mother always 'on air', broadcasting her sermons in various languages and moods with 'active accompaniments'.

The one who shone brightly through this whole sad reality of life was my father. He adapted himself to the situation with grace and fortitude and created a surprising normality for the family within this chaos. He took loving care of Mother in every possible way and in all circumstances for the thirty-three years that her disease lasted.

He tried to behave towards her as if nothing had changed, and she was the same Sofia Khatun he had married back in 1930 when he was only twenty-two. And he taught us to do exactly the same. He was loyal and good to her all the fifty-two years of their marriage until her death in 1982.

But even before Mother's death, with the onslaught of her disease, Father became two persons in one, both a father and a mother in every sense of the term. He never settled for anything but the best for his children's upbringing.

We are what we are largely because of him.

* * *

Father did not mind spending a lot on our education, and later on helping us to make foreign trips, but he kept us to an extremely simple lifestyle and meagre pocket money. Over and above the requirements of books and magazines, Salam and I acquired many new hobbies and interests, as well as a weakness for movies and eating out. Our culinary delights were not highbrow. My favourite dish was fried 'potato chop', or roast potato, with the inside mashed, fried, filled with onion and flavoured with vinegar. We usually ate this with a cup of jasmine tea at a simple tea-stall around the corner from the house. It was not extravagant, but it required extra cash, and Father had no knowledge of any of our interests.

I received a monthly stipend as a result of winning the Competitive Scholarship Examination of all the high schools in the Chittagong District. This provided me with some pocket money, but not enough. I acquired the balance of the cash I needed by taking advantage of Father's simple trust in his sons. During the peak business periods of the day, Father often needed extra help in the shop and gladly accepted it from me, if I was around. During that time, I helped myself to a few banknotes and coins from the drawer where he kept his loose change.

This embezzlement never amounted to much, but it was enough to build up a fund to meet my modest requirements.

Father never detected this.

The first camera that Salam and I bought was a simple box camera. We went everywhere with it.

We researched and planned our subjects like experts – portraits, street scenes, houses, festivities, nature from the roof-top. Our accomplice in this was the owner of a nearby photo shop, appropriately named 'The Mystery House Studio'. He allowed us to go into his darkroom and try our hand at developing and printing our black-and-white film. We tried special effects and even retouched our photos in colour. Eventually we graduated to a folding camera which had a viewfinder closer to our eyes. It gave us a new way of looking at the world.

I became interested in painting and drawing. A friend and I apprenticed with a commercial artist of some repute whom I called my guru ('Ustad'). At home I arranged my easel, canvas and pastels in such a manner that I could hide them away from Father at a moment's notice. As a devout Muslim he believed that reproducing human figures was not sanctioned by

Islam, but also he wanted us only to study and study. So all of our extra-curricular activities had to be done in secrecy. Some uncles and aunts in the family who liked art became my co-conspirators, helping and encouraging me.

As a by-product of these hobbies, we developed an interest in graphics and design. Salam and I also started a stamp collection, and persuaded a neighbouring shopkeeper to agree to keep our display box with stamps for sale in front of his shop.

Together with two uncles, I started to frequent theatres to see Hindi and Hollywood films, and to sing folk songs, steeped in a dream-like atmosphere of romanticism. One then-popular song we sang was called 'Come my heart, let us go somewhere else'.

* * *

Chittagong Collegiate School gave me first and foremost a change of outlook. The atmosphere, in this secondary school, was completely cosmopolitan. My classmates were sons of government officials on transfer from various districts. They were a much more sophisticated lot than the pupils I had been with before and many went on to high stations in life and became government officials themselves.

Chittagong CS offered one of the best educations in the country. But my particular attraction to it was the encouragement it gave to boyscouting. The scout den of the Collegiate School became the hub of my many extra-curricular activities. Along with boys from other schools, we had drills, games, artistic pursuits, discussions, hikes in the countryside, camp life, variety shows around a camp-fire and big rallies. During 'earnings weeks' we raised money by hawking goods, polishing boots, working as tea-stall boys. Apart from the fun, scouting taught me to think high, to be compassionate, to be religious in my inner being if not in outward ritual and to cherish and help my fellow human beings.

It was scouting and my good grades which reconciled my father to my extra-curricular activities. He gave me all the funds required by my scouting adventures and began to have an unshakeable confidence in me. Later on in life he always backed me 100 per cent in whatever venture I undertook.

I especially recall a train trip across India on the way to the First Pakistan National Boyscout Jamboree in 1953, when we stopped to visit important historical sites and relics. The journey became a time-travel through our history, almost a pilgrimage to meet our own true selves. Most of the time we sang and played, but standing in front of the Taj Mahal in Agra, I caught our assistant headmaster, Quazi Sirajul Huq, a man beloved by his students, weeping silently. The tears were not for the monument, nor for the famous lovers who are buried there, nor for the poetry etched on the monument in white marble, no. He said he was weeping for our destiny, the burden of history that we were carrying and not knowing what to do with it.

I was only thirteen, but I was infected by his passionate imagination. Quazi Sahib became my friend, philosopher and guide for life. With his encouragement, scouting began to take over all my other activities. I was a natural leader, and Quazi Sahib soon let me set the pace. I made many of my life friends in the movement, one of whom, Mahbub, worked with me later in the Grameen Bank. But Quazi Sahib electrified my imagination. He had a sublime moral influence on all of us in his care. He taught us always to aim high, and he channelled our passions and restlessness. He did not do this through preaching, but through deeds and heart-to-heart communication which had a lifelong effect on me.

In 1973, in the chaotic days following the Bangladesh Liberation war, I visited him with my father and my brother Ibrahim, and we discussed the turmoil and difficulties through which we were living. A month later, Quazi Sahib, then a frail old man, was brutally murdered in his sleep by his servant, just to rob him of a small sum of money. In those turbulent times, they never caught the murderer. Like everyone who knew him, I was devastated. In retrospect, I understood his tears at the Taj Mahal as prophetic of the suffering that fate had in store for him and his people.

5

Campus Years in the US, 1965–72

For as long as I can remember I have thought of myself as a teacher, and I still do even today. My younger brothers recall that I loved teaching them, and that I insisted that they get only top grades in school. And if my younger siblings did not do well they had to come and answer to me why they were not doing as well as they should.

After finishing high school in 1955, I enrolled myself in Chittagong College where I spent the most exciting two years of my life. I could almost write a separate book on those two years. In 1957 I went to study at Dhaka University, but the four years that I spent there were uneventful and dull. Upon graduating from university in 1961, at the age of twenty-one, I was given a teaching post in my old college at Chittagong. Chittagong College was started by the British in 1936 and was one of the most highly respected in the subcontinent. I remained there from 1961 until 1965, teaching economics to students who were almost as old as myself.

During this time I tried my hand at private business. I noted that all packaging materials had to be brought from western Pakistan, that we in the eastern half of the country had no capacity to make boxes or wrapping material. So I persuaded my father to give his consent to set up a packaging and printing plant. I prepared the project proposal and applied for a loan from the government-owned Industrial Bank. We were among the rare Bengali entrepreneurs who wanted to invest in order to set up an industrial unit. Our loan was immediately approved.

I went through all the hassles of setting up the packaging and printing plant, employing a hundred workers. The biggest packaging industry was located in Lahore, in West Pakistan. But as a nationalist Bengali, I knew we could manufacture it more cheaply in East Pakistan. Our products included: cigarette packages, boxes, cartons, cosmetics boxes, cards, calendars and books. This turned out to be a successful project, making a very attractive profit.

Earning money had never been a concern or a worry of mine. I was never really tempted to become a businessman, but the packaging factory was a way of proving to myself and to my family that I could be a commercial success if I wished.

My father was the chairman of the board, and I was the chief executive officer. My father was extremely reluctant to have us borrow from a bank. He comes from the old school that did not believe in commercial credit. Having a bank loan outstanding made him so nervous and so worried that he made me pay the loan back early. We were probably the only start-up business that ever repaid a loan before it became due. When I went to repay the bank, they offered us a 10 million *taka* loan for setting up a paper plant, but my father would not hear of it.

This experience gave me a lot of self-confidence. It confirmed my belief as a young man that I had no need to worry about money. I was teaching half the time, and being a businessman the other half.

* * *

I dearly loved teaching. So when I got the opportunity to get a Ph.D. in America I jumped at the chance to go there on a Fulbright scholarship.

This was my third trip abroad. The first two times had been as a boyscout. I had gone to the World Jamboree in Niagara, Canada, in 1955 and to Japan and the Philippines in 1959. But this time I was a grown man and I was on my own. And my arrival that summer of 1965 at the University of Colorado campus in Boulder was quite an experience for me.

In Bangladesh, students were so respectful one never dared call one's professor by his first name. One barely dared to address him at all. If one spoke to 'sir', it was only after one had been invited by 'sir' to speak, and even then one spoke in enormously respectful terms. But in America, teachers considered themselves friends and helpers to the students. I often saw faculty and students sprawled out on the lawn barefoot, sharing food, joking, chatting, calling each other by their first names, inviting each other to their homes. Such familiarity was totally unthinkable in Bangladesh.

And as for the young co-eds in Colorado, well I was so shy and embarrassed I did not know where to look. At Chittagong College, female students were still in the minority. Out of a student body of 800, no more than 150 were women. In addition, the girls were very much segregated. Their participation in student politics or in other activities was rather limited. For instance, when we staged a college play, none of the women was allowed on stage, so the boys, wearing women's dress and make-up, played the roles of the women characters in the play. The co-eds were usually confined to the 'women's common room' which was a rather protected area, off-limits to male students.

My female students were extremely shy. When it was time for class, all female students would wait in a group just outside the teachers' common room. And when the teacher came out, without greeting them or even looking at their faces, he would walk to his classroom, and the girls would follow clutching their books and looking down at their feet so as to avoid the stares of the boys. Out of respect for the teacher none of the boys dared interfere with the girls or talk to them.

Our co-eds would sit together in the classroom apart from the boys. They did not mix with the boys at all. As a teacher I avoided asking them questions that would embarrass them in front of the boys. Still, my style was to get to know all my students. At the beginning of each school year, I would memorize their names so that I could develop a personal rapport with them. When class was over, the girls followed me, again in single file, one by one, with their books clutched to their bosom, again staring down at the ground. I never in any way talked to them outside the classroom.

So imagine my dismay arriving in America in the summer of 1965: the campus was alive with rock music; girls would sit on the lawn with their shoes off, sunning themselves, laughing, talking. I was so shy, I dared not speak to any of them, or even look at them. Americans were beginning to experiment with drugs. Alcohol was rife. I never touched drink. It was not out of any great forbearance, but my personality led me to shy away from any parties or places where the behaviour was too raucous. Nor did I study an enormous amount. What I loved best was discovering America itself.

Television appeared in Dhaka only in 1964. Before arriving in America, I had only watched it in friends' houses. But once in the US, I soon became addicted to it. One of my favourite shows was the magazine programme *Sixty Minutes*, but I watched every silly sitcom there was, *I Love Lucy*, *Gilligan's Island, Hogans' Heroes*. I loved the idiot box. I found I could talk and think clearly while my eyes were glued to the box. But if the TV was off, I could not work at all. And that is true even today.

This was at the height of the Vietnam war, and along with other foreign students, I quite naturally joined anti-war rallies and protest marches. But I was extremely shy and never made any speeches.

At sixteen, I had been elected general secretary of the United Students' Progressive Party. This party was confined to our own college, Chittagong College, but it was a dominant party with a good chance of winning the election for the students' union. We were against the government of the day which was oppressively conservative and exploited the religious sentiment of the people, but this did not mean I was ready to take orders from the highly regimented and secretive underground ultra-left party which controlled us as one of their front organizations. On the contrary.

With the support of my central committee, I engineered a *coup d'état* within my student party, and ousted senior functionaries who were manipulating us. It had been quite a feather in my cap to be general secretary, but to use the post to challenge the status quo created a political bombshell in student politics, which sent ripples all through the Chittagong District. Ever since then I had always tried to steer an independent course.

So although while in America I voiced my opposition to the Vietnam war, I always tried to keep an open mind and not merely to spout what was fashionable or to veer into group-think.

What I loved best about the campus at Boulder was the student centre. I could spend hours there watching the students come and go, chatting, laughing out loud, eating, wearing their crazy clothes. The youth of America looked so strong and healthy and full of vitality.

My leftist Bengali friends hated me for my positive opinions about America, but I did not let that bother me. Back in Dhaka there was a lot of anti-American sentiment. Every student on every one of our campuses was calling the US dirty capitalists, and shouting, 'Yankee Go Home!'

But I wrote back to my friends at home: 'The United States is a beautiful country. My life would have been unfulfilled if I had not come here and seen this place, and experienced the personal freedom they enjoy here.'

I was having fun. My studies were going well. I even found time to learn square-dancing, but that was my only experience with dancing. I never tried the Twist, rock'n'roll or slow-dancing. All the other students were, it seemed to me, expert at these, but I was hopeless. I could not even do the minimum part, and I preferred not to go anywhere near a party where there was dancing or carousing. And while I learned to accept that not everyone who drinks is necessarily bad, I never partook of any. I never had any desire to.

Little everyday incidents made big impressions on me. I will never forget entering a restaurant in Boulder and having the waitress say, 'Hi, my name is Cheryl', and giving me a big smile and a glass of water with a lot of ice in it. No one in my country or in South Asia would ever treat you so openly and in such a forthright manner.

The students in our group, West Pakistanis, Latin Americans, Africans were busy charming Cheryl, making small talk with her, calling her 'Hey sweety', and she not only appreciated this banter but handed it right back. I was aghast. Of course there was no question of me doing the same, I was even too shy to look her in the eye. Even listening to the other boys behave like this was extremely uncomfortable for me.

As for American food, I missed my mother's spicy cooking, and as much as I liked French fries and beefburgers, and potato chips, and ketchup, I was heartily bored with American food, and I would have given anything in the world to eat rice and dal, or a Bangladeshi sweetmeat.

Cheryl asked me, 'How would you like your eggs?'

'What do you mean?' I said.

'You want them fried, scrambled, hardboiled, poached, in an omelette?'

'Fried.'

'How would you like them?'

'What do you mean, how would I like them? I just told you.'

'You want them sunny side up or turned over?'

'I don't care.'

By this time all my fellow students were giving me lip, laughing at my indecision, trying to explain to Cheryl that in eastern Bengal people are different.

'Oh well, sunny side up,' I said at last, embarrassed at my indecision and at making a public spectacle of myself.

'You want them well done or wet?'

'Whatever.'

'With toast, muffins or bread?'

'I don't care.'

'You have a choice of side orders: fries, hash browns or mashed potatoes.'

I thought for a while she might be doing this on purpose just to make me look more ridiculous in front of all the others. But later I realized this was the American way – endless choice.

'You want sausage links, ham or bacon?'

The list went on and on, but with the other boys teasing me for my indecisiveness and for my blushing embarrassment, I was sorely tempted to say, 'Look I can cook the eggs myself!'

But I was far too polite and shy to voice any resistance to the onslaught of questions. And I never fully adapted to American openness. I was so timid, I began dreading restaurants.

* * *

After a summer in Boulder, surrounded by students from many different countries, and on a beautiful campus full of sunlight, my scholarship required me to attend Vanderbilt University in Tennessee. Here, I had a completely different experience. Arriving in Nashville, I was so depressed I was almost in tears. It was such a tiny insignificant airport and there was no student campus like the one I had so enjoyed at Boulder. The city looked so unattractive after the wide-open grand vistas of Boulder.

Vanderbilt had only recently been desegregated, and the tiny restaurant I used, The Campus Grill, had been 'whites only' until six months previously. There were few foreign students, and no Bengalis. I was lonely and homesick. The winter was cold, and I was not at all prepared for it. My dormitory, Wesley Hall, was so bad we quickly named it 'Wesley Hell'. It was old and smelly and the heating pipes banged and knocked all night long. The showers were old-fashioned open stalls. But I was so shy and prudish, I could not possibly undress and shower in front of all those strangers. (Even today I would be shocked by such a thing.) So I took my shower wearing a lungi, a full-length skirt to cover the body from the waistline down, as people do in Bangladesh when they take a bath.

I was the only Fulbright scholar at Vanderbilt that year. The first semester classes bored me. My graduate programme in economic development was a 'light master's', superficial compared to the far more advanced master's degree I already had. One teacher of European history actually failed me because he wanted me to spout back exactly what he had said.

After that I was extremely fortunate: they put me in advanced economics classes and switched me onto Ph.D. courses. The one thing which made my stay at Vanderbilt worthwhile was my association with a famous Romanian professor by the name of Nicholas Georgescu-Roegen.

He was known on campus for giving terrible marks. He failed many students. The usual forecast about his marking was, 'when he is extremely polite to you then you should know he is about to "murder" you'. If anyone ever got as much as a B from him, then other students whispered behind his back, 'He got a B from Georgescu.' He had given an A once to a Korean student and that was the only time in living memory.

It was rumoured on campus that he ruined many students' lives, and students generally would not dare cross his path.

I was most fortunate in having such a difficult and unforgiving task master for I don't think I ever had a better teacher.

I now realized that I had previously just memorized formulae by rote. After one two-hour lecture by Professor Georgescu-Roegen, the scales fell from my eyes. It was beautiful how the charm of knowledge just came to me. Through him, I realized there was no need for formulae, one first had to understand the concept. I admired Georgescu-Roegen enormously.

I learned from him certain simple lessons that I never forgot, and which stood me in good stead when building up Grameen.

Though Professor Georgescu-Roegen became my mentor, I can't say we had a close or warm relationship. He was an old-fashioned European teacher who kept his distance. The books he wrote were much too erudite, impossible to understand, but he spoke clearly and concisely. He was a mathematician, a philosopher and had been finance minister of Romania until 1948, when he had to leave and seek political asylum in the United States. He spoke so beautifully that, taken word for word, his classes were a work of art. I studied advanced statistics with him as well as economic theory and Marxism, and he gave me straight As.

As his teaching assistant, I learned to respect precise models which showed me how certain concrete plans can help us understand and construct the future.

I also learned that things are never as complicated as we imagine them to be. It is only our arrogance which seeks to find complicated answers to simple problems.

6

Marriage and the War of
Liberation, 1967–71

I married Vera Forostenko in 1970.

When I left for my Fulbright scholarship in America, I had no intention of finding an American wife. If and when the issue of marriage arose, I assumed that I would marry the way everybody around me had married. The marriage would be arranged by my elders. This may strike Westerners as old-fashioned, but that is our traditional way. I never questioned the propriety of arranged marriages.

In addition, I had no experience of women, and I was terribly shy around them. We are quite prudish and conservative in Bangladesh in general, and all the more so in Chittagong District which is one of the more religious in the country. Until I married I was a total innocent in matters of the heart. And in my family we never discussed intimate things openly.

In 1967, I was seated in the Vanderbilt library one day, reading, when a beautiful girl with shoulder-length red hair and blue eyes came up to me and asked where I was from.

'Pakistan,' I said, rather nervously.

She was friendly, spontaneous and curious about me and my background. Her name was Vera Forostenko, and she was doing her master's work in Russian literature.

Vera was born in the USSR, but she and her family came to America soon after the Second World War. They settled in Trenton, New Jersey.

I had no plans to stay in the US. As much as I admired America, I often felt I was in a prison there because it was not my real life. I wanted to be helping people back home.

Although I had no idea what I would do when I returned to Bangladesh, I always felt I had some sort of mission to fulfil. Studying in America, I felt useless, a vegetable, just sitting in class getting good marks, marks which had no practical application, and I saw this as fulfilling my prison sentence before I could go home.

Because of the expense of the trip, I did not travel to Bangladesh for the holidays, but instead, during the summer, I taught at the University of Colorado in Boulder. My long absence made me all the more eager to return home.

Many of my friends were just the opposite. They were busy exploring ways to extend their visas in order to stay in America.

* * *

I first came face to face with racism in America in the house of an elite local family. The lady of the house said to me, 'Researchers have found that the IQ of blacks is lower than that of whites.'

I stared at her and said, 'What if I told you that the IQ of women is lower than that of men?'

'Do you mean that as an insult?' she said.

'No, but the problem with research is that the questions they are putting are in themselves stupid, or are loaded.'

'You think the researchers are racists?'

'Maybe, maybe not. But researchers might prove that the IQ of the north is lower than that of the south. Or that men over five-feet tall create more crime than men under five-feet tall.'

What surprised me is that in spite of such racism, I felt at home in the United States. Here even the immigration officers treated you like an equal. Everyone in America (except Native Americans) was at one point or another an immigrant, so unlike Europe, even though they might hate you or dislike your colour, no American questioned your right to be there.

In 1969, Vera left Tennessee and moved back to her family's home in New Jersey. I was already making plans to return to Bangladesh.

'I want to come and live with you there,' Vera said.

'You can't,' I said. I was extremely stubborn, almost as stubborn as her. 'It's a tropical country. A different culture. Women there are not treated as they are here.'

'But I will adapt,' she said.

She kept on writing to me and calling to discuss this issue. Every time I found a reason why such a marriage would not work, she would find a counter-reason.

Finally, I changed my mind.

We were married in 1970 and started to live in Murfreesboro, fifty miles south of Nashville where I was teaching at the time at Middle Tennessee State University.

* * *

On 25 March 1971, the Liberation War broke out in Bangladesh, and our plans to return there were abandoned. Immediately, I devoted myself to the cause of the liberation.

Like all Bengalis everywhere I was keeping a close watch on the events in Dhaka. That fateful day, I came back to my apartment to have my lunch and turned on the radio to get the latest news. There was a brief item stating that the Pakistani army had moved in to stop the political opposition against the government of Pakistan, and that Sheikh Mujibur Rahman, leader of the movement, had fled.

I was changing my clothes. I stopped, rushed to the phone and called Dr Zillur at Nashville. I asked him to turn on the radio. I told him I was coming to his house immediately, and that he should contact all other Bengalis.

Within an hour I was at Zillur's house. At that time there were six Bengalis from East Pakistan in greater Nashville (including myself). We all assembled in his house to decide what to do. We carried on collecting the news from all sources. The message was clear: the Pakistan army wanted to crush Bengalis once and for all.

We collected all the information we could. We were terribly frustrated. We tried to sum up the situation and come to some decision. There was no clear consensus on the situation. One of us, a supporter of the conservative pro-Islamic Jamaat party, kept on saying, 'We really don't know what has happened. Let us wait for more details.'

Finally, I could not take it any more and said, 'We have all the details we need. Bangladesh has declared its independence. Now we have to decide whether we consider ourselves citizens of this new country or not. Everybody has the right to choose. I declare my choice. My choice is Bangladesh. I declare my allegiance to Bangladesh. If there is any one else who would like to join me in this, he is free to do so. Those who do not join Bangladesh, I will consider them Pakistanis and enemies of Bangladesh.'

There was silence. Everyone was taken aback by the way I posed the question of allegiance. It was such a charged situation that soon everybody opted for Bangladesh. I suggested that we form a 'Bangladesh Citizens' Committee' and issue a press release immediately for the Nashville print and electronic media.

We decided three things right away:

1. We would try to meet all the news reporters of the local TV stations, and the editors of local daily newspapers to explain our decision and seek support for the Bangladesh cause.
2. We would immediately put $1000 each to create a fund to carry on the struggle.
3. We would put 10 per cent of our salary in the fund every month until Bangladesh became independent. If needed, we would increase the percentage.

Everybody pulled out their cheque-book to write cheques. Those who did not have any, borrowed from others to make the first deposit.

On the next day (27 March), we made appointments with local TV stations and dailies. I was elected secretary of the Bangladesh Citizens' Committee and spokesperson for the group. Local TV stations never get a chance to develop international news stories, so they received us with enthusiasm. For them we represented red-hot international news with a local angle to it. I was a teacher in a local university; the other five were medical doctors in city hospitals, and here we were – declaring ourselves citizens of a country not yet born. What an exciting news item!

We were interviewed by the dailies. Our pictures were taken.

We were also interviewed by all the three local TV channels. We then re-assembled at Zillur's house in the afternoon to watch the evening news. Our guess was right – we were treated with importance. My interview was telecast in full during the local news. The interviewer asked, 'Do you have a message for the Tennesseans?' 'Yes, I do,' I said. 'Please write to your congressmen, write to your senators immediately to stop military aid to Pakistan. Your arms and ammunitions are being used to kill innocent unarmed civilians of Bangladesh. Please ask your president to put pressure on Pakistan to stop genocide in Bangladesh.'

I felt good that we had taken some quick action and that all six of us, from differing political tendencies and socio-economic backgrounds had agreed. We now wanted to know what was going on with other Bengalis around the US. We decided to contact a Bengali official inside the Pakistan embassy. I didn't know anybody. Someone then told me that the second-highest ranking Pakistani in the embassy was a Bengali – Mr Enayet Karim.

I decided to call him. He gave me some important news: there would be a demonstration against the Pakistani army's crackdown on civilians on 29

March on Capitol Hill in Washington, DC. He urged us to join it. He said that the biggest group of Bengalis would come from New York, which was where Bengalis were concentrated.

After the telephone conversation we sat down to discuss the demonstration. My doctor friends could not go, because of their responsibilities at the hospitals. I announced that I would go the next day.

It was decided that I would got at my own expense. The $6000 we had already raised would be given to me to make appropriate use of it while I was in Washington.

Where would I stay in Washington? I didn't know anybody. Enayet Karim sounded like a friendly person. Why not try him? I called him again. I proposed to be his guest the next day – would he mind? He immediately accepted my proposal and said, 'Come right over.'

I was surprised by his openness. He didn't know me, but the crisis had brought all us Bengalis together. We were suddenly one big family.

Until midnight we tried to monitor every single radio station in the world on Zillur's giant short-wave radio. Everyone of us showed off our great skill in taming the radio, and interpreting strange languages around the world. Between the news items we ate all kinds of delicious food continuously supplied by Zillur's American wife Joanne, while we speculated on what might have happened to Sheikh Mujib. Finally, the news came that he had been arrested at Chittagong railway station while he was fleeing from the army (he was actually arrested at his house in Dhaka). We were in tears after hearing the news. Until then we were making up all kinds of scenarios in which Sheikh Mujib was guiding the nation at war from some underground bunker. All the nation needed was his live voice over the radio – Pakistan had no chance against his voice, with all their sophisticated fire-power.

Now what would the Pakistan army do with him? Bring him back to Dhaka and execute him by firing squad? Hang him? Torture him to death?

28 March 1971: With a heavy heart and mindful of all our unanswered questions, I left Murfreesboro in the early hours of 28 March for Washington, DC. I arrived at Enayet Karim's beautiful house in the afternoon. The whole family was very happy to see me. Mrs Karim immediately set the table and soon we discovered that both of us were natives of Chittagong which added some intimacy to our relationship.

I quickly became a family member – that was surprising to me in the context of my experience with government officials who preferred to keep to themselves. The next surprising thing was that everybody was sharing their thoughts as if everybody's opinion mattered. Telephone calls kept coming in. Some were local calls. Some were calls from distant Pakistani embassies around the world; Bengali officials were contacting their counterparts in Washington, trying to find some policy guideline. People were dropping by with messages or questions. It was a busy house.

What excited me was the atmosphere within the house. It felt like part of an already independent Bangladesh. There was no trace of Pakistan in the minds of those inside the house.

While I was enjoying this intoxicating freedom, I noticed a serious-looking man busy writing something. He was Mr S. A. Karim, the deputy permanent representative of Pakistan at the United Nations, who had arrived from New York that morning. Eventually, he wanted to read out what he had written. Everybody became quiet and gathered around him. He had just finished drafting an appeal to all heads of governments around the world to put pressure on Pakistan to stop genocide in Bangladesh. As I listened to the appeal I admired the author's drafting skill.

I kept trying to find out who was in charge of the following day's demonstration on Capitol Hill. What preparations were being made? How could I help? I did not want the demonstration to be a poor show. Was somebody preparing posters, festoons to hold up in front of the TV cameras? Nobody in Enayet Karim's house knew. I thought I should take some initiative myself. I went to a department store and bought stacks of coloured papers, poster colours and brushes. Immediately I prepared as many festoons as I could.

Everybody was surprised to see me doing this. I could feel my spectators had genuine admiration for my work. Writing posters was a skill I had acquired in Chittagong College while I was a student. I was good at it. The skill came in very handy. But brushes were no substitute for *bidi** in creating bold messages, and I missed them.

Shamsul Bari arrived; he was teaching Bangla at Chicago University. I had known him from a distance during our university days in Dhaka. The Liberation war brought us close. We worked together during the entire period of the war.

By evening more people came. All Bengali officials and their families visited Enayet Karim's house at one time or another – some worried about their families in Bangladesh, some tried to find out more information on the Dhaka situation and what needed to be done.

Bidi in Bangla is a kind of hand-made cigarette; instead of wrapping tobacco with a thin piece of paper, it is wrapped in a leaf to make a '*bidi*'.

A new face showed up – a young doctor from Comilla who had arrived in the US less than a year ago – Dr Hasan Chowdhury, from Missouri. He did not know anybody in Washington and did as I had done – he came to Enayet Karim's house and found the doors open to everyone.

The night was spent analysing the situation, and deciding on the strategy for the next day: first, to deliver the 'appeal' to all embassies to be sent to their heads of government; and second, the demonstration on Capitol Hill.

The events in Dhaka had brought three unknown guests to Enayet Karim's house: Shamsul Bari, Hasan Chowdhury, and myself. Mrs Karim treated us as if we were her dearest friends. She kept feeding us while alternately cursing the Pakistani army and reciting Tagore poems.

29 March 1971: I woke up in the morning to some shouting in the house. I tried to understand who was shouting at whom and why, got up, dressed quickly and entered the room where the shouting was taking place. It was around 7 a.m., and I saw a short skinny person with a beard shouting at the top of his voice at Mr Karim who was sitting quietly and listening. It was a very small ante-room, packed with a further five or six people.

I immediately became angry at the person who was shouting at Mr Karim. How dare he treat our good host like this? Who was he anyway? Who were the other people? Who was this tiny man?

Mr Karim tried to explain in a calm voice whenever he could find a way to make himself heard, but the tiny visitor wouldn't listen to anything. He was accusing Mr Karim and all the embassy officials of being 'traitors'. The rest of the people in the room all wore buttons which said 'BANGLADESH' in bold letters.

They had come from Boston, from Harvard and other institutions, and had been driving all through the early hours of that morning. They came straight to Mr Karim's as we had done before. They had come to Washington to join the demonstration on Capitol Hill and inquired about the arrangements as soon as they arrived. During the briefing they found out that Bengali embassy officials had decided not to join the demonstration. That did it. The tiny person – who became one of my closest friends, Dr Mohiuddin Alamgir, a fresh Ph.D. from Harvard – spared no harsh words in attacking Mr Karim. I tried to defend him explaining to Alamgir and his friends that we had discussed the matter on the previous night and were convinced it was a good strategy to stay inside government in high positions so that the Pakistanis would not be free to use the power of the government against the Bengalis in East Pakistan at their will. As embassy officials they would have contacts with the high officials in the US state department and could brief them on the real situation.

Alamgir shouted back by saying that this was only 'sweet talk' by cowards who did not want to join the cause of liberation, who were only busy protecting their cushy lifestyle.

The meeting ended with frustration on both sides. But the issue Alamgir raised did not leave us until 4 August 1971 when Bengali diplomats of the Pakistan embassy defected and joined the Bangladesh government in exile.

That afternoon, we all gathered at the steps of the US House of Congress to demonstrate. I brought all my festoons. Bengalis came from distant places. Washington and New York had the biggest groups until Bengalis from Detroit arrived. I was surprised to see so many Bengalis from Detroit. Most of them were Sylheti workers from Detroit factories.

Nobody knew what was to be done, or who the organizers were. We could not begin our demonstration because we did not have the permission. Fazlul Bari, an employee of the embassy, had applied for permission, but the decision of the Bengali officials not to participate in the demonstration meant that he himself could not go to receive it. Luckily he found another Bari, Shamsul Bari, to help him out and appear to receive it in his place.

We were still wondering how to organize ourselves when Shamsul Bari showed up with the permission. I shouted at the top of my voice: 'Here is our leader. Let's now line up behind him and start our demonstration.'

It worked like magic. The demonstration on the steps of Capitol Hill was a grand affair. We were noticed by US legislators. Congressional aides took time to be briefed on the situation and our demands. The news media was specially active; television cameras covered the rally and took on-the-spot interviews, and news reporters had a field day.

We all met in the evening to decide on the future course of action at the residence of another official of the embassy, Mr A. M. A. Muhith, the economic counsellor. Mr Muhith was everywhere doing everything behind the scenes the whole day. At this grand assembly there was a heated debate on arrangements for the co-ordination of Bengali activities in the US and the immediate transfer of allegiance by Bengali diplomats. The shouting with which my day had begun, was repeated with more intensity at this grand assembly on the same issue – why weren't Bengali diplomats leaving the Pakistan embassy right then?

We left after dinner knowing that we had to find a way to co-ordinate the activities of all Bengalis in the US, convinced that the Bengali diplomats could no longer provide the necessary leadership, and doubtful about the arguments in favour of diplomats staying on with Pakistan.

30 March 1971: Shamsul Bari and I were given the responsibility of visiting all the embassies, meeting the ambassadors or their representatives, explaining our cause, and requesting recognition of Bangladesh as an independent state.

It was a very interesting experience for both of us. We went to many embassies in one day. Each embassy had its own style of receiving us. But there were many common questions: 'Whom do you represent? Do you have a US-based organization? How can you talk about 'recognizing' your country if you don't have a government? Is there any foreign government who is supporting you? What is the position of your diplomats in the USA? Are they supporting you? When are they going to come out in the open? What proportion of the population in 'East Pakistan' want an independent Bangladesh?'

We could give convincing answers to all the questions except one: 'Do you have a government of your own?'

Here we were so enthusiastically asking the world to recognize Bangladesh, and we now found out that this couldn't be considered unless we had a government of our own.

Bari and I decided that we had to have our own government immediately. How can you form a government in Bangladesh while you are in Washington? Probably nobody inside Bangladesh was thinking about forming a government because by now all the leaders were either dead or in hiding.

I had an idea. Why didn't I fly to Calcutta, find a few people to form a cabinet and announce to the world that a Bangladesh government had been formed. Then we would have a country and a government. The issue of recognition could be pressed with vigour. Bari liked the idea. We made up our minds. That's what I would do tomorrow – go to Calcutta to form a government in exile.

I thought of another essential strategy – a radio station to broadcast programmes for Bangladesh, so that the people inside Bangladesh knew what was going on and what they had to do.

A radio transmitter, I thought, should be mounted on a vehicle. It should go inside Bangladeshi territory and broadcast programmes and return to the Indian side of the border whenever chased by the Pakistani army.

I made up my mind. I had $6000. I thought this could be the down payment for a transmitter. It would be a worthy cause to spend the money on.

We had some special discussions with the embassies of three countries. We told the embassy of Burma that we wanted to keep their border open to anybody fleeing from the Pakistani army. Co-operation with the Pakistani army we would consider as an unfriendly act. We would try to find funds for feeding the refugees from Bangladesh. They need not worry about any financial burden on them.

We communicated to the embassy of Sri Lanka that Sri Lanka should refuse to allow landing rights to all Pakistani military and civilian flights between Bangladesh and Pakistan. Pakistan was carrying army personnel, arms and ammunition in civilian flights from Karachi to Dhaka. The Sri Lanka representative was very apologetic. He said that the embassy's power to influence government policy was very limited. But he would definitely communicate the feeling of the Bangladeshi community in the US to his government. He advised us to keep up the pressure on Sri Lanka. The Sri Lanka government had to find a strong reason to change its policies.

The Soviet embassy seemed to know a lot about the Bangladesh situation. They knew all the leftist politicians, and wanted to know if we knew anything about their views on an independent Bangladesh and whether they too, particularly Moulana Bhashani, were strong advocates of an independent state. If they were, USSR would seriously consider supporting an independent Bangladesh.

In the Indian embassy we were treated like highly placed diplomats. They wanted to know about Bengali diplomats in the Pakistan embassy, about the whereabouts of our leaders, whether we had established any contact with them, whether we had a US-based organization. We wanted them to open their border to refugees, to provide free access to Calcutta for expatriate Bangladeshis to be able to visit the city any time they wanted; and a total relaxation of the rules surrounding Indian visas for Bengalis with Pakistani passports.

That night we had an exciting discussion about setting up a government. We slightly rearranged the earlier plan. As we worked out the details it was decided that Hasan should leave immediately for Calcutta and Agartala to make initial contacts with the political leaders who had fled from Bangladesh. He would then send the signal for me to arrive to form the government.

That night Aga Hilali, the Pakistani ambassador, came on a courtesy visit to his number two, Enayet Karim. As soon as it was known that he was coming, three of us who were taking dinner were quickly pushed into the roof-top attic with our food. We sat there for two hours without making a sound, so that the ambassador could not know that his Bengali colleague was harbouring three dangerous anti-state elements in his own house. The ambassador was inquiring politely whether any of Mr Karim's relatives were hurt in the army action in Dhaka.

* * *

Hasan left for Calcutta and Agartala the next day, as planned. From Calcutta, he sent a bitter message of disappointment in the leaders and advised me not to come. Soon the Mujibnagar government was formed. Bengalis in the USA and Canada concentrated on the campaign for Bangladeshi recognition, on stopping military aid to Pakistan and genocide in Bangladesh, and on freeing Sheikh Mujib.

Mahmud Ali, Consul General in New York, defected on 26 April 1971. He became our instant hero. His wife took up a small job to support the family.

The Bangladesh League of America was working from New York under the leadership of Dr Mohammad Alamgir, and the Bangladesh Defense League was created by Dr F. R. Khan in Chicago. Shamsul Bari became its secretary general. He published the first issue of the *Bangladesh Newsletter*. I took it over from him and started publishing the newsletter regularly from my Nashville apartment at 500 Paragon Mills Road. My apartment virtually became the communication centre. The phone would never stop ringing whenever I returned from my long campaigning trips. Calls came from all over North America and the UK. All Bengalis in North America wanted to know every detail of the war every day.

Through the efforts of the Bengalis in Washington, a 'Bangladesh Information Center' was set up near the hill to do the lobbying in the House and the Senate. I took up the responsibility of running the Information Center for the initial period and then went on the road to organize teach-in workshops in university campuses all over the United States, where we also set up Friends of Bangladesh Committees.

During those nine months we drew a very clear picture of the future Bangladesh in our minds, which became sharper and more vivid with each passing day. We wanted to uphold democracy, to establish the majesty of the will of the people which would be expressed in a free and fair election. We wanted to ensure people's right to fashion their lives as they wanted. We wanted people to be free from poverty. We dreamed of a life of happiness and prosperity for all citizens.

We dreamed of a nation which would stand with dignity among all other nations in the world.

* * *

When on 16 December 1971, Bangladesh won its war of independence, I was eager to return and help rebuild my country. The war had taken a heavy toll. Three million Bangladeshis were killed, ten million had left the country to find safety in neighbouring India and this created enormous refugee camps of misery and destitution. Millions more became victims of rape and other atrocities committed by the Pakistani army. By the time the war was over, Bangladesh was a devastated country. The economy was totally shattered. Millions of people needed to be rehabilitated.

I felt that I had to go back and participate in the nation-building. I thought I owed it to myself.

7

Chittagong University, 1972–74

I returned from America in 1972, full of idealism and dreams, bathed in the nirvana of the Western world's rational approach to all problems. I was now more at ease with all the West's social ways and consumer goods; I watched hours of TV a day while working on complex equations.

I was convinced that if East Pakistan could keep its resources rather than being a colony of West Pakistan, our economic situation would quickly improve.

When I returned, I saw bravery and determination among the ruins of war. There were difficulties in every direction, and people faced them resolutely. But as months and years went by, hopes turned into disillusionment. Instead of the country finding solutions, things were getting worse.

As soon as I came back, I was appointed to the government's planning commission, with a fancy title, but I had nothing to do all day except read the newspaper. I was a Ph.D. in economics, fresh from the United States, and the country was in dire need of economic development, and yet they had nothing for me to do.

After repeated protests to the chief of the planning commission, Nurul Islam, my former professor at Dhaka University (at whose insistence I joined the planning commission), I resigned and became head of the economics department at Chittagong University.

* * *

The university campus is located twenty miles east of Chittagong city on 1900 acres of barren hills. Some hills were chopped off at the top to accommodate large red-brick modern buildings for the vice-chancellor of the university, the registrar, and a couple of university professors. Each occupied one hilltop building. On a slice of plain land at the edge of the hills sat the classroom buildings, the dormitories and the teachers' housing.

Built in the mid-1960s and designed by the top architect of Bangladesh, the university had all the amenities of modern construction. Everything was built in exposed red brick, with lots of open corridors. Extremely impressive buildings, but while pleasing to the eye, they were not at all utilitarian. When I started teaching there, I soon found out how impractical all the internal arrangements were. For instance, there was a huge office for the head of the department, but no offices for any of the teachers. One of the first things I did as head of the economics department was to convert the department head's office into a common room for all teachers. I moved my own office into a small room. This made everybody unhappy. They wanted the head to sit in a big room, even if others had nowhere to sit at all.

It was a difficult time at the university. Teachers were refusing to mark examination papers because the students had ignored all the rules and simply copied their answers from books and from each other. The teachers insisted that students should retake the exams, and the students were in no mood to do so. They argued that after returning from the Liberation war (which had just ended in December of the previous year), it was generous of them to have sat for any exams at all.

Many of the students were part of the *Mukti Bahini* (Liberation army) and had fought in the war. They still carried around their wartime guns threatening the teachers with dire consequences if exam results were not announced soon.

I took upon myself the task of mediating between the students and teachers to defuse this explosive situation.

I lived with my parents in town. My father allowed me to use his car to commute to the campus every day. Along the way I noticed how students and teachers were waiting for university buses to get to campus. I gave rides to some of them each day.

I tried to understand what the problem was and how I could make things better.

I discovered that because of a lack of on-campus housing, most students and teachers arrived in the morning and left on the 2 p.m. buses, and so all afternoon and night the university was largely deserted. This seemed to me to be a terrible waste of a great national asset and a shame. I immediately assembled a group of students to undertake a quick research into the problem. The report of our study was printed as a departmental monograph entitled, *Transport Problem at Chittagong University*. These findings were immediately published in the national newspapers. They quoted me as calling our campus 'The part-time university'. This created quite a sensation. I was interviewed by many reporters. No professor or school administrator had ever pointed this out before.

The secretary of education got in touch with me and asked for a copy of the report, which I prepared in detail, giving various solutions that needed to be undertaken in order to remedy the situation. Unfortunately they were not adopted. And the problem of the part-time university subsists today, twenty years later, even though a railway link has been established to bring students from town to the campus.

* * *

Every day I drove through the village of Jobra which stood between the highway and the campus. I saw barren fields next to the campus. I asked my colleague Professor Latifee the reason for not cultivating these lands for a winter crop. He made some guesses for he knew the village well. I proposed that both of us go to the village and talk to the people. We did and soon found the answer.

There was no water for irrigation.

I thought we should do something about it. It was a shame to let the land around a university campus remain barren. If a university is a repository of the world's knowledge, then some of this knowledge must spill over into the neighbourhood and demonstrate that it is indeed useful knowledge.

A university should not be an island where academics attain higher and higher levels of knowledge without sharing any of this knowledge with its neighbours.

* * *

Within a couple of months, I was allotted a house on campus: I was happy because I thought this would bring me closer to members of the community, and I could spend more time on campus.

Our campus housing faced part of the hill range, and every day I looked out over the denuded hills. From the classroom I could also watch the stream of small children, boys and girls, men and cattle walking through the campus to go up into the hills. In the morning as they went one could see them carrying sharp knives. At sunset, each person came down the hill carrying a load of twigs, or a tree that had grown on the hill.

I thought the university community could convert these barren hills into beautiful forests and grow many agricultural forest crops and fruits. This would bring income to the university, employment to the villagers and food and other consumer products to the country as a whole.

I felt strongly that the university should play a role in bringing change to the lives of the local villagers, and that the economics department should take the lead in this.

I wanted to understand the village. Most of what we educators knew about Bangladeshi villages was mere guesswork. No concrete information was available. I thought we should undertake a thorough survey of Jobra. Accordingly, I launched a project, with my students' help, to survey the village.

We wanted to find out:

How many of the families in the village owned cultivable land? How much land did each family have? What crops did they grow? How did landless people make a living? Who were the poor? What skills did the people have? What impediments did they see to improving their lives? How many families could grow food to feed themselves for the whole year? How many could not feed themselves for the whole year? How many months of food requirement could they grow? Ten months? Eight months? Six months? Less than six months? And so on.

I tried to understand Bangladesh by understanding Jobra. Jobra became my Bangladesh. This was the Bangladesh I could feel, I could touch. I could check everything I wanted to, and I could also attempt to make small changes.

* * *

Analyses of the causes of poverty focus largely on why some countries are poor, rather than why certain segments of the population live below the poverty line. Those economists who are socially concerned stress the absence of 'entitlements' of the poor. In spite of plentiful supplies of grain, even during times of famine, the poor have no access to the food. At a time when the most spectacular breakthroughs in science and technology are occurring and when human beings are able to walk on the moon, such human suffering and famine is morally unjustifiable.

What I did not yet know about hunger, I was to find out over the next twenty years, and what I said in Des Moines, Iowa, in my acceptance speech for the World Food Prize in 1994, was that:

Brilliant theories of economics do not take into account issues of poverty and hunger. They tend to imply that these problems will be resolved when the march of economic prosperity will sweep through the nations. Economists spend all their talents detailing the processes of development and prosperity, but none on the processes of poverty and hunger.

I feel very strongly that if the world recognizes poverty alleviation as an important and serious agenda, we can create a world that we can be proud of, rather than feel ashamed of, as we do now.

The 1974 famine dragged on and on, and the worse it became, the more I grew agitated. Unable to stand it any longer, I went to see the vice-chancellor of my university. He was the executive head of the university; the prime minister of the country was the titular chancellor, but had nothing to do with the day-to-day running of the campus.

Abul Fazal was a well-known national figure, an older man, a social commentator and novelist, considered by many to be the conscience of the new nation. He greeted me politely.

'What can I do for you, Yunus?' he said. A ceiling fan turned slowly overhead. Mosquitoes buzzed. His orderly brought tea.

'A lot of people are dying of starvation, yet everyone is afraid to say it.'

Old Abul Fazal nodded and said, 'What do you propose?'

'You are a very respected man, many call you "the conscience of the nation". I turn to you because no one has the guts to protest about what is going on.'

'What would you have me do?'

'Make a statement to the press.'

'Yes, but what?'

'A call to the nation and its leadership to act with full might to end the starvation. I am certain that every teacher on this campus will co-sign his name to your letter if you take the lead.'

'You think it would do some good?'

'It would help mobilize national opinion.'

'Yes.' He sipped his tea and said: 'Yunus, you write the statement, and I will sign it.' I smiled, 'You are the writer, you will know what words to put in the statement.'

'No, no, you do it, Yunus.'

'I am not a writer.'

'Yunus, you're passionate on this. You'll know what to say.'

'But I am only an economics professor. And this document should become a rallying cry, a call to action.'

The more I insisted that he was the perfect man to jolt the country and bring national attention to bear on this terrible famine, the more he encouraged me to write it. He pushed his point so strongly, that finally I had no alternative but to promise I would try a first draft.

That evening I wrote out a statement in long hand.

Then I brought the draft to the vice-chancellor and waited while he slowly read it.

When he was finished, Abul Fazal reached for his pen and said, 'Where do I sign?'

I was stunned: 'But, it is strongly worded, maybe you want to change some things, suggest other ideas.'

'No, no, no, it is excellent,' he said, and with that he signed on the spot.

I had no choice then: I signed the document as well, and I made copies of it and presented it to other faculty members. Many teachers raised objections to one word or another, but because the vice-chancellor had already signed, it carried the full weight of his prestige. All the teachers of Chittagong University ended up signing the declaration. We delivered it to the press, and the next day our statement was carried as a banner headline on the front pages of all the major newspapers.

Our letter started a chain reaction. A series of such calls poured from other universities and other public bodies that had not spoken out against the famine in the country.

* * *

I now focused on the task of unlearning theory, and on learning instead from the real world. I did not have to travel miles to find the real world. It was just outside the doors of the classrooms.

It was everywhere except inside the classroom.

8

Farming: The Three-Share Farm Experiment, 1974–76

The famine of 1974 focused all my efforts on farming.

Bangladesh, a territory of 35 million acres and one of the most densely populated in the world, needed to increase its food production. We had 21 million acres available for cultivation. In the rainy season we produced mainly rice and jute, but there was potential to increase our crops through an extension of irrigation and improved water management during the dry winter season. Specialists estimated that existing crop yields amounted to only 16 per cent of our farm yield potential.

* * *

I decided I should help the villagers of Jobra grow more food. How does one grow more food? Grow more in each crop cycle? Increase the number of times you plant a crop in each plot?

I was not an agronomist. But I made it my business to find out how to grow more in each cycle.

I sat down with my students and explained how important it was to replace the low-yielding local variety of rice with a high-yielding variety developed in the Philippines. We sat down with the farmers to tell them how important this was for them.

The farmers were amused. But we were very serious. We offered our free services to help them plant the high-yielding rice. University students and teachers became volunteer farmers. The whole village and the campus community watched us struggling to plant rice seedlings while knee-deep in mud. Who ever saw a university professor planting rice along with farmers? It was unheard of.

My students and I showed the farmers the importance of spacing each seedling at regular intervals and of planting in a straight line in order to optimize production and land yields. The local newspaper published photos of us, showing local farmers how to use a string to get the rice in a straight line. They laughed at us at first, and many students were contemptuous of my hands-on approach, but we helped quadruple rice production.

I kept looking for new ways for the university to make a difference in the community. My interests and concerns for local farming were entirely practical. An empiricist, I was willing to learn by my mistakes and those of others.

I was trying to bring the academic world and the village together though a university project I championed called the Chittagong University Rural Development Project (CURDP).

Some of my students recall that I was quite formal when I first took up my teaching duties in 1972. I used to require students to sign up if they wanted an appointment with me.

If that was the case, the CURDP which I headed broke down all the stiffness and all the age-old formal barriers that existed in Bangladesh between a university professor and his students.

By now I had almost completely abandoned traditional learning and was conceptualizing many CURDP programmes, including a mass literacy project. I encouraged my students to go down with me into the village and see how day-to-day life there could be improved. They could choose a topic and write a research paper for a course credit.

* * *

In the winter of 1975, my attention fell on solving the problem of irrigation in order to raise an extra winter crop.

When I drove in any direction during the monsoon season, I was struck by the fact that almost every square metre of land was under cultivation, including marshes which appear to be wasteland, but which produce rice and fish. Yet all these lands remained unused during the winter. Why not add a winter crop?

Every day, I noticed an unused deep tubewell sitting idle in the middle of uncultivated fields. It was the dry winter season, the season when the well should have been irrigating the land and allowing a new crop. But nothing was being done. It just sat there, brand new and unused.

When I questioned why the well was idle, I learned that the farmers were angry because during the previous dry season, they had fought with each other over the issue of collecting the money they were supposed to pay for water. They said they had to eat bitter rice, and they did not want any more bitter rice. Since then the farmers would have nothing to do with the deep tubewell, and that was why it sat idle. A waste of capital and of water.

This struck me as a terrible shame. In a country where a famine had just killed many people, here was a 300ft-deep well that could irrigate some 60 acres.

Of all the modes of irrigation then available, deep tubewells were the most capital intensive technology, and perhaps that is why they received the most generous support from the government and the donor community. (Manually operated tubewells, the least expensive and most suitable for the poorest households, have never been featured prominently in any of our government's plans.)

Because of their heavy operating costs, deep tubewells have proved highly inefficient, with corruption and wastage quite rampant in the use of the fuel oil, lubricants and spare parts necessary to make them work. So the problem I encountered at Jobra turned out to be not an exception, but a nationwide problem, and one that became ingrained into the system.

For a deep tubewell to operate efficiently, it needed an efficient water distribution system, and a large number of small farmers with fragmented holdings implementing uniform crop decisions. They needed technical expertise as to fertilizer, plant protection and repair and maintenance of the pumps. They also needed a market outlet for their produce. Coping with all this requires intense micro-level management.

Unfortunately, the government projects never established a link between the end-user and the deep tubewell technology. It was thought that once the deep tubewell was installed and working, that was it. The government, generously assisted by donor agencies, invested in modern irrigation technology, but no one invested time, resources or effort to resolve the people-centred issues.

Because of the perennial management problem, the farmers followed their natural reluctance to take additional risks.

Accordingly, almost half the deep tubewells sunk at the cost of millions of dollars had fallen out of use. The rusting machinery in abandoned pump houses was a testimony of a technology transfer initiative that was simply not relevant to the farmers. Yet another scandal, another failure of misguided development.

I came up with the idea of creating a new type of agricultural co-operative I named the *Nabajug* (New Era) Three-Share Farm.

I called a meeting of the local farmers. I proposed an experiment, in which the landowners would contribute the use of their land during the dry season, share-croppers would contribute their labour, and I would contribute all other costs including the cost of fuel to run the deep tubewell, the seeds for high-yielding crops, the fertilizer, the insecticide and the technical know-how: in exchange each of the three parties (farmer, share-croppers and myself) would receive one-third of the harvest.

The villagers were suspicious of my proposal at first. So much ill-will and distrust had built up between the well operators and the farmers, that they were not ready to listen to me or anyone else. They objected that they had no guarantee that my plan would work, that it could just be an enormous waste of time. Some argued that paying me one-third of the harvest would be paying too much; it should be one-fifth, not one-third! Even my offer to bear all losses and that if the project earned a profit they would divide it amongst themselves, failed to interest them. At this first meeting, they rejected my proposal.

At a second meeting, one week later, I was able to convince them that they had nothing to lose. They would receive irrigation water, fertilizer, seeds, insecticides, all without any upfront payment. All they had to do was to agree to surrender to me one-third of their harvest. Poor share-croppers thought it was a great idea. Rich farmers reluctantly agreed to give it a try. The entire village started buzzing with speculations about what would happen.

* * *

This was a trying period for me. I would lie awake at night, anxious lest anything should go wrong. But I was excited about the outcome, and I was sure that if properly implemented the plan would succeed. I was convinced this would be the solution to the irrigation management problem, but it was not easy.

Every Tuesday evening we visited the farmers and held a formal meeting with the four student 'block leaders' I had appointed as well as my thirteen-strong advisory team. We discussed and reviewed the problems of fertilizer, irrigation, technology, storage, transport and marketing.

Nothing is quite as beautiful as a farmer harvesting his rice. We were used to seeing this during the all-important monsoon harvest, around which rural life revolves, but now it was happening during the dry season.

With what eagerness our Bengali farmers put their energy and labour into sowing rice! They scatter the seed by hand, and new rice shoots up in no time. Then comes the meticulous back-breaking labour of transplanting the seedlings. But practice made this easier for the farmers than for us academics. We quickly forgot our academic egos and social differences as we stooped, ankle-deep in water, pressing in the seedlings.

With proper irrigation, the fields were suddenly full of the emerald green of the standing rice crop. The beauty and promise of a rice crop warms the heart of every Bengali.

It was a learning process for all of us. The first year ended with enormous success. Every farmer was happy. They did not have to spend any cash, and they got a very high yield. I, however, lost 13,000 *taka*, because farmers cheated me on my share. They gave me less than the one-third they had promised me. But I still felt victorious because it had worked. We had grown a crop where no crop had ever grown on this land in the dry season before.

Our Three-Share Farming experiment received the *Rashtrapati Puroshkar* (President's Award) in 1978.

* * *

But I had deep misgivings.

The success of our three-share experiment for the farmers highlighted a problem I had not focused on before.

Once the rice was harvested, manpower was needed to separate the rice from the dry straw. This mindless boring work was, as you would expect, given to the most cheaply paid, day labourers, and these were always destitute women who would otherwise be reduced to begging. They would come early in the morning like beasts of burden and would separate the rice with their feet, for hours on end, holding themselves upright by finding tiny ledges for their fingers to grip the wall so as not to fall over while they worked.

I could not get over the scene I witnessed: some twenty-five to thirty women threshing the paddy produced on the farm. They did this with their bare feet, facing a wall on which they found support. They would perform a continuous twisting motion, wrapping the rice straw around their feet to force the paddy to separate from it. This would go on endlessly from morning to evening. Their wage depended on the amount of paddy they separated during the day's work. They received one-sixteenth of the paddy they separated. This usually meant 4 kilos of paddy a day, which was worth about 40 US cents.

The women would compete to find a convenient position against the wall to make it less tiring. They would race to arrive the earliest. The competition was so fierce that many showed up at the workplace when it was still dark, only to find others already there.

What a terrible life – to earn 40 cents investing the weight of your body and the tiresome motion of your bare feet for ten hours a day!

It was clear to me that the bigger the farmer, the greater the benefit earned from my Three-Share Farm experiment. The smaller and poorer you were, the smaller was your share of the benefit. Worst paid of all were the women who did the threshing of the paddy. This made me extremely despondent.

I was looking for ways to do exactly the opposite – making the maximum benefit go to the poor. I toyed with several ideas, but none appeared to be convincing. I discovered that for the same work, a woman could earn at least four times more than the wage she received if she had the financial resources to buy the rice paddy herself and process it.

'Why should we be happy with your Three-Share Farm?' one woman said. 'After a few weeks of threshing, we are out of work, and we have nothing to show for ourselves.'

These women, many of them widows or divorced or abandoned with children to feed, were too poor even to be share-croppers. They were landless and assetless and without hope.

That is how I came to focus on the poorest of the poor.

In the jargon of international development, 'small farmer' has come to be used to denote the average poor and neglected person, and so rural programmes always focus on farmers and landowners. I object to this for two reasons.

First, the categorization of the landless and near landless as 'farmers' leads us to adopt an almost unconscious gender segregation. As soon as we identify a section of the people as farmers, our thinking process gets drawn into exclusively male issues. One blissfully forgets about the existence of the other half of the population – the women.

If women are remembered at all, it is always in their capacity as minor helpers to the all-important male members of the household. This damages any development programme.

Second, although in rural areas the landless and the near-landless (owners of less than half an acre) provide the bulk of the agricultural labour, this only constitutes one-fifth of their total available labour time. In other words, 80 per cent of their potentially productive time is used in other activities, or in idleness, but not in farming. Farming is a minor part of their life, and cannot be used to categorize them. Not only is this intellectually wrong, but it draws our attention away from looking at potential sources of income and employment for them, and keeps our attention focused on an aspect of their lives – farming – which does not promise much.

* * *

For these reasons it became important to me to begin to differentiate the really poor from farmers.

At this time, government bureaucrats and social scientists were not focusing on the question of who the 'poor' in fact were. No doubt they assumed it was so obvious that nobody could think otherwise. And yet each social scientist can have a changing vision of poverty depending on which suits his or her purpose. A 'poor person' can mean 'a man with a torn shirt' on one occasion, and on another occasion, it may mean 'a man with a dirty shirt'. Who in the list below is poor and who is not:

- a jobless person?
- an illiterate person?
- a landless person?
- a homeless person?
- a person who does not produce enough food to feed his or her family year-round?
- a person who owns less than twenty-five acres of land?
- a person with a thatched house that lets in rain?
- a person suffering from malnutrition?
- a person who does not send his or her children to school?
- a street vendor?

Such conceptual vagueness greatly damages our attempts to alleviate poverty, and a lack of conceptual sharpness in definitions leads to odd situations. The 'poor' is a much larger collection of people than the small or marginal farmers. For one thing, that definition leaves out women and children. In Bangladesh, half of the total population is worse off than the marginal farmer.

I have found it useful to use three definitions of poor* in the context of Bangladesh, each broader than the other:

---

*CGAP (Consultative Group to Assist the Poorest) and the Micro-credit Summit Campaign Committee have adopted the definition of the poor as anyone who is below the poverty-line, and the poorest as anyone among the bottom half of those below the poverty-line.

P1 – hardcore poor/absolute poor, the bottom 20 per cent of the population

P2 – bottom 35 per cent of the population

P3 – bottom 50 per cent of the population

Within each category of poor, I often put subclassifications on the basis of region, occupation, religion, ethnic background, sex, age, etc. Using occupation or region to define the poor is not conceptually as safe as defining them by income–asset criteria. With the combination of these classifications we can build up a multi-dimensional poverty matrix.

Of course the categories are different in other countries where the relative number of poor people is much smaller. Each country should have its own definition of poverty (ownership of twenty-five acres of land can make you poor in a desert country, but rich in a fertile country). And it would be analytically useful for international organizations to identify each nation's standards of poverty for that country, rather than imposing universal ones.

The purpose of defining who is poor and who among the poor are the most in need is not for theoretical perfection or hair-splitting, but for operational strength. Without firm demarcation lines, anyone working in this area and trying to alleviate the worst suffering easily slips from the poverty zone into the non-poverty zone without ever realizing it.

Like navigational markings in unknown waters, definitions need to be distinctive and unambiguous. Any definition which is not clear and precise will be as bad as no definition at all.

In the category of the poor, I would definitely include the women who threshed rice in 1975 for our Three-Share Farm, together with Sofia Begum who made bamboo stools, and Bajlul, a petty-trader who had to borrow at 10 per cent per month or per week sometimes. And others like them who, earning so little making baskets, jute mats, patis (sleeping mats), often had to resort to begging.

Each of these had absolutely *no chance* of improving their economic base and thereby increasing their income

* * *

So my experience with farming and with rescuing Jobra's deep tubewell was crucial to my turning to focus on the landless poor.

Soon I started arguing that wherever a poverty alleviation programme allows the non-poor to be co-passengers, the poor will soon be elbowed out of the programme by those who are better off.

Like good old Gresham's law,* it is wise to remember that in the world of development, if one mixes the poor and the non-poor within a programme, the non-poor will always drive out the poor, and the less poor will drive out the more poor, and this may continue *ad infinitum* unless one takes protective measures right at the beginning.

And what will happen is that in the name of the poor, the non-poor will reap the benefits.

---

*Gresham's law is the theory that when two kinds of money of equal denomination but of unequal intrinsic value are in circulation, the one of greater value will tend to be hoarded or exported; in other words bad money will drive good money out of circulation.

9

Banking: Climbing the Prison Walls of Collateral, 1976

Realizing that my work with farmers had failed to reach the most destitute, I turned my mind to the problem of the landless, assetless people who lived and worked next door.

I always thought that the landless would be more enterprising than small farmers because a life tied to the land, the way a farmer's life is, tends to make people conservative, narrow in outlook, inward-looking. But the landless, who have no ties to the land, are likely to be more mobile, more receptive to new ideas and therefore more enterprising. Their condition of utter destitution makes them fighters. And not being tied to land, they are free from the traditional lifestyle.

* * *

Sufia Begum's story (described in Chapter 1, pp. 6–9) made me sit up. I could not believe anybody could suffer a life of bonded labour because she could not find 20 US cents to carry on her business.

When I gave $27 as loans to forty-two people, I could not believe one could produce so much happiness in so many people with so little money! There was no way I could leave this whole episode at that.

I wanted a better arrangement – an institutional arrangement, so that these poor people could find money whenever they needed it. But how? I thought of asking a bank. A bank could give them money when they needed it. That after all is their business.

* * *

I climbed into my white Volkswagen Beetle, and I drove to my local branch of the Janata Bank, one of the biggest in the country, a government bank.

Its branch at the university was located just beyond the gates of the campus on the left side of the road, along a stretch of tiny stores, stalls and restaurants where local villagers had set up shop to sell students everything from betel nuts, to meals, to paper and pens. It was here the rickshaw drivers congregated when they were not ferrying students from their dormitories to their classrooms.

The Chittagong University branch of the Janata Bank was housed in a single square room. Its two front windows are covered in bars, and the walls were painted dark-green, but they were peeling and dingy. On the right, past the door is the cashier. The rest of the bank was taken up by wooden tables and chairs. The safe was at the back to the right. The manager, sitting at the back to the left, under a ceiling fan, greeted me politely and invited me to sit down.

'What can I do for you, sir?'

The office-boy brought us tea and biscuits. I explained why I had come.

'The last time I borrowed from you was to finance the Three-Share Programme. Now I have a new proposal. I want you to lend money to the poor people in Jobra. The amount involved is very small. I have already done it myself. I have lent $27 to forty-two people. There will be many more poor people who will need money. They need this money to carry on their work, to buy raw materials and supplies.'

'What kind of materials?' The bank officer looked puzzled, as if this were some sort of new game whose rules he was not familiar with. He let me speak out of common respect for a University department head, but he was clearly lost.

'Well, some make bamboo stools, others weave mats, or drive a rickshaw.... If they borrowed from a bank at commercial rates, they could sell their products on the open market and make a decent profit that would allow them to live.'

'I am sure they would.'

'As it is now, they are condemned to work as slaves for the rest of their lives, and they will never manage to get themselves out from under the heel of the *paikari* wholesalers who now lend them the capital at usurious rates.'

'Yes, I know about *mahajons* [money-lenders].'

'So I have come here today because I would like to ask you to lend money to these villagers.'

The bank manager's jaw fell open, and he started to laugh, 'I can't do that.'

'Why not?' I said.

'Well, well,' he sputtered not knowing where to begin with his list of objections, 'for one thing the little money you say they need to borrow does not even cover the cost of all the loan documents they would have to fill in, and the bank is not going to waste its time on such a pittance.'

'Why not?' I said, 'to the poor it is really important.'

'First, of all, these people are illiterate, they cannot even fill out our loan forms.'

'In Bangladesh where 75 per cent of the people do not read and write, filling out a form is a ridiculous requirement.'

'Every single bank in the country has that rule.'

'Well, that says something about our banks then, doesn't it?'

'Even when a person brings money and wants to put it in the bank, we ask him or her to write down how much she or he is putting in.'

'Why?'

'What do you mean, "Why?"'

'Well, how come a bank cannot just take money and issue a receipt saying, "received such and such amount of money from such and such a person?" Why can't the bank clerk do it, why must the depositors do it?'

'Well, how would you run a bank without people reading and writing?'

'Simple, the bank just issues a receipt for the amount of cash which the bank receives.'

'How about if the person wants to withdraw money?'

'I don't know... there must be a simple way. The borrower comes back with his or her deposit receipt, presents it to the cashier, and the cashier gives back the money. Whatever accounting the bank does is the bank's business.'

The manager shook his head, but didn't answer this, as if he didn't know where to begin.

'It seems to me your banking system is designed to be anti-illiterate.'

Now the branch manager became irritated, 'Professor, banking is not as simple as you think.'

'Maybe so, but I am also sure that banking is not as complicated as you make it out to be.'

'Look, the simple truth is that a borrower at any other bank in any place in the world will have to fill out forms.'

'Well, OK,' I said, bowing to the obvious, 'I can get some of my student volunteers to fill out the forms for them, that should not be a problem.'

'But you don't understand, we simply cannot lend to the destitute,' said the branch manager.

'Why not?'

I was trying to be polite. Our conversation had something surreal about it. The branch manager had a smile on his face as if to say he understood I was pulling his leg. And it was a humorous interview, absurd really, but I stared at him perfectly seriously.

'They don't have any collateral,' said the branch manager, not certain whether I am really stupid or only a good actor, but expecting that this would put an end to our discussion.

'What do you need collateral for as long as you get the money back, that is what you really want.'

'Yes, we want our money back,' said the manager, 'but at the same time we need collateral as well, that is our guarantee.'

'To me it doesn't make sense. The poorest of the poor work 12 hours a day. They need to sell and earn income in order to eat. They have every reason to pay you back, just in order to make another loan and live another day! That is the best security you can have ... their life.'

The manager shook his head, 'You are an idealist, Professor. You live with books and theories.'

'But if you are certain that the money will be repaid, what do you need collateral for?'

'That is our bank rule.'

'So only those who have collateral can borrow?'

'Yes.'

'It's a silly rule, it means only the rich can borrow.'

'I don't make the rules, the bank does.'

'Well, I think the rule should be changed.'

'Anyway, we do not lend money out here.'

'You don't?'

'No, we only take deposits from the faculty members and from the university.'

'But don't banks make money by extending loans?'

'Only the head office makes loans. We are here to collect deposits from the university and its employees. Our loan to your Three-Share Farm was an exception approved by our head office.'

'You mean to say if I came here and asked to borrow money, you would not lend me money?'

'That is right.' He laughed. It was evident the manager had not had such an entertaining afternoon in a long time.

'So when we teach in our classes that banks make loans to borrowers, that is a lie?'

'Well, you would have to go through the head office for a loan, and I don't know what they would do.'

'Sounds like I need to talk to officials higher up.'

'Yes, that would be a good idea.'

As I finished my tea and got ready to leave, the branch manager said, 'I know you'll not give up. But from what I know about banking, I can tell you for sure that this plan of yours will never take off.'

'Thank you.' I said.

* * *

A couple of days later, I went to meet Mr Howladar, the regional manager of the Janata Bank in his office in Chittagong.

I explained to him what I needed, and we had very much a repeat of the conversation I had had with his Jobra branch manager. In addition to the arguments I had already heard, I learned a few more norms of banking which my proposal contradicted.

In the coming years I was also to learn many things about the way people think about the poor. A list of the clichés and myths I have been told by people who've never worked with the poor, but who speak with absolute certainty, would include the following:

- the poor need to be trained before they can undertake any income-generating activity;

- credit alone is useless, it must be packaged with training, marketing, transportation facilities, technology, education;

- the poor cannot save;

- the poor are in the habit of consuming anything that they can put their hands on because their consumption needs are so pressing;

- the poor cannot work together;

- chronic poverty has a crippling effect on the mind and on the aspirations of the poor; it is like a bird who having spent his life in a cage, once taken out will not want to fly away;

- poor women have no skills, so it is useless to talk about programmes for them;

- the poor are too hungry and desperate to make rational judgements;

- the poor have a very narrow view of life, and are not interested in anything that will change their lives;

- the influence of religion and custom is so strong on the poor (particularly on women) that they cannot move an inch in any direction;

- the rural power structure is too powerful and too entrenched to allow such a credit programme to succeed;

- credit for the poor is anti-revolutionary; it kills the revolutionary spirit in the poor, so they are bribed into accepting the *status quo*;

- credit is a clever way of mobilizing the poor to gang up against the rich and destroy the existing social order;

- it will be impossible for the women to keep their borrowings or their income to themselves, husbands will torture them to death, if need be, to grab this cash;

- the poor enjoy serving their masters rather than taking care of themselves;

- credit for the poor is counter-productive: it will impose the burden of loans on the slender shoulders of the poor who cannot repay it; so he or she will become poorer by trying to (or being forced to) repay the loan;

- by encouraging the poor to take up independent professions, a shortage will be created in the supply of wage labour; as a result wage rates will shoot up, this will increase the cost of production, create inflation and adversely affect agricultural productivity;

- by extending credit to women, the traditional role of the woman in the family will be adversely affected as will her relations with her husband;

- credit may help temporarily, but it won't do anything in the long run, it won't achieve an equitable restructuring of society.

The list can continue endlessly without ever exhausting the supply of myths and half-truths which are so ingrained in society at large that you hear them today all around the globe.

Each one of the myths or half-truths listed above may have powerful elements of justification. But in general, they overstate their case. Many of the arguments can be levelled against the rich as well as the poor, whether for agriculture, commerce or industry. The relevance of the criticisms will depend on how a loan programme is administered, how the mechanism of giving credit and collecting repayment is designed and implemented.

But some of these myths (such as the need for collateral to ensure loan repayment) are accepted as norms. They have prompted societies to create institutions and policies on the basis of myths which stand as barriers and roadblocks for a significant section of the population, while providing unjustified privileges to another section.

* * *

In the course of our conversation in the Chittagong regional office of the Janata Bank, Mr Howladar said: 'Governments are here to help the poor. Now, if you could find a well-to-do person in the village who is willing to act as a guarantor for a borrower, then I think the bank might consider giving a loan to that person without collateral.'

I considered it – the idea has some obvious merit, but the drawbacks seemed insurmountable to me.

'I can't do that,' I explained, 'what would prevent the guarantor from taking advantage of the person whose loan he was guaranteeing? He could end up a tyrant. He could end up treating that borrower as a slave.'

There was a silence. It was clear from my many discussions with bankers in the past few days that I was not up against the Janata Bank *per se*, but against the whole banking system.

'Why don't I become guarantor?' I asked.

'You?'

'Yes, can you accept me as guarantor for all the loans?'

The regional manager smiled.

'How much money are you talking about?'

To give myself a margin of error and room to expand, I answered, 'Altogether probably 10,000 *taka* ($300), not more than that.'

'Well,' he fingered the papers on his desk and nodded at them. Behind him I would see dusty stacks of papers in old bindings. The vertical filing was made up of huge pale blue binders, some of which rose in teetering piles up to the windows.

The overhead fans created a breeze that played havoc with any filing that was not weighed down by a paperweight. On his desk, all the papers were in a state of permanent fluttering, but they were all solidly anchored, awaiting his decision.

'Well, I would say we are willing to accept you as guarantor up to that amount, but don't ask for more money.'

'It's a deal.'

We shook hands. Then I added:

'But if one of the borrowers does not repay, I will not step in to honour the defaulted loan.'

The regional manager looked at me uneasily, not certain why I was being difficult.

'As guarantor, we could force you to pay.'

'What would you do?'

'We could start legal proceedings against you.'

'Fine. I would like that.'

He looked at me as if I were crazy, but I wanted that, I wanted to cause some panic in this crazy unjust system. I wanted to be the stick in the wheels that stopped the infernal machine. I was guarantor, maybe, but I wouldn't guarantee.

'Professor Yunus, you know very well we would never sue a department head who has personally guaranteed the loan of a beggar. The bad publicity alone would offset any money we might recover from you. Anyway, the loan is such a pittance it would not even pay for the legal fees, much less our administrative costs of recovering the money.'

'Well, you are a bank, you must do your own cost–benefit analysis. But I will not pay if there is any default.'

'You are making things difficult for me, Professor Yunus.'

'I am sorry, but the bank is making things difficult for a lot of people – especially those who have nothing.'

'I am trying to help, Professor.'

'I understand, but it is not you I am blaming, it is the banking rules I have a quarrel with.'

After more such back and forth, Mr Howladar concluded, 'I will recommend this to my head office in Dhaka, and we will see what they say.'

'But I thought you as regional officer had the authority to conclude this matter?'

'Yes, but this is far too unorthodox for me to approve. Authorization will have to come from the top.'

It took six months of writing back and forth to get this loan formalized. Finally, in December 1976, I succeeded in taking out a loan from the Janata Bank and giving it to the poor of Jobra.

All through 1977, I had to sign each and every loan request. Even when I was on a trip to Europe or America, my assistant would send all the documents to me for my signature. The bank did not deal with the borrowers on the spot. I was the guarantor. And as far as the bank was concerned, I was the only one who counted. They did not want to deal with the actual poor who used their capital. In fact, they preferred never dealing with them. And I made sure the real borrowers, the ones I call the banking untouchables, never had to suffer the indignity and demeaning harassment of actually going to the bank.

* * *

I was in the process of discovering the world's basic banking principle, namely that, 'The more you have, the more you get.' And conversely that, 'If you don't have it, you don't get it.'

Perhaps unwittingly, banks have designated a class of people as 'not creditworthy', meaning 'we can't touch you'. Why do bankers insist on collateral? Why is it so indispensable to them? Why have the designers of the banking system chosen to create financial apartheid? I suppose that ideas and concepts are passed on from one generation to the next most often without being questioned.

Out of desperation, we at Grameen questioned the most basic banking premise of collateral. At first I did not know if I was right. I had no idea what I was getting myself into. I was walking blind, and learning as I went along, learning empirically from experience. Our work became a struggle to show that the financial untouchables are actually touchable, even huggable.

To my amazement and surprise the repayment of loans by people who borrow without collateral is much better than those whose borrowings are secured by enormous assets. Indeed, more than 98 per cent of our loans are repaid because the poor know this is the only opportunity they have to break out of their poverty. And they don't have any cushion whatsoever to fall back on. If they fall foul of this one loan, how will they survive?

On the other hand, people who are well-off don't care what the law will do to them because they know how to manipulate it. People at the bottom are afraid of everything, so they want to do a good job because they have to. They have no choice.

* * *

Poverty is not a parade of statistics to overwhelm us.

Poverty is not a Nazi concentration camp where people are locked away to rot until certain death.

Poverty is like being surrounded by high walls around you. And Grameen is not, and should never be, a package thrown into the walled-in existence to make the people inside enjoy a day or two better than the others. Grameen, and all its replications around the world, helps people gather will and strength to make the effort to crack the walls around them, and break them down.

Poverty is a way of life for a huge segment of the population who have learned to accept and live with it.

Poverty is a disease which has a paralysing effect on mind and body.

* * *

The simple way to decapitate the money-lenders, I thought, was to bring in institutional bank credit. Both of them are in the credit business, so let one compete with the other under free market conditions.

Because no formal institution was available to cater for the needs of the poor, the credit market had by default been taken over by the money-lenders who had found a thriving business for themselves. That business was an efficient vehicle creating a heavy rush of one-way traffic on the road to poverty.

The big rush to poverty could have been slowed down, and the traffic need not have been one-way. A two-way traffic flow could have been generated if banks and other financial institutions had taken upon themselves the role they are supposed to play.

* * *

The life story of Ammajan Amina, one of our first borrowers, illustrates what micro-credit can do for a street beggar.

Of Ammajan's six children, four had died of hunger or disease. Only two daughters survived. Her husband, much older than her, was quite ill. For several years he had spent most of the family assets on trying to find a cure.

After his death, all that Amina had left was the house. She was in her forties, old by Bangladesh standards where contrary to the world norm, women have a lower life expectancy than men (58.1 years versus 58.4 years). She was illiterate and had never earned an income before. Her in-laws tried to expel her and her children from the house where she had lived for twenty years, but she refused to leave.

She tried selling home-made cakes and biscuits door-to-door, but one day she returned to find her brother-in-law had sold her tin roof, and the buyer was busy removing it.

Now the rainy season started, and she was cold, hungry and too poor to make food to sell. All she had, she used to feed her own children.

Because Ammajan Amina was a proud woman, she begged, but only in nearby villages. As she had no roof to protect her house, the monsoon destroyed her mud walls. One day when she returned she found her house had collapsed, and she started screaming, 'Where is my daughter? Where is my baby?'

She found her older child dead under the rubble of her house.

When my colleague Nurjahan met her in 1976, Ammajan Amina held her only surviving child in her arms. She was hungry, heartbroken and desperate.

There was no question of any money-lender much less a commercial bank giving her credit. But with Grameen loans she started making bamboo baskets and remained a borrower to the end of her days. Now her daughter is a member of Grameen.

We have more than two million such life stories, one for each of our members.

PART II: EXPERIMENTAL

PHASE

1976–78

10

Why Lend to Women Rather Than to Men?

Traditional banks in Bangladesh are gender-biased and do not want to lend money to women.

When I say this, it irritates my banker friends. They shout at me, 'Don't you see our Ladies' Branches all over town? They are designed to serve women only.'

I answer, 'Yes, I see them, and I see the idea behind them. You want to get their deposits. That is why you make Ladies' Branches. But what happens when one of the ladies wants to borrow money from you?'

In Bangladesh, if a woman, even a rich woman, wants to borrow money from a bank, the manager will ask her, 'Did you discuss this with your husband?'

And if she answers, 'Yes', the manager will say, 'Is he supportive of your proposal?'

If the answer is still, 'Yes', he will say, 'Would you please bring your husband along so that we can discuss it with him?'

But no manager would ever dream of asking a prospective male borrower whether he has discussed the idea of a loan with his wife, and whether he would like to bring his wife along to discuss the proposal. Even suggesting this would be an insult!

So it is not by chance that prior to Grameen, women constituted less than 1 per cent of all the borrowers in Bangladesh put together. To me it was clear that the banking system itself was gender-biased.

Having complained for so long that banks discriminated against women, I wanted at least 50 per cent of our experimental projects' borrowers to be women.

* * *

Once we had reached a sizeable number of women, we started noticing some significant results.

We discovered a new reason to focus on women borrowers. No longer a question of avoiding gender bias, there was now a development reason to favour women.

The more I got involved, the more I realized that credit given to women brought about changes faster than when given to men.

Relatively speaking, hunger and poverty are more women's issues than male issues. Women experience hunger and poverty in much more intense ways than men. If one of the family members has to starve, it is an unwritten law that it has to be the mother. The mother has to go through the traumatic experience of not being able to breastfeed her infant during the days of famine and scarcity.

Being poor in Bangladesh is tough for everyone, but being a poor woman is toughest of all. When she is given the smallest opportunity, she struggles extra hard to get out of poverty.

A poor woman in our society is totally insecure: she is insecure in her husband's house because he can throw her out any time he wishes. He can divorce her by merely saying three times, 'I divorce thee, I divorce thee, I divorce thee.' She cannot read and write, and generally she has never been allowed out of her house to earn money, even if she has wanted to. She is insecure in her in-laws' house, for the same reason as she was in her parents' house: they are just waiting to get her out so they will have one less mouth to feed.

If she is divorced and returns to her parents, she becomes a disgrace and is unwanted there. So given any opportunity at all, a poor woman in our society wants to build up her security. Her financial security.

From our experience, it became evident that destitute women adapted quicker and better to the self-help process than men.

Poor women had the vision to see further and were willing to work harder to get out of poverty because they suffered the most.

The women paid more attention, prepared their children to have better lives, and were more consistent in their performance than men.

Money going though a woman in a household brought more benefits to the family as a whole than money entering the household through a man.

On the other hand, a man has a different set of priorities which do not give the family the top position. When a destitute father starts making extra income, he starts paying attention to himself. So why should Grameen approach the household through men?

When a destitute mother starts making some income, her dreams invariably centre around her children.

A mother's second priority is the household. She wants to buy a few utensils, literally build a stronger roof and improve the family's living conditions. One of our borrowers was so excited she grabbed a reporter and showed her the single bed she had been able to buy for herself and her family.

* * *

If the goals of economic development include improved standards of living, removal of poverty, access to dignified employment, and reduction in inequality, then it is quite natural to start with women. They constitute the majority of the poor, the under-employed and the economically and socially disadvantaged. And since they were closer to the children, women were also our key to the future of Bangladesh.

Studies undertaken by Grameen, comparing how male borrowers use their loans versus female borrowers, consistently confirm this analysis.

So gradually we focused almost exclusively on lending to women. This was not easy. The first and most formidable opposition came from the husbands. Next the *mullahs*. Then the professional people, and even government officials.

The husbands generally wanted the loans to go to them. (I often hear our borrowers say that the worst catastrophe that can befall them is not a natural disaster, a typhoon or a famine, but a man who will steal their money and waste away their capital.)

The *mullahs* and the money-lenders also saw us as a direct threat to their authority in the village (see Chapter 19).

These were objections I had expected. But what surprised me was to hear educated civil servants and professionals argue against us. They said: 'It makes no sense to lend money to women while so many men are jobless and without income.'

Others said, 'Why give money to women, they will only pass it on to their husbands anyway. All you are doing is forcing them to be more exploited now than they were before.'

Of course, our experience was just the opposite: giving the woman control of the purse-strings was the first step in giving her rights as a human being within the family unit.

Many government officials also took a dim view of what we were experimenting with. Indeed, one official of our central bank, who noticed our attempts to get women borrowers wrote me a menacing letter:

Please explain fully and immediately why a high percentage of your borrowers are women.

The tone was so rude, it was almost a show-case notice against us. I wrote back:

> I would be happy to explain the reasons for the high percentage of women borrowers in our Grameen project. But before I do so, I would like to know if the Central Bank ever sent any letter to any other bank asking for explanations as to why they have such a high percentage of male borrowers.

I never received a reply to my letter, and neither did they press me for a reply to theirs.

But from the travels I have made around the world, I believe the problem is not limited to Bangladesh. In most development planning, women are seldom reckoned as an economic force. Why this should be is not clear to me.

In countries like Bangladesh where *purdah* (see pp. 93-4) keeps women inside their houses, their economic value to the man is quite low. And, moreover, because of the dowry her family will have to pay, an unmarried daughter is seen as quite a burden.

* * *

Women having access to credit is not a traditional practice in Bangladesh; indeed many have said it is a social revolution. For poor women to have that access, while men in the family did not, was certainly bound to create many unforeseen social problems. We knew this would be the case, and we tried our best to address it in many different ways.

Initially we made mistakes. Because we did not take enough precautions, our loan programme created enormous tensions between husbands and wives. But gradually, we learned. We prepared our borrowers 'neither to risk the marriage for the money nor risk the money for the marriage'. This was quite a difficult balancing act and the borrowers required a lot of preparation and help before they could face their real-life drama.

We tried to find an institutional solution to this problem rather than seeking it outside Grameen. Once again borrowers' groups played a major role. They invented collective solutions and encouraged individual strategies. We addressed the husbands directly by involving them in collective dialogue with the bank. Individually they might have appeared to be tyrants to their wives, but when the bank invited them in for a discussion as part of a wider group of husbands, they were far more understanding and reasonable. We explained to them everything we did. This generally cleared up many of their misunderstandings about the bank's rules and procedures. Also, and equally importantly, they did not feel neglected any more.

Grameen has come a long way since then. Now Grameen lends money to husbands, but only through their wives. The principal borrower remains the wife.

The husband–wife relationship comes to its most dramatic test when a borrower wants a housing loan. To qualify for a housing loan, a borrower has to have successfully repaid three one-year self-employment loans. Furthermore, her husband must sign over to her the title to the land on which the house will stand. In many cases, this is simply too much to ask from a husband. But Grameen requires it, and we get away with it. We have made well over 400,000 housing loans. In every case the husband has signed over to his wife the title to the land on which the house is built.

Besides institutional arrangements to ensure better husband–wife relationships, the Grameen system of group loans also provides informal forces which work towards bringing this about. Sometimes the group itself works almost like informal marriage counselling.

I noticed it even when I was still struggling to set up the Grameen system in Tangail before 1983. I was walking along a village road alone to get to our branch after attending a centre-meeting. After a while I met a young man (around thirty) who was walking along the same road. He greeted me, I greeted him. We walked side by side.

'Are you with the Grameen Bank?' He asked.

'Yes'. I said. 'But how did you know?'

'I saw you going to the centre-meeting in the village. My wife is also in the group.'

This immediately changed my relationship with him. I became interested in him. He told me his name was Joynal. He was an agricultural labourer. His wife Farida had joined the Grameen Bank eight months earlier, and they had a little daughter of five.

'Farida works very hard to make sure she pays back every single weekly installment on time. She has not missed a single installment yet.'

'Did she have your consent before she joined Grameen?'

'She did. But in the beginning I was not sure whether she was doing the right thing. Then other women in the village were also joining Grameen. She kept on asking for permission. Finally I gave in.'

'Are you happy that she joined? Or, looking back, do you think it would have been better if she did not?'

'No, no, I am happy that she joined. She used to complain that we didn't have enough food, but now she does not complain. We have enough for the three of us.'

For me this was like getting good grades in the final exam. I was pleased that things were working well. Both Joynal and I kept walking silently.

The long silence was broken when Joynal spoke out in a negative tone:

'There is one thing, however. I used to enjoy beating my wife. But the last time I beat her I got into trouble. The women in Farida's borrowing group came to me and argued with me and shouted at me. I did not like that. Who gave them the right to shout at me? I can do whatever I want with my wife. Before, when I used to beat my wife, no one said anything, no one bothered. This is no longer going to be true. Her borrowing group threatened they will get really mean if I beat my wife again.'

I tried to console Joynal:

'Well, maybe it is time you left your wife alone. After all, she is working very hard. She needs your support. You can find something else to do to release your tension.'

* * *

Independent studies have found that the incidence of women being beaten by their husbands is much lower after the women join Grameen.

11

Reaching Women Borrowers

How does one get women borrowers in a country where no poor woman has ever borrowed money from a bank before?

If I had put up a billboard saying,

ATTENTION ALL WOMEN:
WELCOME TO OUR BANK
FOR A SPECIAL LOAN PROGRAMME
FOR WOMEN!

I would get good media coverage for that eye-catching billboard, good free publicity, but it could not actually get women borrowers. Such signs would be ignored because 85 per cent of women in the countryside cannot read, or they are not free to come out of the house without their husbands.

I was having a terrible time getting women interested. At first, we had no women borrowers at all, so we made a conscious effort to seek out female borrowers.

We had to devise a whole series of tricks and techniques.

* * *

Because of the rules of *purdah* (literally a 'curtain' or 'veil'), we never dared enter a woman's house at first.

The term *purdah* refers to a range of practices in response to the Koranic injunction to guard women's modesty and purity. In its most conservative interpretation, it means women are forbidden to be seen by any men except their closest male relatives. Many of these women do not go out of the house even to visit their neighbours.

In rural villages like Jobra, *purdah* is coloured by a belief in spirits which pre-dates Islam. Such beliefs are perpetuated by the village pseudo-*mullahs* who teach in religious primary schools or *maktabs* and interpret Islam for the villagers. These men are looked upon as religious authorities by illiterate villagers, but many of them have a low degree of Islamic education, and their teachings are not always that of the Koran.

Even where *purdah* is not strictly observed, custom, family, tradition, and decorum combine to keep relations between women and men in rural Bangladesh extremely formal.

So when I would try to meet village women, I never dared knock on their doors. Instead, I would stand in a clearing between several houses, so everyone could see me and observe my behaviour. And I would wait. Above all I wanted to be seen respecting their privacy, and their rules of propriety.

I never asked for a chair, or for any mark of respect. The villagers are so used to bowing and scraping before figures of authority, that I wanted none of that distancing between the bank and its borrowers. I would stand outside their door and chat as informally as possible, explaining what we were trying to do.

I tried to say funny things because humour is always a good way to reach people.

I always told my co-workers to show genuine affection for the children for, not only does it come naturally to me, it is an immediate way into the mother's heart. I also told my students and co-workers to avoid wearing expensive clothes or costly *saris*.

* * *

I usually brought one of my female students with me. My go-between would enter the house, introduce me and speak on my behalf. This is how I would initially present the possibility of borrowing from us. My go-between would bring me back any questions the women might have. I would answer their questions, and back into the house the girl would go. Sometimes she shuttled back and forth for over an hour, and still I was not able to convince these hidden women to seek a loan from Grameen.

After an hour or so I would leave, very disappointed, of course. But I would come back the next day.

And again the go-between would shuttle back and forth. We wasted a lot of time with the young girl having to repeat everything I said and all the questions of the other village women. Often our go-between could not catch all my ideas, nor all the problems the women voiced. And again they would send me away, and tell me not to return. Sometimes the husbands would get irritated with me. I suppose the fact that I was a respected head of a university department reassured the husbands. But they always demanded that our loans be given to them, not to their wives.

One day, as I sat in a clearing between the houses of a village, it clouded over and started to rain. As this was the monsoon, it soon started to pour. The women in the house sent an umbrella out so that I could cover myself. I was relatively dry, but then the women took pity on the girl who got wet every time she shuttled back and forth between the house and me. So one woman in the house, said, 'Let the professor take shelter next door, there is no one there. And that way the girl won't get wet anymore.'

That was the first time I was actually invited inside a house.

It was a typical rural Bengali house – a tiny room, without electricity, a dirt floor, and no chair or table. I sat on the bed alone in the dark and waited. There were wonderful food smells I recognized. A bamboo wall and cabinets divided this house from the one next door, and every time my go-between joined the women in the adjoining house, I could hear some of the things they said, but not well, for their voices were muffled. And every time the go-between would return and tell me what they had said, the women next door would crowd against the bamboo dividing wall to hear my answers. It was far from an ideal way of communicating, but it was certainly better than being outside in the rain.

After twenty minutes of hearing each other's voices, but talking indirectly through a go-between, the women on the other side of the wall started by-passing my assistant and hurling comments or shouting questions directly at me in their Chittagonian dialect. As my eyes grew accustomed to the darkness, I could make out human shapes staring at me through the cracks in the partition. The fact that I was fluent in their Chittagonian dialect helped, of course.

Many of their questions were similar to the ones the men asked us: 'Why must we form a group?'

'Why not a personal loan to me right now?'

There were about twenty-five women peeking in at me through cracks in the partition. I could smell *atap* rice being cooked.[*] The pressure on the partition was so great that suddenly part of it collapsed, and they were soon sitting in the room listening and talking directly to me. Some hid their faces behind a veil, others giggled and were too shy to look at me directly. But we

---

*In Bangladesh, people eat rice three times a day – at breakfast, lunch and dinner, like the Japanese. Only the townspeople and those who could not afford rice have it less than three times daily. Experts say we used to grow 10,000 varieties, but of course many of them have now disappeared. Westerners find little difference between plastic vacuum-packed Uncle Ben's or imported *patna* rice. But we Bengalis, nurtured on rice for generations, have our favourites.

had no more need of anyone repeating our words. That was the first time I spoke with a group of Jobra women inside their house.

'Your words frighten us, sir,' one woman said hiding her face with the end of her sari.

'Money is something that only my husband handles,' said another turning her back to me so I could not see her face.

'Give the loan to my husband, he handles the money, I've never touched any. And I don't want to,' said a third.

'I wouldn't know what to do with money,' said a woman who sat closest to me but averted her eyes.

'No, no, not me. We have no use for money,' said an old woman. 'We have all had enough trouble with dowry payments that we don't want another fight with our husbands. Professor, we don't want to get into more trouble.'

It was easy to see the crushing effects of poverty there. Their husbands had no power over anyone except their wives, and to vent their frustrations all they could do was beat their wives and hurl abuse at them, divorce them, treat them like animals. I knew that marital violence was a terrible problem, and that none of these women wanted to get involved in an area reserved traditionally for men – namely the control of cash.

The government was enacting laws to protect women, but even today enforcement of these laws is hindered by tradition. And most rural women are still terribly shy and anxious whenever money is discussed.

I tried my best to encourage them not to be afraid. 'Why not borrow? It would help you to start earning money.'

'No, no, no, we cannot take your money.'

'Why not? If you invested it, you could earn money and use the profits to feed your children and send them to school.'

'No, when my mother died the last advice she gave me was never to borrow from anybody. So I cannot borrow.'

'Yes, your mother was a wise woman, she gave you the right advice. But if she were alive today she would advise you to join Grameen. When she was alive, there was no Grameen project. She did not know anything about this experimental project. Back then there was only one source she could borrow from – the money-lender, and she was advising you rightly not to go to him, because he charges 10 per cent per month, or per week! But if your mother had known about us, she would definitely strongly recommend you to join us and make a decent living for yourself.'

'Why don't you talk to my husband? He knows about money.'

I had heard their arguments so many times I had ready answers, but it was difficult to persuade them to take a chance with us. They had never faced an institution in their lives. So everything that stood in front of them was fearful, and to overcome that fear was quite a task.

This process of breaking down fear was repeated many times over.

At the end of every day, I would debrief my students and discover what they had done that day. Often they would come with the names of potential borrowers jotted down on the back of a cigarette pack. We would exchange stories, names, make plans for the following day.

* * *

One day, a woman called Marium, who was divorced and had three children, wanted to borrow 1000 *taka* ($24). She sold cloth door-to-door, and I was not convinced she should start off with such a big first loan. I was worried that she would have trouble repaying it, and then her entire village would turn against us when things went wrong. We were having trouble convincing her that it was better to start slow, with a 500 *taka* ($2) loan and then to increase later.

My female assistant was going in and out of the house to the courtyard where I was waiting. Finally, I became impatient, and I entered the house to try to break the deadlock. The dozen or so women inside covered their faces with their saris and turned away from me. But an old woman advanced with a small wooden stool for me to sit on. I started talking to them about how when one wants a new untested crop, one starts off slowly by planting a seed in the ground, and then the plant grows and then one plants more seed, and eventually one can have a large harvest. Eventually, the women turned around and we spoke face to face, although they continued to cover their faces.

It was slow going that day. Very slow. And all the days that followed.

We tramped around the village all through the monsoon, and through the month of *Ashar* when people ate lush leafy greens such as *kalmi*, *puishak*, or *kachu shak* a sort of long asparagus which when boiled acquires a delicate flavour and texture. The monsoon vegetables are all tasty. My favourite vegetarian dish is the extraordinarily delicious *kachu shak* made by spicing the boiled *shak* with whole bay leaves, ground cumin, chili and turmeric.

We returned and visited the same houses all through the dry season as well.

* * *

Here is just one of the 12 million lives we have touched in Bangladesh:

Hajeera Begum was born in 1959, in Kirati Kapasia, Monohardi, a subdistrict of Dhaka. Her father, a farm labourer, could not feed his six daughters, and he married Hajeera off to a blind man simply because the man demanded no dowry. Hajeera and her husband survived on what little she earned doing house-cleaning work, but she was unable to feed her three children regularly. One day she asked her husband for permission to join Grameen, but he had heard it was a Christian organization bent on destroying Islam, and he threatened to divorce her if she joined.

Without telling anyone, she travelled to a nearby village and attended some introductory sessions where Grameen workers explained the principles of the bank.

The first time the members of her group took the oral exam to show they knew the rules of Grameen, Hajeera was so nervous that she could not answer the questions: 'All my life I was told I was no good, that I brought only misery to my parents because I was a woman and my family could not pay for my dowry. Many times I heard my mother say she should have killed me at birth. I did not feel I was worthy of a loan, or that I could ever repay it.'

She would have given up had it not been for the support of her group. Her first loan was for 2000 *taka* ($50), and when she received it, tears ran down her face. Her group convinced her to use the loan to buy a calf for fattening and a rice paddy to shuck. When her father brought the calf to the house, her husband was so excited he forgot his threat to divorce her.

Within a year Hajeera had paid off her first loan, taken a second loan and used it to rent a piece of land, planted it with seventy banana seedlings and used the balance to buy a second calf. Today, she owns a rice field with a mortgage, and goats, ducks and chickens.

'We now enjoy three meals a day,' says Hajeera, 'and my children no longer go hungry. We can now even afford some meat once a week. I intend to send all my children to school and college, so that they will not suffer as I did. You ask what I think of Grameen? Grameen is like my mother. No, Grameen is not like my mother, she is my mother. She has given me new life.'

12

Women Bank Workers

In those early days in 1977, through the experiences of Nurjahan and Jannat, our first two female workers, I discovered just how difficult it was for our women workers. Everything in our culture conspired against women working outside the home.

So our fight against the ill-treatment and segregation of women took place not only on behalf of our borrowers, but also for our own bank workers.

We made our workers walk alone through the village. Many parents thought this was demeaning. And parents who might accept their daughter sitting behind a desk did not look kindly upon their child walking all day.

Except for my own students at the very beginning, our women bank workers were recruited locally because we wanted them living at home while they worked for us. (This avoided many problems and rumours spreading about our staff.)

At first when a female bank worker started walking to visit her borrowers, it was not uncommon for a crowd to gather and watch her. When she walked as far as two miles in each direction, she faced a lot of criticism from people who were not used to seeing a young woman anywhere but in her home.

We usually recruit our women workers at a time in their lives when they have finished their studies and either are waiting to be married, or they are married and their husband cannot find a job. Generally, for an unmarried woman, having a job immediately removes the family pressure to get married. In addition, having a job increases her marriage prospects considerably. Having income changes her family status from being a burden to being an asset.

* * *

Another problem was the large area the bank worker had to cover. Men can ride bicycles, but in our society it is not considered proper for girls to cycle.

In fact, even today most of our female trainees do not know how to ride bicycles.

We bought training bikes, and we held classes and tried to make our girls confident bike riders. But in some places, the locals would hurl abuse at her for riding a bicycle. It is all right for a woman to ride a bullock-cart, baby taxi, rickshaw, or even a motorbike. But the religious conservatives would not allow a girl to ride a bike.

Even today, twenty years later, when 94 per cent of our borrowers are women, and in spite of all the societal changes we have helped engineer, we still encounter similar problems.

* * *

Keeping female bank workers is just as hard as ever. Typically if she gets married, her in-laws will exert a lot of pressure on her to leave her job. They do not want a 'decent' girl walking alone around villages. They will also worry that she might not be able to defend herself in case of trouble.

After the first child, the pressure grows to leave her work. And then after the second or third child, the in-laws' pressure becomes almost impossible to resist. Understandably, the woman herself wants to spend time with her children. And the amount of walking that she did as a young woman is not as easy for her.

This is no doubt why more female employees are applying for Grameen's early retirement option whereby after ten years a bank worker can leave with half benefits.

* * *

The story of Nurjahan Begum is typical of many of the pressures to which our young female workers are subjected.

Nurjahan was a graduate student at Chittagong University when we started our Grameen project. She was twenty-three and studying to get her master's degree with honours in Bengali literature. She had lost her father when she was eleven, and came from a conservative middle-class family. Her mother wanted her to get married and have children. But when she did her master's, Nurjahan rebelled: she was the first woman in her village to get a master's, and she had a job offer from a non-governmental organization (NGO). She begged her mother, 'Please give me permission to use all my learning.'

Nurjahan begged her many times, but still her mother refused to give her consent. Girls of good families in Bangladesh are not supposed to work at all. Then Nurjahan tried to convince her brother. He was willing to let her work for an NGO, but he was worried about what others in the village would say. So Nurjahan kept having to delay her starting date. The NGO put back the date three times, but finally they could wait no longer, and she lost the job offer.

After that Nurjahan had an interview with Grameen, and we made her an offer. This time she told her mother, 'You permitted me to live on campus at the university hostel before, well now it will be the same thing. I will live in an all-girls hostel, in a girls' dorm; now you cannot object.'

Her mother said, 'What kind of job will you do?'

'I will work for a bank. Please, mother.'

Nurjahan's brothers ganged up on her mother and finally she relented.

They assumed it was a job with a desk and a phone and a secretary, and Nurjahan did not tell them that in fact she would have no office, no desk, that she would spend her days walking through the poorest areas of the poorest villages, talking to beggars and destitute women. She knew they would be horrified and would force her to quit.

She started working with us in October 1977. And for as long as Nurjahan's family ignored what Grameen was like, they were grudgingly willing to let her work.

The first day Nurjahan worked for us, I asked her to prepare a case study of Ammajan Amina, whose life story I described on pages 82–3. I asked her to do this for three reasons:

First, I believe the best way to inspire a new worker is to let them see and taste first-hand the real-life problems of the poor. And I wanted Nurjahan to have her heart touched by the reality of poverty.

Second, I wanted to see how she would do, I wanted to test Nurjahan. It is not easy to work with the poor, and to do so in a way that will really make a difference to their lives. Nurjahan had a master's degree, but a poverty bank worker needs more, he or she needs a real inner motivation. And for a worker to impart confidence and strength to a borrower requires that they have rare qualities of survival, communication skills, and psychology. It also requires the bank worker to go and spend time with the borrowers, to learn how they live, how they work, how their babies cry, grow up, study, develop, and so on.

Third, I always told our project personnel that they should shift their attention away from the particular product they were offering (namely credit) to the *people* they were serving.

They had to learn to look at their clients as total human beings. It was their job to help change the lives of the borrowers they were serving. They were not there merely to sell a product or a service; this was only an instrument to achieve their objective.

And of course, the best way to try to ensure this easy and fear-free interaction between the poor and their bank was to start with the bank worker finding out everything there was to know about the borrower's life and what her problems were.

For all these reasons I told Nurjahan, 'Try to really see Ammajan Amina and touch her and understand her mentality. For the first day, go there with no pen, no paper in order to gain the woman's confidence.'

She went along with my colleague Assad.

Ammajan Amina asked her, 'Is he your husband?'

'No,' said Nurjahan, 'he is just a colleague.'

'Why are you coming to see us with a man who is not your husband?' asked Ammajan Amina. This went against *purdah* and made her suspicious of Nurjahan.

But little by little, day after day, Nurjahan won her confidence. And part of the training of every new bank worker is writing up a number of such case studies.

* * *

One day, Nurjahan's sister-in-law's brother came to give her some family news. When he arrived at our office (there was only one back then), he saw that it was only a shack with a tin corrugated iron roof, with no telephone, no toilet and no water. That of course shocked him because it was not at all the image he had of what a commercial bank should look like.

The office manager, Assad, told Nurjahan's in-law that she was out in the field. The man went and found her seated in the grass under a tree talking to some village women, and he was extremely astonished. Nurjahan was so embarrassed, she lied and told him, 'This is a special situation, don't worry. Please don't tell my mother a thing about where you found me.'

But he did.

Her mother was furious. Like most conservative religious believers in Bangladesh, her mother felt her daughter should hide indoors, observing the custom of *purdah*. The mother never went out, not even to visit her own children; they always came to her. So she could not imagine Nurjahan working under the open sky, or that such work was decent and becoming for a respectable woman.

Nurjahan told her mother the truth, and eventually her mother, who always tried to help the poor on her own, relented. Today her mother is a big supporter of ours.

One day I asked Nurjahan to travel to the town of Comilla with two junior female bank workers and present Grameen at a cultural festival. I did not make any provision for a male to accompany her because the trip from Chittagong to Comilla is not excessive or dangerous. This was not insensitivity on my part, it was a desire to let my workers fend for themselves. Nothing gives a young person more self-confidence than being able to meet obstacles and overcome them. Also, I thought that the stereotype of a woman not being able to travel alone on a short trip was something Grameen needed to break down.

Although she did not show it, Nurjahan was furious with me for not placing her in the care of a man who would arrange how they would travel and take care of all the details of the road. Nurjahan telephoned a male colleague and asked him to accompany her. Unfortunately, he was busy. She had never travelled alone, and she prayed to Allah to give her strength and courage:

'O Lord, help me travel this alone with two women, I have never gone anywhere by myself.'

And she went. She put on an excellent show in Comilla and everyone was extremely appreciative.

Now Nurjahan goes everywhere and anywhere she pleases with no problem. She is one of the three general managers of the Grameen Bank, heads our training division and helps hundreds of our future young bank workers become self-reliant.

* * *

Poverty is a chronic disease. It cannot be cured with *ad hoc* measures. There may be short-run measures, but one must have a long-term strategy in mind when taking a quick tactical step.

One short programme is totally ineffective in this regard. Continuity of relationships creates an atmosphere of trust which helps to lay down the foundation of a higher level of relationship. Projects can have an impact only when a long-term commitment underlies them.

That is why it is so important to have committed bank workers all the way down the implementing process, ones who are totally serious about holding the line and eventually eradicating the problem of poverty among our borrowers.

13

The Delivery System:
The Mechanics of Joining

We did not know anything about how to run a bank for the poor, so we had to learn from scratch.

In January 1977, when we started, I looked at how others ran their loan operations, and I learned from their mistakes.

In Bangladesh, conventional banks and credit co-operatives always demanded lump sum repayments. This caused severe repayment problems because a lump sum repayment was a psychological hurdle for borrowers, and rather than ensure repayment, they tended to delay the day of reckoning for as long as possible, in the process getting into further debt, which compounded the difficulty of repayment. In the end they often defaulted totally on the loan.

In structuring our own loans, I decided to do exactly the opposite: I made the payments so small that the borrower would not miss the money, would not even notice it. This was a way to overcome the psychological barrier of 'parting with all that money'. I decided to make it a daily payment. The monitoring would be easier, I would be able to tell right away who was paying and who was falling behind in their payments.

I also thought it would enhance self-discipline among people who had never borrowed before in their lives, and would give them the confidence that they could manage it.

For ease in accounting I decided to ask that the loans to be paid down fully in one year. Thus, a 365 *taka* loan could be paid down at the rate of 1 *taka* a day in a year.

A *taka* a day makes people laugh, but I kept on reminding myself of that wonderful story of the power of small steady incremental gains.

The story goes like this: a prisoner who was condemned to death was brought before the king and was asked to make a last wish. The prisoner pointed to the chessboard which was to the right of the king's throne, and he said, 'I wish only for a single grain of rice on one square of the chessboard, and that you double it for each succeeding square.'

'Granted,' said the king, not realizing the power of geometrical progression. For soon the prisoner had the entire kingdom.

* * *

Slowly we developed our own delivery–recovery mechanism, and of course we made many mistakes along the way. We adapted and changed as we went along.

We discovered that the formation of a group was crucial to the success of our operations.

Individually, a poor person feels exposed to all kinds of hazards. Group membership gives him a feeling of protection. Individually, a person tends to be erratic, uncertain in his or her behaviour. But group membership creates group support and group pressure and smoothes out behaviour patterns and makes the borrower more reliable.

Subtle, and at times not so subtle, peer pressure keeps the group members in line with the broader objectives of the credit programme.

A sense of inter-group and intra-group competition helps everyone try to be an achiever. It is difficult to keep track of individual borrowers; but if he or she is a member of a group, it is much less difficult. Also, shifting the task of initial supervision to the group reduces the work of the bank worker and increases the self-reliance of the group.

The group dynamic is important: because the group approves the loan request of each member, in the process it feels morally responsible for the loan. So if any member of the group ever gets into trouble, the group usually comes forward to help out.

We therefore required an applicant to form a group of people, other than family members, who should be like-minded and should have similar economic and social status.

Loans were given to the individuals. Although we put a system of interlocking responsibilities in place, formally each borrower was personally responsible for his or her loan.

We also decided that a borrowing group should form itself rather than being formed by us. Group solidarity would be stronger if the group came into being through the borrowers' own negotiations.

* * *

It is not easy to form a group. What happens is that a prospective borrower has to take the initiative to form a group and to explain how the bank works to a second person (not a member of the family), and she has to convince the second to want to join.

If this is the first time Grameen has entered the village, it will not be easy. Usually, the first will have to try various friends who will be terrified, or they will have excuses, or their husband will not allow them, or they are simply against the idea of being indebted to any one, 'No, I can't, this is terrible.' But eventually a friend will have heard what Grameen did for other households and will say, 'Okay, let me think about it, come back tomorrow.'

Then the two will go out and each one will seek out a third member, and a fourth, and a fifth. And finally when they are ready, it often happens that one of the five members comes to her friends and says, 'No, my husband has changed his mind, he won't let me.' So the group falls back to four, or three, or sometimes back to one. And that one has to start all over again.

Then each prospective borrower has to go through a lot of training so that they fully understand what we are about.

Often the night before a borrower is accepted into Grameen she is so worried and nervous that she goes and prays to Allah to help her out; she promises to light a candle in some saint's shrine. And some are so nervous that they cannot stand the pressure, and even the night before passing the entrance test, it often happens that a prospective member will tell her friends in the group, 'No, I cannot do this, I want to drop out.'

And then the four remaining ones have to request that Grameen give them a later date for the test by which time they will have a fifth member for the group.

But finally on the day selected, each of the five in the group are separately tested on what they have learned about Grameen. They know that if they fail, they will let down not only themselves but also the others in their group. They have to answer questions like:

'What is the group fund?'

They don't have to write anything down – most of them don't know how to read and write – but it must be clear that they understand what they are saying.

If a prospective borrower fails to answer correctly, the bank worker will tell the group to study some more. Others in the group will tell her, 'For God's sake, even this you cannot do right! You have ruined not only yourself but us as well.'

This process assures us that only those who are really desperate and tough will become members of Grameen.

Some critics say our rural clients are too submissive, that we can intimidate them into joining. Perhaps this is why we try to make it hard to join Grameen. We wanted our members to overcome hardship and harassment, so that only those who are genuinely poor come to us. Better-off women will not find it worthwhile to go through with it.

Some critics say this gives us an unfair advantage than if we just took all the poor regardless of personal qualities. But I disagree. As a pioneer, you need more courage, more ambition. Once destitute borrowers have proven how successful they can become with micro-credit, then it will be easier for their neighbours to join. For those who come later, it will not be like stepping out into the unknown.

* * *

We focused on helping women to form groups and on initiating the loan process. Awareness-building and leadership development would follow the delivery of credit, rather than precede it.

The time it took for a group to form until it was recognized as such by the bank project, could be anywhere from a few weeks to a few months. Members first had to participate in training and learn our rules. Once the members had demonstrated their knowledge of how our project worked and once the group was recognized, they attended weekly meetings for about a month.

Then finally the day would come when a group member would muster her strength and ask for a loan; usually the first loan is about $12, or $15. She cannot imagine larger amounts than that, it is the largest amount she can possibly think about. When all the preparations are completed, and she is about to receive the loan the next morning, will she be excited about it? Far from it. She is totally terrified. She cannot sleep all night. She struggles with herself as to whether she should go through with it or just pass up and say, 'No, I cannot do this. I am too scared.'

What is her fear?

Fear of being a failure, fear of being condemned, fear of the unknown. Just plain fear of something new.

In the morning she almost decides that she cannot take the pressure. The $15 loan puts too much responsibility on her shoulders. She has severe doubts about whether she will ever be able to repay it. No woman in her entire extended family has ever done this.

So her friends come around to persuade her: 'Look, we all have to go through it. We will support you. We are here for just that. Don't be scared we will all be with you.'

When she finally receives that $15 loan, she is literally trembling, shaking. The money is burning her fingers. Tears roll down her eyes because she has never seen so much money in all her life. She never imagined it in her hand. She carries it as she would carry a delicate bird or a rabbit, until someone tells her to put it away in a safe place lest anyone steal it. (And theft does occur, as our borrowers discover.)

She cannot believe such a treasure has been put in her hands. This generally is the beginning for a Grameen borrower.

All her life she has been told she was no good, that, being a woman, she only brought misery to her family, because they now had to pay for a dowry, which they could not afford. She has heard her mother or her father tell her many times that they should have killed her at birth, aborted her, or starved her. In fact, she has never heard anything good about herself, or about her being in the world. To her family she has been nothing but a mouth to feed; another dowry to pay.

But today, for the first time in her life, an institution has trusted her with all this money. She is stunned. She promises herself she will never let down the institution which has trusted her so much. She will struggle to make sure every penny is paid back. And she does it.

* * *

At first we extend loans to only two group members. If these two repay regularly for the next six weeks, two more members can become borrowers. The chairman of the group is the last borrower of the five.

When the first-time borrower pays back her first installment, there is enormous excitement because she has proved to herself she can earn the money to pay it. Then the second installment, then the third. It is an exciting experience for her. It is the excitement of discovering the worth of her own ability, and this excitement seizes her; it is palpable and contagious to anyone who meets her or talks to her. She discovers that she is more than what everybody said she was. She has something inside of her that she never knew she had.

The Grameen loan is not simply cash, it becomes a kind of ticket to self-discovery and self-exploration. The borrower begins to explore her potential, to discover the creativity she has inside her.

I would say that with Grameen's two million borrowers, you get two million thrilling stories of self-discovery.

* * *

We also decided to set some funds aside as a fallback to protect the borrowers in case of emergency.

We automatically put 5 per cent of each loan into a so-called group fund, into which members were also required to make weekly payments of 2 *taka*.

If a member defaulted, no other members of that group could get a loan. In practice, when a member has difficulty repaying a loan, the other members of the group work out a solution that assures repayment to the bank.

The organization of up to eight groups in a 'centre' was another way we found to develop leadership skills and to improve on self-help techniques. Centres meet in the village with a bank worker at a regularly scheduled time, usually early in the morning so as not to conflict with work commitments. At these weekly meetings, members make repayments, they make deposits to savings accounts and discuss new loan requests and any other matters of interest.

If the group has trouble with one of its defaulting members, then the centre can help to work out a solution.

All business, especially the exchange of money and the discussion of loans, is carried out openly. This reduces the opportunities for corruption and increases the opportunities for members to assume responsibility. Each group elects a chair and a secretary. The centre elects a chief and a deputy chief. These serve for one year and cannot be re-elected.

The self-reliance of the group, the reduction of work on the bank agent and a strong savings programme are all essential.

The existence of a common group fund gives members experience in money management.

14

The Repayment Mechanism: The World Upside Down

At Grameen we have always tried to maximize operational simplicity. Today we have arrived at this simple repayment mechanism that all our borrowers understand almost immediately:

- one year loans

- equal weekly installments

- repayment starts one week after the loan

- interest rate of 20 per cent

- repayment amounts to 2 per cent per week for fifty weeks.

- interest payment amounts to 2 *taka* per week for a 1000 *taka* loan.

We decided that if Grameen was to work, we had to trust our clients.

From the very first day, we decided that in our system there would be no room for the police.

We never use the judiciary in seeking repayment of our loans. We assume that we know how to do our business. If we don't, we should get out of banking and go into some other venture. We do not involve lawyers, or any outsiders.

It is our business, and we try to ensure repayments as best we can. That is our job.

There is no legal instrument between the lender and the borrower. We feel our relationship is with people, not with papers. We build up the human link based on trust. Grameen succeeds or fails depending on how strong our personal relationship is with the borrowers. We place trust in people, and the result is that they in turn trust us.

The meaning of the word 'credit' is 'trust'. And yet over the years as commercial banking has become institutionalized, it has built its entire edifice on the basis of mutual distrust.

Today banks tend to assume that every borrower is going to run away with their money, so they tie him or her up with all kinds of legal papers, and all kinds of lawyers pour over the documents to make certain the borrower cannot escape the reach of the bank. In some cases the borrower does end up cheating the bank, but in most cases this is not so.

If one of our bank workers is robbed (which is a very rare incident), usually all the borrowers in that village will find out who did it and will hunt them down. Their power, when acting together in a concerted effort can be very considerable. And more often than not they force the thief to return the money.

Grameen on the other hand assumes that every borrower is basically honest. We may be accused of being naive, but it saves us having to fill out all those endless documents. And in 99 per cent of the cases our trust turns out to be vindicated.

Our experience with bad debt is less than 1 per cent. Even then, Grameen does not conclude that a defaulting borrower is a bad person. Rather, that their personal circumstances were so hard that they could not pay back their tiny loan. So why should we run after lawyers for them to give us the blue pieces of paper, the yellow pieces of paper, the pink pieces of paper? Bad loans of 0.5 per cent is the cost of doing business, and it also represents a constant reminder of what we need to improve in order to succeed.

* * *

As for the repayment mechanism, I decided that we should keep it simple.

I went to visit the *pan* (betel leaf) seller, in his tiny stall in the middle of Jobra village. He was a small man with a toothy grin, often unshaven; his shop was open day and night, and he knew just about everyone in the village. Certainly everyone knew him. He was enthusiastic about what I was proposing to do, and he agreed to be the collection point. He did not ask for any fee.

We told the borrowers:

'Every day as you cross the road, or go about your ordinary business, just give your daily installment to the *pan* shop-owner. It's easy, you see him every day.'

This proved to be a short-lived experiment. Soon borrowers were claiming they had paid their daily installment, and the *pan* shop-owner said they had not.

'Don't you remember,' a borrower would say, 'I came at midday and bought some *pan* from you. I gave you 5 *taka*, and when you gave me my change I told you keep my installment of the loan repayment, don't you remember?'

'No, you didn't give me 5 *taka*.'

'Yes, I did; I remember it very well.'

'No, you paid me with a bill and I gave you back full change.'

Arguments were unending. My God, this is mad, I thought. We must simplify it. So I bought a notebook, and on the left I wrote the borrower's name, in the centre I had three columns showing amounts paid per installment and the date:

Name of Borrower   Installment amount   Dates (Installment no. 1, 2, 3 etc.)

I made it simple so that all the *pan* shop-owner had to do was to make a tick in the appropriate column each time a borrower made a payment.

But after a few days even this system broke down. The borrowers claimed that the *pan* shop-owner had forgotten to put down the tick. Or else he had written in down next to someone else's name.

We soon realized that the simplified streamlined system we had tried was worse than not having any system at all. Something had to be done about my accounting system. But what? I didn't know. I believe that every problem has many solutions, and that all we had to do was to select the best possible alternative.

So we abandoned this daily repayment system and moved to the next best thing, a weekly repayment system.

And today, some twenty years later, our loans are still paid in the same way, in weekly installments.

* * *

Our repayment rate has remained high all along. Generally, it is our success with repayment that most people find unbelievable.

In Bangladesh the richest who borrow from the banks make it a habit not to pay back. I am always amazed by the mockery that goes on in the name of banking. Public deposits go through the banking system, through the government banks, through private banks, to people who will never pay back the money.

So how do we manage? What is our secret? Money is a sticky substance. It has the habit of clinging to the person who is currently in possession of it. So it requires enough 'pull' power to detach it.

If the repayment time were to come six months or one year after the loan has been taken, even if the borrower had the cash ready in his pocket, he or she would hesitate to give it back because it is such a large amount, and large amounts are difficult to part with.

Borrowers find a million opportunities not to pay back. A psychological barrier arises: 'I have the money. I know this is my obligation. But I will wait for an opportunity not to pay back.' And life provides us with many such opportunities.

In Bangladesh, people expect that when a new government comes into power, the first thing it does is to write off current debts. In fact, politicians promise as much during the election campaign: 'If you vote for us, we will write off your loans.' When one party promises this, the other party does the same.

So the borrower remains confident that whoever comes into power, he will not have to repay his debt. Borrowers wait for the next general election not to have to repay.

How were we to fight against this?

The psychology of the borrower is extremely important: we decided to make the payments small, small enough for the psychological barrier never to come into play.

I asked the borrowers to repay their loans in daily installments. So obviously they needed to invest their loan in something that had immediate payback: a cow they could milk, a rickshaw they could pedal as a taxi, cloth they could turn into clothes and sell, bangles they could fashion into jewellery.

The asset purchased, when associated with their labour, would yield them a product that could be immediately sold at a profit, and the profit could give them enough to live on as well as pay back the original loan.

* * *

At first when we were working only with ten or fifteen borrowers, it was easy to collect installments every day. But as the number of borrowers increased, it became messy.

Then we moved on to weekly installments.

Psychologically, nothing is more important than imparting confidence: if you have repaid your weekly installments three months in a row, you feel encouraged to pay back the rest because already one-quarter of the money is paid back, and there is only three-quarters to go. If you hit the half-way mark, you feel elated – only half way to go! It is encouraging. And within a year the entire amount plus interest is paid back. Our borrowers did not mind paying tiny amounts because it did not hurt them. On the contrary, it comforted them.

All of these tricks are confidence-building measures. But they are also real, because it is hard to take a huge wad of bills out of one's pocket and pay the lender. There is enormous temptation from one's family to use that money to meet immediate consumption needs. But to part with a few *takas* every day, that is easy.

Borrowers find this incremental process easier than having to accumulate money to pay a lump sum because their lives are always under strain, always difficult.

If there is going to be non-repayment, we can monitor the situation and know of it almost immediately. There is no need to wait until the end of a long period when the borrower has disappeared or is no longer in a position to correct his or her economic circumstances.

So Grameen's repayment system was designed not only to help, encourage and strengthen the borrowers' psychological resolve but also to increase the likelihood that we would be repaid.

* * *

What made us succeed even at this early stage was patience, innovation, moving with slow but steady steps, and the willingness and ability to correct our mistakes, for we made many mistakes.

Early on, we decided not to influence the borrowers on their choice of income-generating work for we thought they would know best what to do in the locality, and if they did not know, their friends or group members could help them better than we could.

From the very beginning, we introduced a system of annual workshops for centre-leaders in each branch. These workshops aimed at getting the centre-leaders to spend a week together to review their problems, progress, learn from each other, identify areas of concern and look for solutions to social and economic problems.

This worked well. They learned from each other, and we learned a great deal about their lives and their worries.

In our second year, we arranged for a 'national' workshop of selected centre-leaders to allow a wider group interaction.

The first national workshop was held in 1980, in Tangail. At the end of it, we wanted to write down some of the decisions they arrived at. We listed four such decisions which we wrote down and gave a copy of to each participant to take home.

We did not expect these to be taken more seriously than the proceedings of the meeting, but we soon started getting requests for more copies.

We held the second national workshop in 1982, and this time we concluded the workshop with 'Ten Decisions'. These Ten Decisions became very popular in all the Grameen centres.

The decisions were increased to 'Sixteen Decisions' in our 1984 workshop of a hundred Grameen centre-leaders, held that year in Joydevpur.

We never imagined how deeply these Decisions would sink into the hearts of our members. Today, anywhere in any Grameen branch, our members take enormous pride in reciting these Sixteen Decisions and telling visitors how many of them they have implemented in their personal lives, and they feel guilty if some have not been fulfilled as they would wish them to be.

Now in our national workshops, we plead with the participants not to increase the number of decisions. Let us do a good job implementing the existing Sixteen Decisions rather than keep adding new ones.

The Sixteen Decisions help give meaning and purpose to the lives of our Grameen members. They make Grameen a closer part of the borrowers' lives than it would otherwise be. The Sixteen Decisions are as follows:

1. We shall follow and advance the four principles of the Grameen Bank – discipline, unity, courage and hard work – in all walks of our lives.

2. Prosperity we shall bring to our families.

3. We shall not live in a dilapidated house. We shall repair our houses and work towards constructing new houses at the earliest opportunity.

4. We shall grow vegetables all the year round. We shall eat plenty of them and sell the surplus.

5. During the plantation seasons, we shall plant as many seedlings as possible.

6. We shall plan to keep our families small. We shall minimize our expenditures. We shall look after our health.

7. We shall educate our children and ensure that we can earn to pay for their education.

8. We shall always keep our children and the environment clean.

9. We shall build and use pit-latrines.

10. We shall drink water from tubewells. If it is not available, we shall boil water or use alum to purify it.

11. We shall not take any dowry in our son's weddings, neither shall we give any dowry in our daughter's wedding. We shall keep the centre free from the curse of dowry. We shall not practice child marriage.

12. We shall not commit any injustice, and we will oppose anyone who tries to do so.

13. We shall collectively undertake larger investments for higher incomes.

14. We shall always be ready to help each other. If anyone is in difficulty, we shall all help him or her.

15. If we come to know of any breach of discipline in any centre, we shall all go there and help restore discipline.

16. We shall introduce physical exercises in all our centres. We shall take part in all social activities collectively.

Local branches of Grameen also take local decisions which deal with problems in their own areas.

* * *

At the very beginning, Grameen was really like a family. Today, twenty-two years later, in July 1998, we have over 12,000 employees and we have lost some of this family feeling. Right now we have 1112 branches in the country. The staff meet more than 2,300,000 borrowers face to face each week, on their doorstep.

Each month we lend out more than $35 million worth of Bangladeshi currency in tiny loans. At the same time almost a similar amount comes back to us in repayments.

Some of my colleagues from this early period are nostalgic for the old days, but I see growth as an inescapable part of success.

* * *

In spite of our numbers we are still 'small' compared to the massive work that needs to be done in Bangladesh and worldwide.

The success of a credit programme lies in how it builds up a rapport with its clientele and how well it can draw out its borrowers' dynamic human qualities.

So no matter how large we grow, we must never lose that close relationship between the borrower and the bank.

15

A Comparison with Conventional Banks

Today, when people ask me, 'How did you come up with all your innovative ideas? You are not a banker by training, how did you set up Grameen?' I tell them: 'We looked at the conventional banks, and we turned everything around.'

They laugh, but, in a way, it's the truth. And it is interesting to step back and draw comparisons between how they run their business and how we run ours.

Conventional banks ask their clients to come to their office. An office is a terrifying place for the poor and illiterate. They find an office threatening. It creates yet another distance. We wanted to remove that barrier. So we decided that we would go to the clients. The entire Grameen Bank system runs on the principle that people should not come to the bank, the bank should go to the people.

This is not just a public relations gimmick, it is crucial to our marketing operations, particularly if one wants to attract women clients in a country as conservative as Bangladesh. So early on, one of our principles was not to make people come to the bank, but that the bank should go to the people.

If you visit any Grameen Bank branch in Bangladesh, you will not find people standing in line at the counter. You may see staff working there, but originally, we used to put up the following notice in all our offices:

If any staff member is seen in the office, it should be taken as a violation of the rules of the Grameen Bank.

When we tell this to our new recruits, some clamour, 'So where are we supposed to be then?'

We tell them, 'Go away. Do not come to the office. Sleep under a tree or gossip in a tea-stall, but do not come to the office.'

Then some complained, 'The staff need to come to the office to safeguard the money and to keep proper records.'

Our solution was simple: 'Display your office hours. When you are seen in the office within those hours, we will forgive you. But if you are beyond those hours, we will punish you. You are not paid to sit in an office, but to be with people.'

* * *

Our clients do not need to show how large their savings are and how much wealth they have, they need to prove how poor they are, how little savings they have.

In a commercial bank, bankers are only answerable to the shareholders to maximize the bank's profits within the limits set by government and industry-wide regulators.

We too are answerable to our shareholders. With the exception of 8 per cent of our stock owned by the government, our shareholders are our borrowers. In this respect we are more like a *banque mutuelle* in France, or a building and loan society in England.

A successful commercial bank is one that has high profits and provides high dividend returns to its shareholders.

We too want a high return for our shareholders, but this is often a return in kind to our borrower/shareholders in terms of housing and increased standard of living. Paying a cash dividend to our owner/borrowers in something we hope to do one day. But the dividend in kind, that is changing their day-to-day lives, is far more important. We can also benefit them directly by reducing our interest rates.

In Grameen, the people's needs and their welfare is not a sideline, it comes first and foremost. All the rest is merely a means to advance our goal of transforming the lives of our borrowers and their dependants.

Our success is measured not by bad debt figures or repayment rates – though we need to keep these records for the internal records of the bank – but by whether the miserable and difficult lives of our borrowers have become less miserable, less difficult.

Only a very small part of Grameen's training is classroom training. The best training for our workers comes from working with the people.

A Grameen annual report, unlike that of conventional banks, lists very small economic activities, many of which may never have been heard of before, but which represent gainful self-employment for our borrowers. See Appendix II, page 299, for listings from the most recent (1996) Grameen Annual Report.

Grameen exerts no pressure on what economic activity its borrowers should undertake. The loans are extremely diverse.* Our annual reports lists over five hundred different categories, everything from photo-binding, to tyre repairing and manufacturing cosmetics, toys, perfume, mosquito nets, hair lace, candles, shoes, pickles, bread, quilts, boats, clocks, umbrellas, cold drinks, spices, mustard oil, firecrackers, and so on.

A commercial bank will ask at the start of its loan whether the borrower has collateral to repay it. Then it will forget about that borrower completely. Only if the loan is not repaid will it concern itself again with the borrower.

Grameen keeps regular checks through weekly and monthly visits at the borrower's house to make certain that her economic health is good and that she can repay the loan, and that the whole family is benefiting.

Conventional banks have built their credit institution on the base of distrust. But for Grameen 'credit' means 'trust'. We went back to the basics of the borrower/lender relationship and built an institution based on mutual trust. We have no legal instrument between the lender and the borrower in Grameen. All the millions of dollars that we give out as loans every day have no legal cover.

The borrowers of commercial banks are all living well above the poverty line. Our borrowers are all initially below the poverty line. We would like our borrowers to rise above the poverty line. Grameen has decided that, in our own national context at least, rising above the poverty line in rural Bangladesh means meeting the following criteria:

– the household must have a rain-proof house
                              a sanitary toilet
                              clean drinking water
                              the ability to repay 300 *taka* ($8) a week

– all school-age children must be in school

– the entire household must eat three meals a day
                              must have regular medical checkups

We at Grameen spend a lot of our own time making certain that Grameen borrowers are better off than others with regards to sanitation and quality of life. Special housing loans have provided sturdy leak-proof homes for 425,000 families; while another 150,000 have built houses with incomes from their Grameen-funded enterprises.

*For a brief description of Grameen loans available, see Appendix II.

At Grameen we are trying to generate not only economic change, but social change as well. We want women who were second-class citizens to now make decisions about their fate and that of their families.

* * *

Some banks in the developing world have a pitiable loan repayment record. The repayment on loans from the Bangladesh Industrial Development Bank is about 10 per cent.

I once had the following conversation with a friend of mine who was president of the government-owned Bangladesh Industrial Development Bank. I asked him:

'Why do you call yourself a bank?'

'What do you mean?' he said.

'Well, the repayment rate of your borrowers has been less than 10 per cent over the last twelve years; how can a self-respecting banker go on making millions of dollars of loans to rich clients who never bother paying back?'

'Well, these have been hard economic times, a lot of new ventures have gone bankrupt,' he explained. 'It is difficult to get new industry going in a country like ours.'

'Why don't you take the sign Bangladesh Industrial Development Bank off the building and put up a new sign that says Charity Organization for the Rich?'

He laughed, but I kept pestering him: 'How does it feel to dole out bundles of money to the rich, knowing full well they will never repay it?'

'Not too comfortable,' he admitted.

I shook my head: 'Bankers keep telling me how indispensable collateral is, but in fact it does not protect the banks' investment. What it really does is push the poor away from the banks.'

I opened a newspaper and showed him the recently published list of the rich who did not repay their loans. All the biggest families were there. He nodded.

'Would you like to know how I would run the Industrial Development Bank if I were given responsibility for it?'

'You would hire more expensive lawyers to engage legal actions that take years and that remain inconclusive for technical reasons?' he suggested.

'Not at all,' I said. 'I would simplify the whole thing. I would take loads of money, put it in a helicopter and go around the country throwing it out the window. And the next day I would run a big ad in the newspaper and on radio saying that it was the Industrial Development Bank raining money down on them, and if anyone picked up some of the cash, could they please return the money within such and such a period, adding an interest charge. And I would add, "We'd be grateful if you make good use of it."'

He laughed. But I was being quite serious.

'I bet you that by using my method of distribution and recovery, repayment rates would far exceed 10 per cent. And you would save the cost of appraising loan requests, all the salaries of staff, engineers, technicians, loan officers, lawyers, all that would be saved. You'd need no documentation and hardly have any overhead costs whatsoever, just the cost of the helicopter and the ads.'

This tongue-in-cheek proposal illustrates the difference between how institutions view the rich and the poor. Instead of repaying their debts, the rich in Bangladesh plead: 'Our industries are sick, we want to improve them. Please give us more credit!'

Because the defaulters are their friends, relatives, political supporters, backers, dignified financiers, in short the backbone of the society's upper class, the government hesitates to put them all in jail.

16

Grameen as an Experimental Branch of the Agricultural Bank

(1977–79)

In October 1977, on a trip to the capital city of Dhaka, I had a chance meeting that radically changed and boosted our efforts to bring credit to the poor of Jobra.

I was in the offices of one of our biggest national banks for personal reasons that had nothing to do with Grameen, when I bumped into an acquaintance of mine, the managing director of the Bangladesh Krishi (Agricultural) Bank (BKB). It was one of those chance meetings, a fluke like so many unplanned things in life, which was to change the fate of our tiny experiment.

Mr Anisuzzaman is an extremely talkative and outgoing man. When he saw me, he immediately launched into a tirade, a long monologue against me and other academics who were not doing enough for their country and preferred to hide in their ivory white towers. It was a blistering attack, and although I listened in absolute silence, I could not have agreed with him more:

'You academics are failing us. You are failing in your social duties. And the banking system of this country stinks. It is all corruption and embezzlement and filth. Millions of *takas* are stolen every year from this bank without any trace. I should know, I am its managing director. No one is accountable to anyone for anything. Certainly not you lily-white-handed academics with your cushy jobs and your cushy foreign jaunts. You are useless all of you. Useless, I say! I am absolutely disgusted by what I see in this society. It is everyone for himself. No one thinks of the poor. So the poor only get poorer. And no one tries to do a damn thing for them. And as for my own Agricultural Bank, it too stinks. I tell you this country is a disgrace, and it deserves all the problems it has.'

Mr Anisuzzaman went on and on like that. He is a big energetic man, and when at last he had finished telling me how useless I was, I said: 'Well, sir, I am happy to hear you say this because I just happen to have a proposal that may interest you.'

I told him what I was doing on an experimental basis just around my university, and how I was using my students on an unsalaried basis: 'They donate their time, and I use the budget from my field research to pay for expenses. The loans are being repaid and the situation of our borrowers is improving by the day, but I worry for my students. They need to be compensated, even in a small way for doing this work. The entire experiment is holding only by a thread and needs institutional support.'

He listened carefully to my story, and as I spoke I saw his whole face become transformed with excitement and enthusiasm.

'What problems do you have with the Janata Bank?'

'They insist that I guarantee each and every micro-loan. I will be in America for three months, attending UN General Assembly sessions, and they will mail the loan documents for me to sign there. You can imagine how practical that is!'

He shook his head, 'Tell me what I can do to help you.'

I was delighted. I could have gone on for years and not have run across a banker so wholeheartedly on our side. I went on to explain:

'The Janata Bank cannot raise objections because there has been no loan default. But to process a new micro-loan requires anywhere from two to six months because every single one has to be sanctioned by the head office in Dhaka. Every time they have a question, it takes months to go up the chain of command all the way to Chittagong and to come back again. It is impossible to operate like this.'

Mr Anisuzzaman waved away all my concerns: 'You cannot go on like this. That is absurd. Now tell me what would you want from me?'

'From the Krishi Bank?'

'Yes.'

'Well,' my mind was racing and I smiled. 'I guess I would like the Agricultural Bank to set up a branch in Jobra and leave it at my disposal. I'll frame its rules and procedures. And you'll allow me to grant loans up to a total of 1 million *taka*. I'll recruit my own staff.

'Give me a 1 million *taka* limit, give me one year, then close the lid and let me go to work. A year later, open the lid of the bank, just as you do after you have left a dish to cook on the stove, and see if I am still alive. If you like just one thing that I have done, pick it up in your bank and use it

In 1952, aged 12.

My father in his jewellery shop in Boxirhat Road; my brother Jahangir is standing on the right.

First US apartment, Nashville, 1966.

With my daughter Monica, 1990.

With my wife Afrozi at our wedding reception, April 1980.

With my father and brothers on my wedding day, April 1980. *Back row, left to right:* Moinu, Jahangir, Azam, Ayub. *Front row, left to right:* Salam, my father, myself, Ibrahim.

Three generations of my family, 1993. *Back row, left to right:* Tani (Moinu's wife), Raushan (Ayub's wife), my sister Mumtaz, Jahangir, Afrozi, myself, Huda (Tunu's husband), my sister Tunu, Salam, Azam, Bithi (Tunu's daughter), Ibrahim, Ayub; *middle row, seated, left to right:* Kanta (Tunu's daughter), Shaon (Tunu's son), Kushal (Ibrahim's son), my father, Jion (Azam's son), Tisha (Azam's daughter), Shanta (Tunu's daughter); *front row, kneeling, left to right:* Ridoy (Moinu's son), Imon (Tunu's son), Nazia (Ayub's daughter), my daughter Deena, Ujal (Ibrahim's son).

With my wife Afrozi, my father and my daughter Deena, 1998.

House built with Grameen's housing loan.
(Credit: Salahuddin Azizee)

Grameen borrower with her cows.

Another example of a Grameen house showing our logo. *(Credit: Salahuddin Azizee)*

Grameen borrower in her kitchen garden.

Rice-husking: a popular business with our borrowers.

Above: A Grameen family in a new house financed by the Grameen housing loan programme. *(Credit: Salahuddin Azizee)*

Left: Anwara Begum, a Grameen 'telephone lady'. *(Credit: Nurjahan Chaklader)*

With Grameen borrowers preparing yarn for weaving.

With former President Jimmy Carter, Afrozi and Deena, receiving the World Food Prize in Des Moines, Iowa, 1994.

Hillary and Chelsea Clinton in Grameen village Rishipara, Bangladesh, 1995, with Grameen staff and a borrower.

With Afrozi, Deena and the Lord Mayor of Coventry, receiving a Doctorate of Law from the University of Warwick, 1996.

Jim Wolfensohn, President of the World Bank, after being received by Grameen children in Banaripara, Bangladesh, 1997. *Back row, left to right:* Jim Wolfensohn, myself, Mrs Wolfensohn, Minister Tofail Ahmed, State Minister A. K. Faizul Huq. *(Credit: Nurjahan Chaklader)*

Above: The first Microcredit Summit, 2–4 February 1997.
Left to right: Tsutomu Hata, former Prime Minister, Japan; H.E. Pascoal M. Mocumbi, Prime Minister, Mozambique; H.E. Alberto Fujimori, President, Peru; H.M. Queen Sofia, Spain; H.E. Sheikh Hasina, Prime Minister, Bangladesh; Hillary Rodham Clinton, First Lady, United States; myself; Elizabeth de Calderón Sol, First Lady, El Salvador; Ana Paula dos Santos, First Lady, Angola; H.E. Dr Siti Hasmah, First Lady, Malaysia; H.M. Queen Fabiola, Belgium. *(Credit: Joe Vericker, PhotoBureau Inc.)*

Right: Speaking at the Microcredit Meeting of Councils, June 1998.

countrywide, or if not, then just close the branch down and forget about it. Use me as an experiment. If no one repays any of our loans, then all you have lost at most is a million *taka*.'

I was still thinking of my efforts only as the experiment of an academic, which would be taken over by the banks once we proved that it could work.

'It is done,' said Mr Anisuzzaman. 'Now what else?'

'Well, if you give me all that I want, I have nothing more to ask. You have already made me "managing director" of a branch. What else can I ask for?'

'Are you certain?'

'Yes, this gives me all the support I need. How can I ever repay you?'

'Well, wait until it is done. Now I have to get the bureaucracy to heel. That is not always so easy. We're not out of the woods yet.' Mr Anisuzzaman picked up the telephone and told his secretary, 'Get me the manager of the Chittagong District.' He covered the receiver and said to me: 'When are you going back to Chittagong?'

'Tomorrow afternoon.'

'By the afternoon plane?'

'Yes.'

When Mr Anisuzzaman got his district manager on the line, he said: 'My friend, Professor Yunus, is flying back from Dhaka tomorrow. He will arrive tomorrow at 5 p.m. at the university campus. I want you to be waiting for him at his residence, and I want you to take orders from him. Whatever he says, whatever he wants, those are orders from me. Do you understand?'

'Yes, sir.'

'Have you any questions?' said Mr Anisuzzaman into the telephone.

'No, sir.'

'Perfect, and I don't want to hear anything going wrong, I don't want Professor Yunus complaining to my office that his orders are not being followed. Do you understand?'

As I came out of his room, still trying to add up what it all meant, I saw a girl sweeping the street outside. She was extremely thin, barefoot and wore a ring in her nose, exactly like thousands of cleaners one sees in Dhaka streets. This woman could work all day long, seven days a week, and she would never earn more than what was necessary for her bare subsistence. She worked just to feed herself and her children. She was one of the so-called lucky ones, for she had a job. It was for women like her, and for all those women who could not even aspire to a job of cleaner, that I wanted to develop my credit programme.

* * *

The next day I met the Chittagong regional manager of the Agricultural Bank, exactly as Mr Anisuzzaman had set it up. He was waiting for me in my drawing-room. The man was understandably nervous for he was worried I would take his job in the bank.

I told him the story of how I had met Mr Anisuzzaman, what this surprising man had said and how enthusiastic he was for the type of work that I and my students were doing in Jobra.

'But I know nothing about how to go about it. So I must rely on your help as to how this is to be put into practice.'

The manager said I would need to write a project proposal, and when I asked him to help me write it, he said he would bring several of his colleagues to my house, and that they would write up my oral answers into a formal written request.

The following Monday five people showed up at my home. The district manager asked me a million questions, things I had never considered or thought about: how many borrowers I wanted; how many employees; what salary levels I would hire them at; how many safes I would need, etc. I answered as best I could.

Then they went back to Chittagong and a few weeks later I received an envelope from him. I read the document patiently and to my shock and disgust, I found that nothing of what I had said was written there in black and white. Instead, the document was a long and complicated thick tome, full of bureaucratese and jargon. Reading even a single page was almost impossible.

So I took a pen and jotted down in my own words what I wanted to do. It was a direct and short proposal, and to the point. The first thing I changed was the very name of my branch. I wrote:

Krishi Bank uses the word 'Krishi' in its title which means 'agricultural' and I do not want this branch to be about agriculture. Farmers are not the poorest people in Bangladesh. On the contrary, those who own farms are relatively well-off compared to the destitute landless who make a living by selling labour. I want this branch to cover all aspects of rural lives such as trading, small manufacturing, retailing and even selling door to door. I want this to be a rural bank, not a bank merely concerned with crops and farms. So I choose the word 'Grameen'.

Grameen comes from the word 'gram' and means 'village'. So the adjective 'Grameen' can mean 'rural' or 'of the village'. In my proposal, I named the new branch, 'The Experimental Grameen branch'.

* * *

Several months went by, and then Mr Anisuzzaman called me for a meeting in his office in Dhaka. It was a six-hour train ride. When I arrived, he said:

'Well, I had to place your proposal before my board of directors, and they say I have no authority to do what I am trying to do. I cannot delegate my banking authority to you because you are an outsider, not an employee of the bank.'

Mr Anisuzzaman paused for a while to frame his question.

'Yunus, you really want to open a new branch of our bank, do you?'

'No, not at all. I just want to lend money to the poor.'

'Do you want to remain a professor?'

'Well, teaching is the only thing I know how to do. It's what I love.'

'I am not pressuring you, I was only thinking out loud.' He blew smoke up to the ceiling. 'Otherwise, you could give up your job at the university and simply become an employee of our bank. Then it would be easy for me to make you my deputy. I could delegate any of my powers to you without anyone complaining.'

'I have no real interest in becoming a banker. I would rather remain a professor. But thank you. I have a department to run, students and professors to oversee, university politics to contend with. I am doing this poverty alleviation work with my left hand as it were. I am doing it in between other assignments.'

'I will find a way, don't you worry,' said Mr Anisuzzaman staring out the window of his office. The smoke from his cigarette curled at the window.

I could see his mind toying with various ideas.

'What if on paper I do not make you responsible for the branch. So officially the district manager oversees the branch, but unofficially he does everything you tell him?'

'It's up to you Mr Anisuzzaman, you know best.'

'I will tell him to take his orders from you. You would instruct him on everything you want. And if there is anything out of the ordinary, then he can come to headquarters, to me here and I will approve it.'

'That sounds fine to me. Will the board accept it?'

'I will handle that. But you should submit a list of your students who are currently working for you in Jobra. One of them can become the branch manager, others can become formal employees of the bank.'

'Thank you. Those are good jobs.'

'Yes, and no competitive civil service exam for them.'

I smiled because my associates, Assad, Nurjahan and Jannat would finally have good paying jobs for the first time in their lives.

'I would call it the Grameen Branch.'

Mr Anisuzzaman nodded, 'OK, the Experimental Grameen Branch of the Agricultural Bank. How does that sound?'

'Perfect.'

We were both smiling now. He got up, and we both stood by the window. Outside there was endless city traffic. We watched a familiar sight: barefoot beggars with babies in their arms, children sleeping on the pavement, kids with terrible deformed limbs and horrible diseases that no longer shock us because in order to live here you have to become almost blind to the human suffering around you.

'The urban poor are another problem ...,' he said with a loud sigh.

'If we can alleviate suffering in the countryside, that will reduce the pressure on the poor to rush here and clog the cities,' I said.

He nodded slowly. 'Good luck, professor.'

How unexpectedly and quite randomly our lives proceed. You just happen to drop in on the right person at the right time, and everything clicks into place. A few months earlier, I had no possibility of achieving my plans for the poor, but by chance I happened upon the right man, and it transformed our tiny university research project into a banking experiment that would catch national attention.

17

Eid-Ul Fitr

(1977)

In 1977, the first year of our rural banking experiment, I joined my family in Chittagong for our traditional annual get-together.

I make a point of joining my family for every holy festival, especially the *Eid-Ul Fitr*. My mother and father were extremely religious. They inculcated a respect for tradition in their children, and our presence at these religious festivals meant a lot to them.

Eid-Ul Fitr marks the end of the month-long fasting of Ramadan. Offices close one day before and open one day after the *Eid* and it represents our most joyous festival.

It is a three-day holiday, but like most Bangladeshi families we take a week off to celebrate it. This is an opportunity to gather with relatives we have not seen for a long time, to bond and to catch up on the year that has elapsed.

We all congregate at 'Niribili', a house my father built in 1959, in the then-new Pachlaish residential area of Chittagong. Its name means peace and quiet. It was the first house built in the neighbourhood, and it has so many memories for us, so much personality, you could almost say that 'Niribili' has become a member of the family.

My father has his own old-fashioned way of doing things. For several days he walked around town examining which building struck his fancy. He fell in love with a large modern two-storey block of flats and hired a master craftsman to make a drawing of it. Then he hired an engineer to supervise the translation of that drawing into reality.

The result is a huge transatlantic steamer of a house. It rises behind a protective garden wall, surrounded by lush green mango trees, beetlenut trees, banana trees, teak, guava, coconut and grenadine trees. 'Niribili' boasts huge verandahs and great unused spaces. The house has many faults: the rooms are too big, the hallways too lavish and not functional enough, and many things could be improved, but we love the place. Today, four separate apartments in 'Niribili' are occupied by my brothers. And so my father who lives on the ground floor is surrounded by half of his sons, which is what he likes. The house is a source of family strength and unity.

My brothers were all there, Salam, Ibrahim, Ayub, Azam, Jahangir and Moinu, and their wives, as well as my sisters, Mumtaz and Tunu. And all their children. We visited Batua, my father's ancestral village where I was born, where the family spent most of the Second World War, and where my father still owns land.

My father spends the entire Ramadan paying his religious tax (*jakat*) which the Koran requires him to give. As prescribed by *Shariah* law, first he donates to family relatives who are in need, then to poor neighbours and finally to the poor at large.

On the day of the *Eid*, our family's ritual is fixed according to custom. We rise early and wash.

At 7 a.m. we head for the *eidgah* (an open field prepared for accommodating a large number of people who will say their *Eid* prayer). The women stay behind. But led by our father, Muhammad Dula Mia, all seven of us brothers walk together. It is an exciting time to be reunited. Our father is more devout than all of us, and we know how much this means to him; but also it is an important family ritual, and none of us would miss it for the world.

In the *eidgah*, we pray. We say our *namaz*. The *Imam* gives his *khutbah* (sermon). Several thousand people line up behind the *Imam* to say the prayer. It is an open football field. There is no cover to protect us from the sun. After the prayer we embrace each other, with the greeting '*Eid mubarak*' (Happy *Eid*). All of us brothers line up to touch the feet of our father as a mark of respect and greeting.

Everybody is dressed in their new *Eid* clothes. Children display a whole range of new *Eid* fashion. The smell of perfume and traditional scents is everywhere. We walk slowly as we leave the *eidgah*.

Then we go to the cemetery and pray for our loved ones. We pray that the souls of the dead may find peace. Father leads the prayer, and our prayers are in Arabic.

Back at the house at about 8 a.m., we show the same mark of respect to our mother and other elders. We also pay the compulsory *fitra* tax, which amounts to the price of 1.25 kilos of wheat to the poor.

After this begins a long round of visits to relatives' houses. After a month-long period of fasting, this is a joyous occasion and marked by endless eating. Mostly we eat sweetmeats; especially popular on this occasion is *semai*, a sweet noodle dish, prepared in a variety of ways.

As at every *Eid-Ul Fitr*, my mother would read the holy Koran out loud. This gave her strength and security. She was devout, and as her disease worsened, she used to retreat into the repetition of these holy words.

My father gave up trying to find a medical answer to her illness. Quacks of all sorts had been through our house and charged him a fortune for miracle cures that were of no avail. My father had sought the help of psychiatrists, faith healers, chiropractors, neurologists, surgeons, biologists, traditional healers. Nothing helped.

We loved her and surrounded her with love, but for Mumtaz, Salam and me (her three eldest children) who knew her in her prime when she was the source of strength, pride and family honour, it was heartbreaking to see her so reduced, and was extremely hard to accept. How difficult it must have been for my father.

My father never once spoke ill of our mother or complained about his fate. He was strong, loyal and loving, and we all took inspiration from his example.

* * *

One of our *Eid* rituals is to visit our eldest sibling, our sister Mumtaz. We always look forward to this visit. She prepares the best sweets of all.

Mumtaz is twelve years older than I. She has an oval face and warm eyes. She married and left the house at seventeen, but she always made it her business to oversee and protect her siblings as if she were our substitute mother.

At the *Eid-Ul Fitr* of 1977, all around us, my brothers and their children were calling out to each other, kids were laughing, eating, playing, screaming, running. But Mumtaz took my hands in hers. How good she is. How caring and loving she has been to me, to all of us. As I stared into her eyes I recalled the day in 1950, when I raced by bus and rickshaw all the way to her house to announce the birth of my brother Ayub. How out of breath I was, how excited at ten. She laughed and embraced me, and immediately called her neighbours to tell them the good news.

We ate and celebrated long into the night, and the next day Mumtaz prepared her bag and moved into our house to help mother take care of little Ayub.

I also recalled a day in 1947, when my brother Ibrahim and I came to sleep over at Mumtaz's house. I left Ibrahim behind and went to a movie. When I returned, he was drowning in tears, his red puffy face and open mouth screaming that I had betrayed him by racing off, and there was no way to calm him down. He was just three years old, and we had no alternative but to take him home in a horse-drawn carriage.

We ate my favourite sweetmeats: the wonderful *rasho-malai*, a kind of milk-based sweet made in Natore. I enjoyed the *semai*, and of course there was the rich delight of mango pulp mixed into *kheer*, a sort of rich, thick evaporated milk.

But what was different about this *Eid* in 1977 was that my wife Vera and my daughter Monica were not with me, and their absence was sorely felt by all of us. We are private about personal matters so no one asked me anything about what was going on, but they all knew. Mumtaz came up to me and held my hands as she said: 'They have gone back to America, haven't they?'

I nodded and explained that it was only temporary, but we both knew that there was something far deeper that I was not ready to acknowledge, a huge cultural abyss that made it impossible for Vera to feel at home sharing my life in Bangladesh.

From the moment of Monica's birth on 7 March 1977, Vera insisted on having every American amenity for the baby – bibs, nappies, toys. She also became determined to leave the country, saying that she could not raise Monica there because Bangladesh was not a good place to bring up a child.

I saw no solution. Vera and I still loved each other, but the problems I had foreseen before our marriage had proved too great. So Vera and Monica departed for the US, and for months afterwards I kept the baby's crib and toys and clothes exactly as Vera had left them, hoping that they might come back. It was the saddest sight in the world, but I could not bear to get rid of them.

In the fall I went to the US as a member of the Bangladesh official delegation to the United Nations general assembly. During my stay in the States, I tried my best to see if I could convince Vera to return.

The Agricultural Bank proposal had not yet been accepted, so the Grameen project loan requests still had to be processed through the Janata Bank. Each micro-credit loan request had to be forwarded to me all the way from Bangladesh to New York, and I still had to guarantee each one personally. It was an absurd, time-consuming procedure.

In New Jersey, Vera continued to pressure me to stay in the US and live with her.

I could not do what she asked, I could not abandon Bangladesh. We had reached the end of our decade-long relationship. We got divorced in December 1977.

Looking back on it, I can see that my sister Mumtaz was right – she had advised me not to marry an American girl. But I do not regret it. I respect Vera and cherish my time with her.

And, ever since her departure, I miss my child, Monica, terribly.

PART III: CREATION

1978-90

18

Taking Our Time
At the Start

(1978–83)

When I returned from my three months in the United States, newly divorced, I threw myself into my work. I was still a full-time professor at the university. Under the Agricultural Bank our Jobra branch was entirely staffed by my ex-students. We could go faster than we had with the Janata Bank, and I no longer needed to guarantee the loans personally, but it was frustrating that we still had less than five hundred borrowers.

A few months later, in 1978, I received an invitation to a seminar on 'Financing the Rural Poor' organized by the Central Bank, and was asked to preside over a session. It was under the aegis of the United States Agency for International Development (USAID) and was attended by a number of experts from Ohio State University.

The US experts argued that the key to lending to farmers was setting the interest rate at a higher level. At higher interest, the repayment would be better. This made no sense to me. I protested: 'If you lend to farmers, they will borrow regardless of what interest you charge. They are so desperate they will even go to a money-lender who threatens to take over all their possessions.'

I went on in that vein, picking a quarrel with everyone in that large conference room. They all looked at me as if I were mad.

'I would pay farmers a negative interest rate.' I explained: 'I would lend them 100 *taka*, and if a farmer returned 90 to me, then I would forgive him the repayment of the 10 *taka*, because the real problem with lending to farmers is getting the principal back, not the interest.'

I was being intentionally provocative because I wanted to get a message across and to spark some discussion on a national level. Experts were arguing for making credit difficult so that, they argued, only genuinely capable borrowers would borrow. On the other hand, I was arguing in favour of making it easier for people so that they would be encouraged to pay back.

I told them how we achieved the full repayment of loans with the Grameen experiment in Jobra, and I challenged them to achieve the same results.

One elderly banker exploded: 'Professor Yunus, your Jobra experiment is nothing, only a pin-prick compared to the big national banks we manage. Our hair did not turn grey for nothing. We have a lot of experience. If you want to prove your point, do so over a whole district, not just a single village.'

I readily accepted the challenge. Most of the bankers did not take me seriously. They glossed over my desire to extend the programme and remained entrenched in their belief that it was unworkable on a national level.

During this discussion, the deputy governor of the Central Bank, Mr Gongopadhaya was in the audience listening. Afterwards, he called me into his office and asked me if I was serious about wanting to extend my experiment.

'Of course.'

'Do you really think your little Jobra experiment can work nationwide?'

'I am 100 per cent convinced of it.'

'What would you need, tell me?'

Although I always accused commercial banks in Bangladesh of being anti-poor, anti-women, anti-illiterate, I cannot forget that it was thanks to Mr Gongopadhaya of the Central Bank that Grameen got its first break over a wide area.

A month later he invited me to a meeting of all the managing directors of the state-owned banks. He convened this meeting to discuss my proposal.

They greeted my proposal with the indulgent and patronizing attitude with which one would greet any crazy academician. When Mr Gongopadhaya asked them for their support, they said, 'Of course, no problem at all,' but it was only lip-service to please the deputy governor of the Central Bank.

The two reservations they kept uttering were first, that our borrowers were repaying because I was a highly respected university professor, and that second, it worked in Chittagong because I was a native of that city, and that it would not have similar success in another district.

I tried to explain that the poor did not go to my university, that none of their families could read and write and therefore I had no power over them in the classroom sense. But around the table they all agreed that if I was serious about demonstrating that this project could be replicated by any other bank, I should resign my professorship, should become a banker and set up in another district.

I said I was willing to take a two-year leave of absence and would let them select a district where I was not known and had never played any academic role. To make certain it was a neutral choice, I would let them pick the district.

They selected Tangail because it was relatively small and close to Dhaka, and it would be easy for them to judge if the programme was having any impact.

On the basis of this discussion, I prepared a proposal for the Grameen Bank Project. I submitted it to the Central Bank for approval, and this they soon granted.

* * *

The University of Chittagong gave me a two-year leave of absence. I officially joined the Grameen Bank Project in Tangail on 6 June 1979.

Each national bank had to make available to us at least three branches in Tangail, that gave us a total of nineteen branches (one small bank offered only one branch), plus six branches in Chittagong including the Agricultural Bank branch we had already created in Jobra – twenty-five bank branches in all.

I brought my young associates from Jobra with me to Tangail: Assad, Dipal and Dayan and I left Mohammad Ali and Shamim in charge of our ongoing Chittagong operations.

Tangail District was in the midst of a war-like situation. Armed guerrillas in an underground Marxist dissident movement called The People's Army (*Gono Bahini*) were terrorizing the countryside. The guerrillas would kill with little compunction. In every village you came to, you would see a dead body lying in the middle of the road, or a body hanging from a tree, or shot by a wall. To save their lives, most of the local community leaders had run away and were hiding with neighbours or had moved into hotels in the main city. There was no law and order.

What could we, a fledgling new bank project, do about all this bloodshed and killing? We became worried for the physical safety of those we were recruiting as branch managers and bank workers. They were hired on the condition that they would go and live by themselves in distant villages. It was a terrible situation.

For no reason at all, men would point a gun and fire. The countryside was awash with arms and ammunition left over from the Liberation war. What made matters even more dangerous for us and what we were trying to do, was that many of the young workers we hired, who were ex-students, were leftists themselves, and could therefore easily sympathize with the aims of the leftist armed guerrillas.

It was the hottest, driest part of the year. During the day, the roads were deserted, and people stood under trees waiting for rain that never came, or for a sudden *kalbaisakhi* (summer storm). Even the slightest effort left you completely exhausted. The villages we passed through seemed so God-forsaken, and the people so poor and emaciated that I felt that, in some strange way, I had come to the right place. This is where the challenge lay.

The bureaucracy of the banks through which we were supposed to operate resented us being there and adding to their workload. Countless times they refused to provide services or actively opposed us. The situation got so bad that one of our own officers aimed his gun at the manager of the local commercial bank through which he operated and threatened to kill the man on the spot if he did not make more funds available to Grameen borrowers. We sacked the officer, but this precipitated a grave crisis. The assaulted manager asked to be sent back to Dhaka, and no one in that bank wanted to work with us anymore.

We did not give up. We recruited among the local poor. We tried to do as much of our work as possible ourselves because whenever we had to rely on the national banks, it would not get done. The underground fighters were young – eighteen, nineteen or twenty. Basically they were good, hard-working, dedicated kids, and provided they gave up their guns, we tried to hire them as bank workers.

The ex-*Gono Bahini* turned out to be excellent Grameen staff. They had wanted to liberate the country with guns and revolution, and now they were walking around the same villages and roads extending micro-loans to the destitute. They just needed something to believe in, some cause to fight for. We channelled their energies towards something far more constructive than terrorism. What is business if not using your courage and despair to make things happen? The *Gono Bahini* in Tangail had a lot of fighting spirit waiting to be channelled in the right direction, why not give them a chance to do something constructive for society?

In these first difficult days in Tangail, my spirits were kept high not only by the excitement of the work itself, but by the generosity of the poor people we met. Often an old man would step forward under his badly thatched roof and invite us to eat *pantabhat** with him and his family. But Grameen had made it a rule early on not to accept any food or gift from any borrower or villager.

The Central Bank gave me a white Toyota micro-bus, which I used to drive all around Tangail. This allowed me to work full-time. At first we just had our skeleton staff who came up from Jobra: myself, Assad, Dipal and Dayan. Later, when we thought it was safe, we brought two of our female colleagues who had also worked in Jobra, Nurjahan and Jannat.

I was still a teacher, a teacher with exciting groups of students. I held classes with the borrowers, and with our bank staff.

I moved into a building which was still under construction, and lived in a single room, with all the building labourers working around me. During Ramadan I ate the traditional light meal of *iftaar* in the evening: soaked *chira* with ground coconut and sugar, brown chickpeas fried with one or two red chillies, mango slices and flat discs of fried ground lentils seasoned with green chilli and onion.

I had no toilet in my office. When I wanted to relieve myself during the day I had to go and disturb the neighbours or else hold it in. This situation lasted for an entire year. Then at night I would go back to my temporary home, a tiny little unfinished room on the third floor of a building still under construction.

Each tiny decision I made had to be reviewed at the regular monthly meeting of the Central Bank of Bangladesh in Dhaka with the managing directors of all the commercial banks present. This was a slow and ponderous process.

Decision no. 37 'Give a flashlight to each bank worker so that they can walk between villages at night' ran into trouble. We wasted two hours discussing this with all the managing directors of the banks because of the opposition of one single managing director. The problem was not the cost of the batteries, but the fact that he felt that village life in Bangladesh ought not to be 'ruined' by the importation of flashlights. He wanted our bank workers to use old-fashioned lanterns and kerosene lamps. Finally, the banks voted for our way of doing things, but not without a struggle.

Some social anthropologists criticize Grameen for social engineering and changing society. But why is this negative? Some processes are irreversible.

Pantabhat is left-over rice soaked in water and kept overnight where the heat will ferment it by morning. For a destitute person who has a hard day's work, it is a substantial meal especially if seasoned with hot fried chillies, raw onions and some left-over vegetables. When you're hungry and it's 30°C in the shade, nothing tastes better.

I am all for change. In the process of changing, old yields to new. If you take it in its totality, you cannot bring change without changing, possibly even sacrificing the old.

However, I am not for changing the old ways, when the old ways prove good and useful for the people.

* * *

We began disbursements of loans to the landless in Tangail in November 1979.

In April 1980, I married Afrozi. There was a big ceremony in Dhaka to which we invited many of the ministers I knew and bankers with whom I worked. Afrozi and I met several years earlier when we were introduced by mutual friends. She was a Bangladeshi teacher and researcher in advance physics and was then working at the University of Manchester. She was as comfortable in the Eastern and Western worlds as I was.

For a few months Afrozi remained in England finishing her work and I worked in Tangail. Soon she joined me in Tangail and we lived on the third floor of our office building. Since then, we have always lived close to the office, and even today we live within the office complex. The only real difference now is that we have our beloved daughter Deena Afroz Yunus who was born on 24 January 1986, but I am getting ahead of my story.

By November 1982, the Grameen Bank membership stood at 28,000 out of which less than half were women (11,000).

How did we achieve this jump from the less than five hundred members we had in Jobra in 1979? The secret can be stated in one word: slowly.

Whenever Grameen starts functioning in a new location, it is never in a hurry to do anything. This is important for our success. First, we do not want to offend anyone who might be antagonistic towards us or suspicious of us. But also, we believe it is better to progress slowly and steadily and get things right, than to go quickly and make mistakes.

No branch should try to reach more than a hundred borrowers in the first year of its operation. Go as slow as you can! The slower the better. One can pick up speed only when everything is in order.

A guiding principle to our work is to start low-key and in a small way.

When a branch receives the full repayment of the first one hundred loans and does so without the slightest hitch, only then can one feel satisfied that things are moving in the right direction. (Usually it takes two years to detect any structural faults in a programme.)

Why hurry? If poor people have survived without Grameen for all these centuries, they can survive without us for many years to come. Our objective is to develop a system that works, not to rush out a service at breakneck speed.

Grameen is a self-help organization. We only want to liberate the genius of individuals to create a better life for themselves. We are not an organization bent on forcing anyone to do anything they do not want.

* * *

In our Tangail expansion we developed a procedure we would use later on over and over again:

The manager, usually accompanied by an associate manager (a trainee who would soon be given the responsibility of setting up a new branch) arrives in a village where Grameen has decided to set up a branch. It is most important that these two have no office, no place to stay, and no one to get in touch with. They arrive without knowing anyone, and without an introduction. Their first assignment is to understand and document everything about the area.

Only two persons with modest belongings? At first every villager looks at them in disbelief because they look like two helpless babies. They don't even know where they can spend the night.

The reason we do this is to make us as different as possible from government officials who arrive in a village creating an aura of tremendous importance around them. Any official takes it for granted that the village leaders will make all the necessary arrangements for him. They know they will find delicious meals awaiting them at the houses of the rich. Grameen tries to do all it can to differentiate itself from 'officials' whom villagers may have seen in the past. We are a new breed with new ideals and a new way of doing things, and we want to show them that from the start.

So our manager and his associate have to pay for a room, and they are not permitted to stay in fancy surroundings. They can find shelter in some abandoned house, school hostel, or local council office. They decline offers of food from the well-to-do, explaining to them that this is against Grameen rules. What they cook is so rough and ready that often it does not even look like food to the villagers.

At first no one believes they are bank officials of any kind, and certainly not managers. If they do represent a bank, how come they not have an office or staff? If they really are bank managers, why do they live like peons, cooking for themselves? Why don't they tell the *Union Parishad* (Local

Council) chairman to do the things needed to be done? Why do they have to walk miles to do these things themselves?

After a few days, the villagers learn that both of these strangers who have moved into the village have master's degrees. They are highly-educated university graduates. Local schoolteachers are usually the first ones to recognize their educational status. None of these teachers have ever made it to the university. They cannot believe that after completing a university education anybody would ever come to work in such a miserable village with such poor people, walking several miles every day; no big chair, no big tables, no big office. No glamour. So usually, the teachers are the first to support the new branch.

From their appearance everybody gets the impression that not only are our young university graduates quite willingly living in the village, but that they are also enjoying their work. We have never had any experience where villagers did not notice this aspect of Grameen and failed to show genuine admiration for the young managers.

Locals try to recall if any 'son of the soil' ever finished university. If they ever knew of a local graduate, it is always someone who never came back to the village again. It is not uncommon for us to discover that the only person with a master's degree within a radius of ten miles is the Grameen manager.

As soon as the manager gets into action, he becomes the subject of rumours and allegations – especially from interested quarters such as money-lenders and religious leaders.

* * *

The manager and his associate walk for miles every day to talk to villagers and answer their questions. They explain the procedures for forming a group. In order to make certain that we favour the most disadvantaged, it is our policy to accept only women's groups which are located the farthest away from the proposed location of the branch. Mixing up the poor and the non-poor is a sure path to failure. Entry into a group is quite an elaborate process. We make so many checks on the way, that it is quite tough for a non-poor to get in.

People see how hard Grameen managers work. Come rain or shine, they never stop visiting the poor. They never try to take short-cuts by appointing some of the villagers as their agents, which is the usual practice of government officials and of commercial bankers. Locals soon find out that their understanding and knowledge is deeper than that of most villagers.

But ultimately, it is not their words, but their hard work which softens the attitude of the villagers. Even if you don't like their ideas, their ways of doing things, you become convinced that they are here to help the poor; at least they are not doing all this in order to reap some huge personal benefit. So the attitude of the locals gradually turns in their favour, and people come to accept that they really want to improve the condition of the poor.

When a young manager gets the opportunity to set up a branch, it is his or her first chance in life to make a reputation for themselves. There is a sense of adventure. Their training has prepared them to climb a difficult mountain. Now they want to conquer the highest peak. They know that nothing is impossible.

The manager alone decides whether to go ahead and start the process of setting up a branch or to abort it. While deciding, they recommend the general location of the future office and draw a map of the area. They write reports on the village's history, culture, economy, and the poverty situation in the area.

To give Grameen maximum exposure, the manager invites the village leaders, religious leaders, teachers and government officials, to a 'projection meeting' at which some high-ranking Grameen official explains everything in detail, giving the villagers the option either to accept Grameen with all its rules and procedures or, within a specified time frame, to tell it to leave the village. So far, no village has ever asked us to leave, but giving people the option makes it clear there is no compulsion.

* * *

Towards the end of 1981, after our two-and-a-half year experiment in Tangail was coming to an end, the Central Bank asked the managing directors of its member commercial banks to give an assessment of Grameen's work and to suggest where we should go from here. Their reaction quite puzzled me. They said: 'Yes, Grameen works beautifully, but its success is due to the fact that Professor Yunus and his staff work day and night. He has worked until midnight day after day.'

This made me very unhappy. This is the ultimate rejection, I thought. Why should we be penalized for our hard work?

'Grameen is not really a bank,' another banker said. 'Grameen's staff does not sit in their office or keep bankers' hours. They go door to door like boyscouts.'

'Grameen has results that we could never imitate,' said a third commercial banker. 'It is not a model we could replicate. It depends too much on Professor Yunus's personality. We can't have a Yunus in every branch.'

I was angry.

Rather than admitting that we had come upon a new banking structure, a new idea which could revolutionize the structure of banking (and question how banking had operated for so many years), they kept trying to assign our success to the individual qualities of myself and my staff. This was the same reaction I had heard two years earlier when we were only experimenting on a tiny scale in Jobra village.

Many other facets of our work seemed difficult to commercial bankers: we were committed to a clientele which was relatively expensive (at least initially) to serve. Our annual Tangail report listed hundreds of different kinds of businesses initiated by our borrowers, everything from husking rice, to making ice-cream sticks, trading in brass, repairing radios, processing mustard oil or cultivating jackfruit, and for each activity we had to list the number and amounts of loans disbursed.

Classical bankers would prefer to lend a large amount of money to one business, since serving that debt is simple and easy. We, on the contrary, prided ourselves on the number of our customers. This generally depresses bankers. Thousands of tiny, short-term loans are much more cumbersome to manage than a few big, long-term loans.

'O.K.,' I said accepting their challenge, 'why don't you spread our experiment over a large and geographically spread-out area. Choose the worst places you can find, and make certain that they are so wide apart, that I cannot possibly be in all those areas in person at once, so that my personality will have a limited impact.'

On a sheet of paper with a pencil, I drew up right there and then a five-year expansion plan for the Grameen experiment. I also promised it would not cost a penny, that I would find some international donor to guarantee the funds that were lent.

They agreed to the plan because the deputy governor of the Central Bank, and our big backer, Mr Gongopadhaya, was there. If they wanted solid evidence on which to base their decision, they only needed to look at our performance in Tangail.

* * *

One international organization always came up with unhesitating support whenever I asked for help, ever since my days at Chittagong University. This was the Ford Foundation. In the past, Lincoln Chen, Stephen Biggs, Bill Fuller, had each came up with flexible ways of assisting our work. At this particular time, the Foundation was studying our experiment to provide us with support in a way which would help us overcome the opposition of the traditional bankers.

Adrienne Germain, was Ford's resident representative in Bangladesh. 'I need a flexible fund,' I told her late in 1981, 'a fund that I can use to cope with the problems we face every day in our work. I want to offer a guarantee fund to the commercial bankers who are sponsoring our proposed expansion so that they cannot back out of the expansion by arguing that it is too risky.'

The Ford Foundation agreed. I asked them to set aside $800,000 for Grameen and promised them that with our record we would never need that guarantee fund. 'The fact that it is there,' I said, 'will do the magic.'

And that is how it in fact worked out. We put the funds in a London bank account and earned interest on its rollover, and we never drew any of it down.

To reduce the cost of our funds, we negotiated a loan of $3.4 million from the International Fund for Agricultural Development (IFAD), based in Rome. This amount was to be matched in a 50:50 way by a loan from the Bangladesh Central Bank for expanding Grameen's programme in five districts over the next three years.

So in 1982, we launched our expansion programme to cover five widely-separated districts: Dhaka in the centre of the country, Chittagong in the south-east, Rangpur in the north-east, Patuakhali in the south, and Tangail in the north.

At the end of 1981, our total cumulative loan disbursement was US $13.4 million. During 1982 alone, our disbursements increased by an additional US $10.5 million.

19

Against the Mind-Set

When people are finally ready to believe that micro-credit is effective in eradicating poverty in Bangladesh, one of the most frequent comments I hear is, 'But no doubt it requires the special cultural background that you have in Bangladesh to succeed.'

And I have to laugh: because in order to succeed in Bangladesh, Grameen has had to struggle mightily to create a counter-culture. That is why so many observers say we are engineering a social revolution.

Not only does micro-credit not follow the general culture of our nation, but it works actively to oppose some of our most pernicious practices, such as dowry payments, under-age marriages and the maltreatment of rural women.

We help destitute women earn a living and gain control over their lives in a way which would be totally unthinkable in our society if Grameen did not exist.

* * *

Often when we enter a new village, conservative clerics actively oppose us. They scare uneducated, gullible people by telling them that a woman who takes a loan from Grameen trespasses into a forbidden area of the men's world. And for her punishment, when she dies, they will not bury her in consecrated ground in an Islamic ceremony. That is a terrifying prospect for a woman who has nothing. She thinks to herself: 'Not only have I nothing, but now if I die, I won't get the last religious rites for my own funeral. I'd better not accept their money.'

Even when religious opposition is extremely tough, we tell our bank workers to avoid all violence, and even the threat of violence.

We tell them to go slowly and quietly about their business in one tiny corner of the village. And if just one handful of desperate women take the money we offer, then the others around will be able to see for themselves that nothing terrible has befallen the first batch of borrowers.

We find that after the initial period of resistance things change quickly. Women who said 'no' to us before, now say, 'Why not? I need the money too, in fact, I need the money more than the others need it.'

And gradually this attitude of acceptance spreads throughout the entire village, and the opposition against us thins away and soon disappears.

But in every new village, it is a new battle all over again.

Opposition from religious leaders causes the most ludicrous rumours to float around the village: Maharani Das, aged thirty-five, from the coastal region of Patuakhali, was told that Grameen would turn her into a Christian; her family beat her repeatedly to prevent her from joining in 1987. But now she laughs, 'Those who forecast those terrible things, are themselves asking to join Grameen.' Musammat Kuti Begum, aged twenty is from Faridpur. Her mother and grandmother were starving part-time housemaids, and she joined Grameen in spite of being warned that the bank would take her to the Middle East and sell her there to a slave-trader. Mosammat Manikjan Bibi, thirty-five years old, from Paipara, says, 'The money-lenders and the rich people told me if I joined Grameen, I was a bad Muslim, and the bank would take me out to sea and drop me at the bottom of the ocean, and I would never come back.' Sakina Khatun, aged thirty-eight, from Dariash Mirershorai in Chittagong District, was told she would never be buried in consecrated ground if she joined Grameen. Manzira Khatun, also thirty-eight, from the Rajshahi District, was told she would be tortured, have a number tattooed on her arm and be sold into prostitution.

Other lies spread about us declare that Grameen

– will convert you to Christianity;

– will steal your house and property;

– is a secret front organization for slave-traders;

– is a front for a Christian missionary Church;

– steals women borrowers away and no one ever sees them again;

– will run away with your money;

– has no intention of giving any money;

– is part of a big international smuggling ring;

– is a new East India Company and part of a Western conspiracy to re-colonize us as the British did two and a half centuries ago;

– makes its staff take a secret pledge to convert the rural poor to Christianity;

– wants to destroy Islam by taking women out of *purdah*;

– will make you a bad Muslim;

– managers run after women because they have some evil design;

– borrowers are branded with a cross, which you'll find if you dig up their corpses.

As soon as such rumours start (and the above list is by no means exhaustive), the situation very quickly becomes tense. Both sides get ready for a showdown.

Usually the women who are the most desperate, who have nothing to eat, have been abandoned by their husbands and are trying to feed their children by begging, and have no one else to turn to, stand by their decision to join Grameen no matter what the *mullah* threatens them with because they have no other choice.

In some cases it is either borrow from us, or watch their children die.

And those on the sidelines who watch but dare not ignore the terrible remours about us, soon find out that even on religious issues, the Grameen manager's understanding and knowledge is deeper than that of most of the people accusing him of being anti-Muslim.

* * *

As soon as any serious physical threats are made, our bank workers have orders to leave and go to another location. One example that occurred in a particularly conservative village is quite typical of how we proceed.

In one village, a religious leader came to our Grameen manager and told him: 'If you enter this village, you will do so at your own risk. We cannot guarantee your physical safety, or the safety of your workers.'

The manager tried to reason with the religious leader, but when he saw there was no way to get him to soften his position, he left the village. When potential members came to ask him what was going on, the manager explained:

'I have been told by so and so that if I enter your village, my life may be in danger. So if you want to become members of Grameen, you will have to go through your orientation meetings in the neighbouring village.'

Some women made the daily trek to the neighbouring village to form a group and join Grameen. But others, more determined than ever as they had seen Grameen change the lives of neighbours in other villages, went to visit the religious leader, and argued with him:

'Why did you threaten that Grameen manager?'

'You want to go to hell, is that what you want?' answered the *mullah*.

'Grameen was coming here to our village to do nothing but good.'

'It is a Christian organization!'

'The Grameen manager is a Muslim, and he knows the Koran better than you!'

'Grameen wants to destroy the rules of *purdah*, that is why it has come.'

'Not at all, we can work at home, husking rice, weaving mats, making bamboo stools or fattening a cow, and raising children, without ever going out. The bank comes to our house. How is that against *purdah*? The only one who is against *purdah* here is you, by making us travel miles to a neighbouring village in order to get relief. You are the one who is destroying our lifestyle, not Grameen.'

'Go to the money-lender, he is a good Muslim.'

'He charges 10 per cent a week!'

'Your souls will rot in hell forever!'

'If you don't want us to borrow from Grameen, then you lend us the money.'

'Leave me alone, I have had enough of your harassing me day and night.'

'It is you who harass us by not letting Grameen come here.'

'I am doing this all for you, so that one day you can be buried in consecrated ground. Now get out, all of you.'

'We will only go when you let Grameen into our village.'

'Get out, and leave me in peace!'

'We will come every day and harass you until you let the bank in.'

'Oh, O.K. then, to hell with you all. If you want to damn yourselves to perdition forever, go ahead, join Grameen. I have tried my best to save you. No one can say I didn't try my best to warn you. So go, borrow and be damned!'

The women were overjoyed. They rushed in a group to the neighbouring village, and they told the Grameen manager the good news:

'You can come back now. We have talked to the religious leader who threatened you and he says he has no objection if you come back!'

The manager thanked them for their persistence on his behalf but he said,

'Since some people in the village threatened me with physical violence, I will enter only if the person who threatened me comes and requests me to enter the village, only then will I enter. I don't want any misunderstanding, or any physical threats hanging over me or my Grameen colleagues.'

And so the women returned to their village. And again the village women went and confronted their religious leader. Again they argued with him and argued with him until he was so disgusted and tired of the whole matter, he wished he had never become involved. Finally, at his wit's end, and in order to have some peace from these women who gave him not a day's peace, he agreed. The religious leader came to the Grameen office in the neighbouring branch and he invited our representative back into his village. It was not an extremely courteous invitation, but everyone heard it. That was the important part. Everyone heard the *mullah* say, 'Now listen, forget about what I said earlier. You can come back to our village. I will try and make certain that no harm befalls you or your property. The women want you to come, and I have no objection to it.'

And as usual, Grameen moved in a slow deliberate manner, not hurrying anything or anyone. Time is on our side.

* * *

We believe that Islam has no objection at all to the eradication of poverty through micro-credit programmes; indeed it is not inherently against women making a living for themselves, or improving their economic situation.

In 1994, the Adviser on Women's Affairs to the President of Iran came to visit me in Dhaka, and when I asked her what she thought about Grameen, she said, 'There is nothing in *Shariah* law or in the Koran against what you are doing. Why should women be hungry and poor? On the contrary, what you are doing is terrific. You are helping to educate a whole generation of children. And thanks to Grameen loans, women can work at home, instead of sitting around.'

In addition, the Grameen Bank is owned by its borrowers. Many Islamic scholars tell us that under *Shariah* law the ban on charging interest cannot apply to Grameen where a borrower is also the owner of the bank. The purpose of the religious injunction against interest was to protect the poor from usury, but where the poor own their own bank, the interest paid is in effect paid to the company they own, and therefore to themselves.

We believe that nothing good can come from a confrontation with conservative religious leaders – an us-against-them view. This only freezes an already difficult situation, prevents people from shifting their views and causes positions on all sides to harden.

Grameen is about personal economic development, and wherever there is development there is change. People improve their lives, their lives change, and suddenly the situation is fluid. The change which occurs is not a victory over another person, but over the condition of abject poverty.

Improving one's living standard is intrinsic to the process of change.

* * *

We are not fighting against anyone or any philosophy, Grameen is only trying to liberate people from the tyranny of poverty and the injustice of a life without hope.

But while everyone knows of our success in fighting poverty, there is an untold side of this story, and that is the social and political dimension of micro-credit. Not only does it liberate the poor from hunger, it liberates them from political slavery. A case in point centres on the elections held in Bangladesh on 12 June 1996.

It convinced me that micro-credit is not only a tool against poverty but turns out to be an effective tool for change against those forces of paternalism and extremism that would keep the poor in a downtrodden state.

Voter turn-out in the 1996 election was 73 per cent. The official records on the exact percentage of women voters casting votes is not published, but Grameen's information compiled across the country indicates that in most constituencies more women voted than men.

Because usually the turn-out of women voters was below that of men, election officials had set up voting booths for men with twice the capacity of voting booths for women. The result was that women voters waited in line an average of three hours, while men waited less than an hour. The women did not have to be told whom to vote for. Many, if not most, of them suffered enormously at the hands of the conservative paternalists and fundamentalist clerics who threatened them with all sorts of dire punishments for violating rules set by them.

To fight their way out of the clutches of money-lenders, to stop begging in the street, to borrow from Grameen, takes an enormous amount of personal courage, will power and discipline; so it is not surprising that they had the courage to cast a vote. For them it was just one more cry for freedom and justice.

The fundamentalist Islamic party had seventeen seats in the previous parliament. In the 1996 election they lost fourteen seats. One of the explanations offered for this debacle of the party was the large turn-out of female voters throughout the country. They voted not just for a candidate, but for a house, a subsistence income, a sanitary toilet and fresh water.

* * *

In 1995, I was in New York at a meeting where geostrategists, little concerned with the alleviation of poverty, peppered me with questions about how to combat Islamic zealots. I pointed out that Grameen was not at war with anyone, certainly not with any zealots. What I said was that micro-credit gives the poor and the barefoot access to credit that normally only the wealthy enjoy. This allows what was once frozen, fixed and unmovable in society to become unblocked. By economic development our borrowers suddenly bypass a whole series of rules and orders of extremists they disavow.

My audience listened to me because their primary interest was to contain a religious threat, but I see this as a natural outcome of the eradication of poverty and the human liberation of the poor.

What is amazing is how smoothly and 'biologically' micro-credit works: just as investment capital of much larger amounts creates dividends, so does its smallest and least significant form. It is the natural well-spring of creative and economic life, so that people can add investment capital to their human capital to improve their lives and the world around them.

Some of the West's great geostrategists and thinkers see the world locked in future cultural struggles, such as Christianity versus Islam. They seem to think it is inevitable and are quite pessimistic because of the militancy of certain extremist regimes.

We at Grameen do not look at the world this way. We make loans to Muslim, Hindu, Christian and Buddhist women alike, all religious and cultural groups are represented on our board of directors.

There is no reason for religious or cultural wars if the poorest can, through their own self-help, their own micro-capital, develop and become independent, active, thinking and creative human beings.

Let us hope that the West, champion of capitalism, will see and learn the lessons we have learned here in Bangladesh.

The side-benefits of micro-credit are not only political, but also social: thanks to economic activity, the poorest women in Bangladesh who were not allowed to go out of their houses because of *purdah*, now have the mobility to travel and talk to other women. In Norway's Arctic region, micro-credit has been used to repopulate islands where women had lost their social context. In Chicago and Arkansas, it has helped women who were second and third generation welfare recipients get off welfare. On Native American reservations in North America, it has helped alcoholics stop drinking and start working for themselves.

Why should we be surprised that in Bangladesh it has helped defeat religious fundamentalism at the ballot box?

Micro-credit may not be a cure-all, but it is a force for change, not only economic and personal, but also social and political.

20

Natural Disasters:
Our Other Enemies

Bangladesh is a land of natural disasters, so this is unfortunately an important factor in our doing business here.

But no matter what cataclysm, weather disaster or personal tragedy befalls a borrower, our philosophy is always to try to get that person to pay back the loan even if it is only at the rate of a halfpenny a week. The purpose here is to boost the borrower's self-reliance, pride and confidence in her own abilities. To forgive a loan does just the opposite and can undo years of difficult work in trying to get that borrower to believe in her own ability.

If a flood or a famine decimates a village and kills a borrower's crops or animals, we immediately and always lend her new money to start up again. We never wipe out the old loan, we convert it into a very long-term loan and try to get the borrower to pay it off ever so slowly.

In the extreme case where the borrower dies, we pay a grant from the Central Emergency Fund (a life insurance fund for borrowers) to the deceased's family as soon as possible. We then ask the group or centre to replace the deceased member with a new member from that same family.

Bangladesh has so many natural disasters that often an area will be hit by several disasters in the same year. It has happened that a village, a district or a whole region is hit by floods as many as four times in a year, which completely wipe out all the savings and assets of a family.

Grameen's operational procedures in such situations are always the same.

First, we suspend all rules and regulations of the bank; and the local bank manager and all bank personnel are directed to go out immediately and scour the region to save as many lives as possible, provide shelter, medicine, food, protect children and the old.

This may sound simple, but in fact it is extremely important and difficult. After a catastrophe such as the 1991 tidal wave that killed some 150,000 people in the Cox's Bazaar region of southern Bangladesh, survivors were completely paralysed with fear and psychological trauma.

They had heard the warning alarms given at midnight, but rather than heed them, many thought the situation would not turn out to be so disastrous, as they had heard many such warnings in the past. The tidal wave hit at 2 a.m. catching much of the population completely unawares. Grameen bank workers and managers were badly hurt. After recovering from their shock, they went out in boats looking for survivors. Bloated bodies of dead animals and dead humans lay everywhere.

The survivors had to be taken by the hand and led to safety. Many of them just sat still, not knowing what to do. Often they sat next to their devastated houses afraid looters would steal what few belongings they had left. In the hours immediately following such a cataclysm, many lives continue to be lost because the traumatized survivors do not immediately make provisions for shelter and food.

Second, the bank workers immediately visit the houses of our members and try to re-establish the victims' confidence by letting them know that their bank and other fellow members are ready to support them. We then find out what the survivors need to start again and make provisions to give it to them.

Emergency food as well as water and saline solution to prevent dehydration and diarrhoea are delivered to the families affected by disasters. Emergency seeds for planting and cash for buying new cattle and new capital assets are distributed.

The importance here of new loans is above all else psychological. We want to give time to our members to mourn their loved ones, but we do not want them to sink into apathy and lethargy from despair.

We want them to start right up again thinking of surviving and rebuilding what they have lost. Since national and international relief is usually late and inadequate, the only way they can get through the pain, suffering and devastation is by going on and rebuilding what they had.

What other choice have they, or we as the bank committed to helping them? Short of letting our members die, we must get them back on their feet again.

Third, the old loans are rescheduled and a long grace period is accorded for repayment. The local centre is given the authority to decide in a special meeting how long to give for the victims to pay back their loan after the disaster.

Fourth, we look into longer-term plans that will make their area safer, such as building cyclone shelters and training the villagers and their children to take advantage of the shelters.

Grameen keeps no overall statistics on how many natural catastrophes we have had to overcome regionally, or as a nation. But I estimate that about 5 per cent of our loans go to survivors of natural catastrophes.

This is something we have become expert in handling. So much so, that many of our Grameen branch offices along the coastal belt are now built in solid, reinforced concrete, tall cyclone and tidal wave shelters.

It has almost become our national habit to claim we are helpless and need hand-outs from the international community. In the past, one of the ways the government got aid was by playing up our natural disasters. As this book goes to press, severe floods in Bangladesh have made millions of people, including Grameen borrowers, homeless and incomeless. A big disaster is in the making, but it is not getting enough international attention.

Policies pursued by past governments were in this regard counter-productive.

If governments offer subsidized loans or interest-free loans and criticize the interest rates charged by banks for the poor, it becomes impossible to run a self-reliant micro-credit programme. It makes it extremely difficult for independent organizations such as ourselves to continue to do business and to provide the services at a rate of return necessary to keep us in existence.

Equally, when governments forgive loans extended by nationalized banks, it creates an almost untenable situation for micro-credit programmes to recover their money.

* * *

Here, as described in Pramila's story, one can see the kinds of disasters that confront our borrowers. In June 1971, during the Liberation war, Pramila's house was burned down as it was again in October of the same year by the Pakistani army. She joined Grameen in 1984. In 1986 she contracted enteritis, and went into Tangail hospital. She was operated on and was told not to work for a couple of years. Her fellow group members suggested she take a loan from their group fund to pay for the operation, but as there was not enough she sold her cow and her grocery shop.

She was given a new loan with which she bought milking cows. When these died of an unknown disease, she went to her weekly centre and took out a tiny loan of $60 from the group fund with which she bought a new cow.

During the floods of 1988, the village of Chabbisha was under water and her house was destroyed. She lost all her crops. Grameen stopped all meetings for three weeks as disease and epidemic had broken out in the village. The bank staff visited the village daily to give water purification tablets and guidance in how to survive because the drinking water was highly polluted. Pramila received 40 kilos of wheat and vegetable seed from Grameen which she paid back at cost price into the centre's disaster fund. She started her grocery store up again three weeks later when the situation in the village became normal again.

In 1992, the fire from an oil lamp spread and burned down her house. Neighbours and villagers tried to help her put out the fire, but in the ensuing blaze, she lost all her stocks, crops, food, her entire grocery store and her two cows. All that was left were the clothes she and her husband had on their backs.

The Grameen staff visited her the next morning and organized a special meeting at which they offered her a loan from the centre's disaster fund. Instead, she decided to take a seasonal loan and a loan from her group fund. Part of the loan she used to start up a small grocery store and the rest she invested in fertilizer for her irrigated land. With the help of her three grown sons, she was able to start paying off the loan. Three months later Grameen gave her a housing loan, and she constructed herself a new house.

She is currently in her twelfth loan. She owns and leases enough land to sell about 10 mounds of rice paddy a year, after feeding her whole family.

21

Training Grameen Staff

There is no one secret to our success, but surely the hard work and dedication of our bank workers is a most important part of it.

To build this level of motivation and commitment, we have found it is important to pick fresh young people to run our branches. Those who have no previous work experience of any kind are the best suited.

Previous work experience always distracts people from the kind of things we want them to do at Grameen.

Grameen has a policy against hiring from other banks or other organizations because lateral hires do not have the same feel for the organization as those employees who have come up through our ranks. We believe in fanning the motivation and loyalty of our personnel as they work their way up. These are people who might never have an opportunity at top jobs without Grameen.

If we hired 'experts', the likelihood is they would ask the same old questions, using the same old tools, and they would arrive at the same old conclusions as in the past, perhaps verbalized differently.

Old experts using new language to fit the new mood in the organization that hires them would be a blueprint for disaster. That is why we have made it a cardinal rule of Grameen never to hire anyone who has worked in a traditional bank, for it would take too much time to reprogramme them to our iconoclastic ways.

If one needs five people to run a branch, then we recommend starting training with ten and gradually selecting the best five on the basis of performance during the training.

Working in a bank for the poor is, and must be recognized as, highly specialized work. This is true from the planning and designing down to the person-to-person contact in the field.

If one accepts that banks for the poor are an entirely new breed of creature then it stands to reason that one has to find a new breed of worker.

* * *

What makes a Grameen worker or manager so different from other young people? A willingness to work under such harsh conditions?

I believe part of the answer lies in the training.

Our training is simple, but tough and rigorous. It is simple because the bulk of it is self-taught. There are no pages of reading material to go through. There are no books to read. We find that the villages of Bangladesh teach young people more about life than the pages of any book could ever teach them.

Anyone who has a master's degree in any discipline with at least a 'second class' (a B average or better) in all final examinations, and of an age not exceeding twenty-seven years, is eligible to apply for a job as one of our bank managers.

We advertise in the national newspapers and receive a large number of applications. We have always felt that if we had the facilities we should take them all. Half of them would make first-class bank managers for Grameen. But since our training facilities are limited we screen the candidates through interviews to pick only a selected few.

Those we select are asked to report to our Training Institute. Here they receive a two-day briefing on the format of their training, and then we send them off to various branches for six months. Before they go, the Institute tells them: 'Observe everything carefully. When your training is over, your task will be to create a Grameen branch of your own which will be better in every respect than the one in which you spent your first six months.'

So trainees discover for themselves what Grameen is all about by watching others run one of our branches. During this time, they are encouraged to criticize and to come up with proposals for modification or improvement of any work procedures. They then present them to their assembled colleagues at the Training Institute in the Dhaka headquarters, in order to convince them that if the proposals were accepted and introduced, Grameen would function better.

Each batch of trainees meets for one week at our Training Institute, three times during the six months, after a two-month segment. During this week back at headquarters, each trainees tries to outwit the other by raising intricate operational problems, proposing new rules and procedures and convincing their colleagues that these would make us more efficient. They criticize the branches with whom they are attached for not doing enough, or for not doing things properly. Issues are raised and debated, but not resolved. They are asked to go back to their branches to find answers to the questions they themselves have raised.

During these six months in the field, the young university graduates come face to face with the reality of Bangladesh for the first time in their lives.

Nobody has taught them any of this before. At first they want to run away from this intolerable situation. They regret taking the job with Grameen. But then they see that some of their friends are taking the matter seriously. They do not want to fall behind their friends. They look seriously at everything around them. What they see impresses them. They see their predecessors from their own university, even their own department, working hard to bring changes to the harsh reality that surrounds them.

Above all they notice that all this hard work is producing results. They can see the changes, they can feel them, touch them. What they see excites them. It is not a promise for change in the distant future. It's right here and now before their eyes. This attracts them. They want to be instruments of change themselves. They can see the respect commanded from borrowers.

Often a trainee can feel the self-respect and confidence that such work brings. Each wants to do better than others who have gone before.

* * *

When our trainees return for a week after a two-month spell in the field, they always bring in a breath of fresh air. They have a lot of keen observations to report.

While we, the old guard inside headquarters relax in self-admiration for doing such a superb job, our trainees report all kinds of terrible things directly from the field. They tell everyone how our dependable and sacred rules are routinely violated, how the process we imagined was working like clockwork, is in fact disintegrating. They come with major plans for overhauling our operations, and terrible punishments for those who violate our rules. And we old fogies at the top have to sit up straight and grab our latest reports from the field, our latest trend analyses and everything else we can lay our hands on, and hold on to our chairs to meet this onslaught.

In the ensuing open debate that we encourage, many of the sharp edges of the trainees' criticisms are softened, but there are elements of truth in what they report.

We may feel a little reassured, but we still send all the information to our Monitoring and Evaluation Department to keep an eye out for these problems and to check up on them from time to time.

Not only do we allow diversity of personal opinions and styles, but we actively encourage them. Innovation can sprout only in an atmosphere of tolerance, diversity and curiosity. In a regime of rigidity, creativity has no chance.

Some of the things that our young managers have experimented with in the field, and which we then picked up nationally in the bank, include, an annual athletic meeting by each branch, each year for the children of the members; an anniversary meeting of the branch organized on the branch's birthday; and physical exercises, which one of our staff had himself learned while in the University Training Corps.

At first, many in Grameen, myself included, believed such exercises would be too regimented and would be resented by the members. But we discovered that our male members were voluntarily gathering every week in open ground to exercise and parade with members from various centres and branches, because it strengthened their self-discipline and their resolve to get out of poverty. So we decided to expand this practice in a modified form to the entire bank.

Generally, Bangladeshi young men and women have a strong sense of social responsibility. Students have always been at the forefront of social and political movements in our society. They were in the front lines of our war of Liberation. And they still make enormous personal sacrifices for national causes.

We offer our young workers a lot of responsibility with a lot of flexibility.

* * *

Unlike any other commercial bank workers, our staff members are above all else teachers. They are teachers in the sense that they help their borrowers to unfold their full potential, to discover their strengths, to push their horizons and their capabilities further than ever before. We give our staff an opportunity to use all their knowledge, imagination and experience to become true teachers. The job of manager is a personal adventure, the type of challenge a student has never had an opportunity to take up before.

I am a teacher by choice. Many of the senior officials at Grameen were my students at Chittagong University, and I am happy that they look upon me more as a teacher than as a boss. You have to be formal with your boss but with a teacher the relationship is more informal, even spiritual.

One can discuss one's problems and weaknesses freely with a teacher. One can admit one's personal mistakes more freely without fear of triggering any official sanction.

An official needs his office, his papers, his desk, his telephone to remain an official. And often he feels lost without his props. But you can strip everything away from a Grameen employee and still at heart he remains a teacher.

* * *

Our bank workers, unlike our managers, do not have master's degrees. They have only two years of college education and at least a second division (a B average) in both high school and college. If they were to enter government, they might become junior clerks or office boys, and they would be at the bottom of the office hierarchy.

We receive thousands of applications each year for such positions. But unfortunately we take only about one in ten applicants. I say unfortunately because I believe that 75 per cent of those interviewed would make good bank workers. We feel sorry that we cannot take them all and give them something worthwhile to do. Many of them are desperately in need of a job. And job-hunting can be an expensive and brutalizing experience in Bangladesh.

Almost all organizations require a non-refundable deposit with each application. Each job interview costs about ten times what the application cost. Some fake organizations advertise job openings just to collect money from the candidates. In Grameen, applicants can expect to get a job without offering some sort of bribe. In Bangladesh, a bribe can range anywhere from twice to twenty times the monthly salary the job will bring. It has even happened that a candidate may have to marry somebody's daughter in exchange for a job! It shocks many of our applicants, but we screen them based solely on merit. We do not require any application fee or deposit.

The overwhelming majority of our job applicants (85 per cent of men, 97 per cent of women) who come for an interview with us have never visited Dhaka before. To raise the money they need to pay for their interview trip, many parents sell crops, standing trees, cows, goats, ornaments, anything they have. The parents of at least half of our applicants borrow money to finance the trip, many from money-lenders.

Over half of our candidates arrive in Dhaka on the day of their interview, as they don't know anyone in Dhaka to spend the night with and staying in a hotel or a guest house is too expensive.

Nearly one-quarter of our candidates spend the night at the railway station, if they cannot avoid a night in Dhaka in order to catch a morning train.

Nearly all who appear are good people imbued with a strong sense of traditional values. Most of them pray five times a day as a Muslim is expected to do.

The bank is hard work, but those we select get to like their work because it gives them security, respectability, self-confidence and a chance to move up the career ladder either with us, or in some other job should they one day leave us.

Their career prospects after working at Grameen are excellent. But although we pay the wage that an equivalent government worker would get, we find that commercial banks and NGOs (non-governmental organizations) which offer higher wages than we do rarely entice our workers away from us.

What makes our staff so committed? Is it the work itself? Their training? The friendships they have formed, their youth, the sense of personal challenge, the high sense of self-worth, the conviction that they are pioneers helping their country? I suppose that every worker has his or her own personal reasons.

* * *

We always make it clear to our trainees that our primary objective is people, not rules and procedures.

Our overall objective to help the poor is far more important than any regulation we may adopt to further that objective. In fact, the first thing we ask our trainees is to give us their opinions and suggestions for improvements. This achieves two things: first, they pay far more attention to our procedures to find fault with them than if we merely asked them to learn them by rote.

Second, we do not want our trainees to adopt a single mould and to all be alike. We want them to retain their individuality and diversity, for diversity brings strength. In times of crisis, an organization in which everyone's thinking follows the same pattern is far more likely to collapse.

So we hire trainees who come from a wide variety of socio-economic backgrounds. We encourage them to be politically and socially aware. And we trust them to analyse the objective reality and come up with their own conclusions.

Above all we want to develop a problem-solving attitude among our workers. Poverty is the greatest problem facing mankind today. In wrestling with this on an everyday basis, a multitude of problems will arise.

We firmly believe that every problem has a solution, in fact it may have many solutions, and it is our job to select the best.

If you go deep enough into the problem and immerse yourself in it, you can begin to touch the surface of the solution, and then find or create another configuration so as to make the problem disappear.

* * *

Here is a typical Grameen bank worker's day, a composite of the 12,000 workers we now employ:

Name:	Akhtar
Age:	27
Monthly salary:	2,200 *taka*, including housing allowance, medical subsidy and commuting allowance
Bonus:	Two months salary paid during two *Eid* holidays.
6 a.m.	Wake up, wash, pray, have breakfast.
7 a.m.	Akhtar goes to the branch, gets his bicycle, documents and carrying bag and pedals to a centre.
7.30 a.m.	Forty bank borrowers await Akhtar; they are seated inside the bamboo hut which they have constructed in their own time and by their own efforts.
	The borrowers sit in eight rows, each with their own group members. Each group chairman holds the passbooks of her group's five members including her own. They start the meeting with exercises. Akhtar collects the loan repayments and deposits from each group.
9.30 a.m.	Akhtar bicycles to another centre for his second meeting. During the course of the week he attends ten different centres that he is in charge of, thus each week he meets all four hundred borrowers for whom he is responsible and collects repayments for general, seasonal, housing loans and savings deposits.
11 a.m.	Akhtar visits the homes of members and offers advice. This is an important part of his duties, a practical part of teaching and keeping track of the borrower's needs and problems.
12 noon	Back at the branch office, Akhtar fills out all the reporting forms and enters all the records in the ledger. After the branch manager signs off, Akhtar's duties are complete. But as not even a *taka* discrepancy is permitted, he cannot relax until everything is processed.

1.30–2.00 p.m.	Lunch break, a cup of tea with his fellow workers.
2 p.m.	Funds collected in the morning are disbursed as new loans in the afternoon. The workers all help the branch manager with this task.
3 p.m.	Once the loan disbursements are finished, Akhtar and his fellow workers record the loan information in the ledgers.
4.30 p.m.	Akhtar drinks tea and talks to his fellow workers.
5.00–6.30 p.m.	He visits a centre which is experiencing difficulties with some loans, or organizes an educational programme for the children.
7.00 p.m.	Akhtar returns to the office, does some paperwork and retires for the day.

This is the daily routine of a Grameen worker. The headquarters in Dhaka is our administrative centre. Work here is more like any other office.

22

Birth of Grameen as a Separate Corporate Entity

(1982–83)

Bangladesh has 120 million people, but it is sad to say that just a handful of people run things, and most of them are college or university friends. Time and again this unfortunate feature of Bangladesh has helped Grameen overcome impossible bureaucratic hurdles.

* * *

A. M. A. Muhith was an official in the Pakistan embassy in Washington, DC when I was teaching in the United States. During the Liberation war, I worked with him in lobbying the US government and in trying to create public support in America for our cause. This gave me a chance to get close to him.

Slightly over a decade later he was appointed finance minister of Bangladesh quite unexpectedly. This chance event opened the door for creating the Grameen Bank as an independent institution.

In 1982, we met in the Bangladesh Rural Development Academy in Comilla where I was supposed to present a paper outlining the future options for the Grameen Bank Project. As we assembled in the conference hall, we were given the news that a *coup d'état* had toppled the civilian government, and that the army chief-of-staff, General Ershad had assumed power. Martial law was declared. All day, Mr Muhith and I sat in the cafeteria of the Academy with all the other delegates and talked informally since under martial law all meetings were banned. No traffic was allowed to move all day. We could not move either. We sat and speculated about the political situation. It was a day of high anxiety as wild rumours swept through the Academy.

A. M. A. Muhith had become an admirer of Grameen when he was still a civil servant. He had even planned to start a Grameen programme in his own village through his own initiative. So that day, I spent most of the day explaining to him my dream of making Grameen a separate banking institution, and how government civil servants and the bureaucracy of the Central Bank were against me. By the end of the day, the military relaxed its restrictions against public movement, and we returned to Dhaka.

In the following few days, Muhith was made finance minister in the new government. And so it turned out that my day 'wasted' in the Academy had a determining influence on the future of Grameen.

Several months later, I met Muhith and asked for his help. He called me back some time later and said, 'Yunus, at the next monthly meeting of the Central Bank, I want to say a few words to help Grameen gain its new status.'

'Expect a lot of resistance,' I said.

'Yes, I know, but I will put it on the agenda.'

He did. He faced a storm of opposition from the chief executives of all the government-owned banks. All those in the room that day came up with a dozen reasons why it would be unwise to turn Grameen into a separate bank.

After the meeting, Muhith took me aside and asked: 'Yunus, do you have patience?'

'Yes, that is all I have,' I said.

'Good, well let me handle this my way.'

A couple of months later, Muhith again convened a meeting in his office for the managing directors of the seven banks through whose branches we had been administering the Grameen Project, and again he raised the issue of the future of Grameen. Again, all said that the work which Grameen was doing was great, but that converting us into an independent bank would be disastrous.

One managing director said: 'Yunus will have to bear a lot of administrative costs that right now he can pass on to us. He doesn't realize the time and expense his type of poverty banking takes.'

Another said: 'Yunus, you can create a division of our banks and work through us, wouldn't that suit you better?'

'No it would not,' I said, 'because I would have to adapt to the rules and procedures of your bank, and we have seen in Tangail that is extremely difficult. I would say it is impossible.'

'You will lose money.' said another managing director.

'It will never work,' said another.

'The staff will start cheating you. You don't know what it is to have internal controls. You are not a banker, you have never run a bank. You are a professor.'

Fortunately for us, the Secretary of the Finance Ministry, Mr Syeduzzaman, was another friend of Grameen. Muhith enlisted his support and took my proposal directly to the president. I had never met the president. As a military dictator he had no political legitimacy, and maybe he saw in Grameen a chance to score some political points by creating a bank for the poor. Whatever his thinking was, it worked in our favour. Muhith knew exactly how and when to present the proposal to him, and he must have given him the right sales pitch, for the president gave it his blessing.

When you already have the president's approval, it is a mere formality to present it in the cabinet which he presides over and which was created to aid him in discharging his duties. So the cabinet approved the proposal without raising any new issues, and the ministry of finance was given the responsibility of implementing the decision.

My plan was to have the Grameen Bank 100 per cent owned by the borrowers. That is how I had been presenting my case all along. But Finance Minister Muhith indicated that my proposal would have a better chance of passing if I offered a block of shares to the government.

I was asked by the finance minister to submit a draft of the legal framework for the new bank.

I approached Dr Kamal Hossain. A former foreign minister of Bangladesh, Dr Hossain was one of the closest aides of our first president, Sheikh Mujib, when he was negotiating the political future of Pakistan after Mujib's landslide election victory in East Pakistan. When Bangladesh became an independent country, Dr Hossain played a central role in drafting our country's new constitution.

My colleague, Muzammel, knew Dr Hossain very well. Muzammel was a former student of mine during my college-teaching days in the early 1960s. It was Muzammel who directed me to seek Dr Kamal Hossain's help and who got him interested in our plight, for Muzammel had studied at Oxford University when Dr Kamal Hossain was a resident scholar there, and he knew him well.

Dr Hossain, who was also a great admirer of Grameen, immediately immersed himself in the detailed drafting of our by-laws. He suggested we offer 40 per cent of our shares to the government, keeping 60 per cent for our borrowers. Without much enthusiasm, I went along with this. We went over countless drafts discussing each paragraph, each line, each word in exhaustive detail. Then we submitted our final draft to the ministry. After that, all we could do was wait.

At the end of September 1983, while I was on a tour of Rangpur, I received a call from Muzammel in Dhaka saying that the president had signed the proclamation and that the Grameen Bank was born.

This was a day of great rejoicing, and we all celebrated. The tiny project in Jobra had now become a recognized financial institution!

Back in Dhaka when I read the full text of the proclamation, I was shocked – the ownership percentages had been reversed – the government had kept 60 per cent of the ownership and the borrowers got only 40 per cent. In effect, it had become a government-owned bank which was exactly what I did not want. I felt betrayed and deeply hurt.

I immediately called the finance minister to tell him how unhappy I was. He was a patient man and invited me to his office to explain what his strategy had been. I was too upset to accept his invitation. For some time, I pondered what to do. What should I do? Accept his offer of a meeting, or reject it? What were the implications in each case? I finally decided the damage was already done, and I had nothing to lose, so I accepted his invitation and listened to what he had to say.

Mr Muhith sympathized with my position. But he used all his skills of persuasion to convince me that the situation was not as bad as it appeared. He explained that this was only the first step to move towards my desired goal:

'Yunus, I know you are angry at me. But you wanted to have a bank, didn't you? This was the only way I could get it for you.'

'But this is contrary to everything I was working for,' I said.

'No, it is not. I have a very clear plan for your bank. I didn't want to get shot down. If I presented the proposal your way, my guess is that it would never have gotten through the cabinet. So I changed it in order to make it easy for the cabinet to approve it. Now you go ahead with the task of setting up the bank. Once it is established, you can come back to the finance ministry to change the ownership structure. That will be a much easier task. I promise you that within two years, I'll get the ownership ratios reversed. You have my word of honour.'

I was not quite convinced. Once you are born as a government bank, I couldn't see how you could ever change the attitude of the bank workers. I went back and discussed the issue with my colleagues – Muzammel, Mahbub, Dipal, Nurjahan and others. We all felt we had no choice, and that like it or not the Grameen Bank was born. We had better take what we had and steer it in the right direction, rather than leave and give the government the option of really taking it over.

Our staff at the grass-roots level were rejoicing. The fact that it was a government bank meant job security for them and a relatively easy life.

So instead of looking unhappy, we decided to put on a happy face, and we joined in the celebrations with full enthusiasm, trying all along not to let our staff start feeling like government employees.

We chose an immediate date to start Grameen's operations as a fully-fledged independent bank. We signed loan agreements with all the commercial banks to take over their assets and liabilities effective from 1 October 1983. Actually 1 October was a weekend; so our first working day fell on 2 October. And we decided to have an opening ceremony.

We invited Finance Minister Muhith to be the chief guest at our opening festivities. But when we told the ministry the ceremony would be held in a branch located in a Tangail District village, they immediately said that it would not be an appropriate place to launch a bank, that it should be done in Dhaka so that all the top government officials could attend.

We tried to explain to them that as we did not work in urban areas, it made no sense to have a ceremony in a place where we had no borrowers.

'If the ceremony were held in Dhaka, what about the participation of our borrowers, those who were now 40 per cent owners of the bank,' I asked. 'They cannot be transported to the city simply because government officials do not want to go to a village!'

We stood firm in our conviction that we wanted the function held in a rural setting – where we worked, surrounded by our borrowers, near their homes and their villages. We were a bank of the rural people, for the rural people, and the symbolism of where we opened would not be lost on anyone.

The finance ministry official responsible for the Grameen Bank told us that if we insisted on holding the opening ceremony in a village, the minister might not find the time to attend. I told him that it was up to him to decide whether he found the time or not, but that we would go ahead with our ceremony as planned.

As the deadlock continued, I called Muhith and told him about our date, the place and the order of events. He immediately confirmed that he would attend and he gave me the names of friends of his that he wanted us to invite for the occasion. It now became clear to me that it was never the minister, but the ministry officials who thought the ceremony should be held in the city. When I mentioned this, Muhith said: 'They are crazy. Why should the Grameen ("Village") Bank have its opening ceremony in the city? I cannot even imagine such an absurd thing.'

* * *

As we were drafting the legal framework of the bank, I was also thinking about a logo for it. As it would be the successor to the Grameen Bank Project, I thought that if the logo could be among everything else it would inherit from the project, we could avoid lengthy debates in the newly created board of directors – where the majority of members would be government officials – about which logo to adopt.

Often, when I am in a meeting and not participating in a conversation, I scribble or doodle. Now all my doodles concentrated on a possible new logo. Three themes occupied me, all of them rural. One involved weaving, particularly weaving with cane which is such a beautiful allegory and symbol, for each tiny piece is small on its own, but together the whole can become as big as you want to make it. I tried many designs with weaving patterns, but none really attracted me.

Another theme was the number five, since all our groups are made up of five people. I tried many arrangements with five sticks, five people, five hands, five faces.

The third theme I wanted to include in the logo was the typical village hut: it is simple and it speaks eloquently for all that is 'rural'.

During this time, whenever I visited a Grameen village, I carefully noted all the unfinished cane-work, the rice-husking, the different types of work people did, their houses, their implements and decorations, to see if I could pick up some detail that I could use or turn into our logo. How cane is arranged at the early stage of making a cane bowl caught my imagination most, and I tried many variations with it.

I was attending a seminar in Bangkok when the outline of a logo hit me. I was not paying attention to the lecture, but was scribbling in my note-pad, working on the theme of a hut. And suddenly out came a design. I drew several versions of it. One I liked right away, and I knew I had found my logo; I even wrote down its colour scheme.

As soon as I returned to Dhaka, I got it drawn and coloured and showed it to my immediate colleagues – Muzammel, Mahbub, Dipal, Nurjahan and Dayan. They were polite about it. As I had designed it, they could not reject it out of hand. They asked many questions. What did it symbolize? What did its colours mean? I gave my own interpretations: it was a hut to signify 'rural'. Also, it was an arrow shooting upwards, and the red colour of the arrow signified high speed. Green stood for new life, and that was the goal the arrow was aiming at.

Initially my colleagues were not too enthusiastic. I argued that we should adopt it and put it everywhere, on our letter-head, envelopes, and all other stationery so that it would become part of the project, and the new bank would simply inherit it.

My colleagues agreed to go along with me, and we started using it immediately on all our pamphlets and stationery (see p. 305). To make the logo an even more inseparable part of Grameen, we used it for our opening day ceremony. We built an enlarged logo out of bamboo and coloured paper. It stood as a gate through which one entered the Grameen branch. The green part of the logo was the door one needed to open in order to enter the branch.

Our logo was never questioned by the board. It became familiar to everybody as an integral part of Grameen, and over time it has become an immediately recognizable and well-liked symbol of our bank.

* * *

On 2 October 1983 the Grameen Bank Project at last became the 'Grameen Bank'.

Until then our staff had been recruited on a temporary basis, and they always worried that sooner or later the project would terminate, and they would be out of a job. As soon as Grameen became an independent bank, they automatically became permanent staff of the new organization. This was the biggest piece of good news for all of them. They were jubilant.

We held the opening ceremony in a big open field in the village of Jamurki in Tangail. We invited selected groups of borrowers from several branches to participate in the ceremony, and we invited all the staff from the nearby branches. They filled the field. Other guests came from Dhaka. Minister Muhith, representatives of the borrowers, and sat on the podium.

It was a wonderful day, full of bright sunshine. It began with recitations from the holy Koran, as is customary on such occasions. Speeches from the women borrowers were quite emotional. For all of us who had laboured so long and so hard to achieve this, it was a dream come true.

I stared out at all those women seated in their colourful red, green, ochre and pink saris – a sea of saris – hundreds of barefoot borrowers who had travelled from near and far to join our celebration. They had voted with their feet. There was no doubt about their commitment, their determination to break free from poverty. It was a beautiful spectacle, powerful in all respects.

Jorimon, from Beltoil Village in the District of Tangail, is one of the members who was with us that day. She was born around 1952, suffered a terrible skin rash that almost killed her at the age of six and which still scars her today; as a child she also suffered terribly from ringworm. At the age of ten, she was married off to a poor house worker, Rustom Khan, twelve years her elder. She had two sons and a daughter. During the famine of 1974 she and her children spent the year in near starvation. Her husband used to beat her up on the slightest pretext and was always threatening to divorce her. In spite of working non-stop, her husband and she knew nothing but suffering, hunger and sorrow.

On 20 December 1979, she and four other women joined the Grameen Bank Project and in January, her group received its very first loan of 600 *taka*. With the paddy-husking business that she started, Jorimon was able to repay her first loan by 1 January 1981. During this first year, she and her family never went hungry thanks to the earnings generated by the Grameen loan, she also had enough to buy new clothes for the whole family and had a profit left over. At first her husband was very worried about her joining the group, but once it worked without problems, he accepted. She went on to buy a cow and to build a house with her profits.

In her words, 'Previously, we went hungry for days on end; I worked like a slave in other people's houses; I walked from village to village with a heavy load of firewood on my head, trying to get some money in return. We had no home of our own. People used to ignore us all the time. No one ever looked at us with grace or favour … But today God has shown us the path to happiness through the bank loan.'

23

Full Independence of the Bank

(1985–90)

Unfortunately for us, Finance Minister Muhith resigned in 1985 before he had a chance to keep his word to me on Grameen's corporate structure.

Luckily for us, the permanent secretary of the finance ministry, Mr Syeduzzaman was a friend of Muhith. They had both been in the civil service together, and Syeduzzaman shared Muhith's enthusiastic views as far as Grameen was concerned, and he knew about the promise Muhith had made to me. When I reminded him about this unfinished business, Syeduzzaman assured me that he would stand by the promise Muhith had made.

And he did. He quietly changed the ownership structure of Grameen by giving 75 per cent of the shares to the borrowers and keeping 25 per cent for the government, the government-owned Sonali Bank and the Bangladesh Krishi (Agricultural) Bank.

* * *

In 1986, the composition of the board of directors was changed to bring in the majority members from the borrower shareholders.

We now found ourselves in a strange situation. Grameen became a private bank run by a 'government official'. According to our legal framework, I was a government-appointed managing director. I had to follow all the rules of a civil servant, including asking permission from the president before I could leave the country to attend any meetings. (For instance in 1985, I was not able to attend the UN Women's Conference in Nairobi because my request for permission to leave the country was rejected by the president who raised the question, 'Why should a man go to a UN Women's Conference?')

My appointment also hung on a very weak thread, for my appointment letter said that I was 'managing director until further orders'. This meant I occupied the position as long as the government was not unhappy about me. I could wake up one morning and read in the newspaper that somebody else had been appointed as managing director of Grameen in my place. The government was not required to explain why I would have been sacked, or what I was supposed to do with myself.

This organizational arrangement did not ensure stability. I kept worrying about the provision and became convinced I should have it changed before one government or another ousted me from Grameen.

I consulted Dr Kamal Hossain, the lawyer. We worked out a request for an amendment of the Grameen legislation by the parliament. I had to take it to the floor of parliament through the finance ministry. But officials in the ministry were in no mood to amend this provision. Why should they help to change a provision which gave them unlimited power over the appointment of the managing director without being required to give any explanation?

I sent in my proposal for amendment anyway, and the finance ministry paid no attention to it. I then manœuvred to place it with a higher body called the Executive Committee of the National Economic Council – a body of ministers. They recommended that my proposal be adopted.

However, Mr Syeduzzaman's successor as permanent secretary of the finance ministry paid no attention to this recommendation. When I raised the issue with him, he argued that the Council was not the government, and that the ministry of finance was not required to take instructions from the Council. For me this was an unforgettable lesson in the functioning of the government machine: it became another demonstration of how the government likes to cling to power and not give it up.

I kept on knocking at any door that I could find. Finally, I raised the issue with President Ershad himself. He ordered his finance secretary to put this up for consideration at his next cabinet meeting. But the finance secretary sent the papers to the president with a recommendation not to amend the provision. I did not give up.

I explained my case through the secretary in charge of the presidential secretariat. This senior bureaucrat happened to have been a student in my maths class while I was teaching at the University of Colorado in Boulder. Because of our past history, he always addressed me as 'teacher'. And when I asked for his help, he did everything possible. He organized a high-level meeting on the issue, inviting the vice-president, the governor of the Central Bank, the finance minister, the finance secretary, the planning minister and myself. The president was to preside over the meeting.

I argued my case as forcefully as I could. Everyone in the room expressed support for my position, except for the finance secretary who built his case around the fear that government would lose the ability to properly supervise the bank. He said that when Professor Yunus was no longer the managing director, the government would have to step in and hold the reins of the bank.

This meeting approved the amendment proposal, but even after this decision at the highest level, the finance ministry delayed its implementation. Luckily for us, the amendment was passed by the parliament at its last meeting just before it was dissolved, and the Ershad government was brought down by the people's uprising.

Under the law's new provision, a managing director had to be appointed by the board of directors, not by the government any more. When the board went through the legal steps and appointed me managing director of Grameen, I stopped being a government official and became an employee of the bank.

More importantly, the Grameen Bank was now free to choose its own chief executive officer (CEO) who could serve the interests of its shareholders. It no longer had to remain at the mercy of the government in order to find a CEO who would remain ever watchful to make sure that the party in power, or that some government bureaucrat in the finance ministry, was happy with his performance, instead of the bank's performance.

That amendment was the most crucial amendment of the Grameen Bank legislation. Without it, Grameen could have ended in disaster at any time.

To ensure the future safety of the Grameen Bank, there is another vital amendment which needs to be enacted. This relates to the appointment of chairperson. At the moment, the government appoints the chairperson of a bank which is privately owned. This is unnecessary, and holds the doors open for many future troubles. Again, sometimes, in usual government style, the appointment is valid only 'until future orders', in other words, the chairperson can be changed any time the government wants. This does not promise stability. On our board of directors, the role of the chairperson is very important, particularly as nine out of thirteen members of the board are representatives of the borrowers who are usually illiterate.

I hope that all the friends of Grameen will appreciate the urgent need for this amendment, and I hope we will be able to amend the provision before we face a crisis. I think the best way to protect the Grameen Bank is to allow the board to choose its own chairperson.

PART IV: REPLICATING THE GRAMEEN PRINCIPLE

24

International Replications

Grameen replication simply means 'reproducing the essential features' of our approach in different national contexts.

There are many things in Grameen which are important to us but not essential for the success of our replication programmes. In this respect, we believe in practical innovation and change. For example, the Sixteen Decisions are not essential: in some countries it may make no sense to resolve to plant vegetables year-round, or not to pay a dowry. In desert regions or in the polar Arctic year-round planting may be impossible. As for dowries, many cultures do not have that problem at all. But replicators may invent their own version of the 'Sixteen Decisions' if they want to.

In replicating Grameen, one must remember right from the beginning that, if the recovery rate is not near 100 per cent, no matter how good it looks, it is not Grameen. All the strength of Grameen comes from its near-perfect recovery performance. It is not merely the money which is reflected through the recovery rate, it is the discipline which speaks loud and clear through this recovery experience.

Replications of Grameen should also not compromise on the target population. We would advise any replicators to start their experiment with the bottom 25 per cent of the population, and to focus on the poorest women.

It is essential to have a thorough understanding of how Grameen works, of our philosophy and our procedures. This can be achieved by going through an intensive dialogue and exposure programme with existing Grameen units. Any one who will be running a Grameen programme in a new country should go through the Grameen training programme to prepare themselves to face possible problems.

The International Dialogue Programmes of the Grameen Trust, which are held four times a year in Bangladesh, provide a good introduction to Grameen for would-be replicators.

* * *

Today, Grameen-type credit programmes are being replicated in fifty-nine countries, both in the developing and in the developed world.

In Africa, there are replications in twenty-two countries: Burkina Faso, the Central African Republic, Chad, Egypt, Ethiopia, Ghana, Kenya, Lesotho, Mali, Malawi, Mauritania, Morocco, Nigeria, Sierra Leone, Somalia, South Africa, Sudan, Tanzania, Togo, Uganda, Zanzibar, Zimbabwe.

In Asia, in sixteen countries: Afghanistan, Bangladesh, Bhutan, Cambodia, China, Fiji, India, Indonesia, Kyrgyzstan, Nepal, Pakistan, the Philippines, Lebanon, Malaysia, Sri Lanka, Vietnam.

In Australasia: Papua New Guinea.

In the Americas, fifteen countries have replications: Argentina, Bolivia, Brazil, Canada, Chile, Colombia, Dominican Republic, Ecuador, El Salvador, Guatemala, Guyana, Jamaica, Mexico, Peru, the US.

In Europe, five countries: Albania, France, The Netherlands, Norway, Poland.

Africa

We still face old mind-sets everywhere, those of government planners, donors, bankers, etc. At international meetings I am often attacked by social scientists and intellectuals who say that micro-credit cannot work.

Recently, at Unesco's headquarters in Paris, an intelligent and outspoken Malian attacked Grameen saying that the poor in Bamako were simply too poor to use micro-credit, that they first needed training and social services, free water, free schools, free medical care, free clothes. Rather than point out that she had never tried to administer micro-credit herself, I let Abou Tall, Technical Manager of FAARF, a successful Grameen replicator in Togo, answer her. He explained that his Grameen replication had 18,000 members in the poorest slums and countryside of Togo, that it had 97 per cent repayment rate, $1 million in loan turnover, and it was working well and expanding.

My friend Maria Nowak was able to help Grameen replication programmes start in Guinea and Burkina Faso with the support of the governor of the central banks. She had first heard me speak at a conference in 1986 and then came to visit us in Bangladesh to see how the bank works in the villages. Excited by what she saw, she went back to replicate our programme in equatorial Africa.

As in Bangladesh, we discovered that the rate of interest is not as important as the fact that credit is available to the poor. The poor can pay 20 to 30 per cent interest without problem. The liberating force of credit is so enormous, that the borrowers soon had a million activities which no planner or social scientist had ever dreamed of before.

In 1994, Maria Nowak had the following conversation with a shoe-shine man called Moussa in the town of Bobo Dioulasso:

'And what do you do with the money you earn?'

'Well, half of it I keep in order to buy rice for me to eat, and the other half I give to my boss.'

'Who is your boss?'

'Oh, he is the owner of the brush and the shoe box that I use.'

Moussa's statement exactly echoed the lesson in the added value of capital that I learned in Jobra two decades earlier. It shouts out to anyone who knows the importance of allying capital to the work efforts of the destitute. A loan of just $40, or 5000 CFA francs in local currency, would be enough to change Moussa's life forever. Without such a loan, the owner of the shoe box would keep Moussa's earnings as low as possible just to keep him alive and slaving away.

In the Yatenga, the most deserted and driest region of Burkina Faso, borrowers used their loans to fatten up a sheep for resale, then bought a calf and did the same, and pretty soon built up a whole herd; others bought and sold soap, or cooked fritters ('*beignets*') which they sold as snacks in the market; others went into gold mining, using their loans to buy digging tools; still others joined together and bought up the old grain mill in the village. The region came to life, thanks to micro-credit.

* * *

I had occasion to visit Grameen replications in South Africa, Ghana, Kenya, Ethiopia and Egypt.

When I arrived in Mombasa, Kenya, it was the middle of the holy month of Ramadan. My hosts said that no one would be interested in discussing micro-credit, that the villagers were too religious, they were weak from fasting, and that it was the hot dry season, not the right time of year, far too hot for serious work, and our concepts were far too strange to their mentalities. They also assured me that I would hurt their religious sensibilities. Well, I am a Muslim, and I saw nothing wrong with trying to talk about how to improve one's life, even in Ramadan. As soon as I began to discuss money, I found the village women forgetting their hunger from the Ramadan fasting, forgetting their reserve, and soon, they were all asking a million questions.

As I was leaving the village, the local women followed until we arrived at the waterfront where our boat was waiting to ferry us back to the mainland of Mombasa. And all the time they kept asking me and chanting: 'When are you coming back, Yunus?' and 'Bring money with you next time'.

I am always surprised by how relatively easy it in fact turns out that one can replicate the Grameen model in different cultural contexts.

* * *

In South Africa, the Grameen projects have been especially useful.

I had a chance to fly in a small six-seat aircraft to the land of Tzaneen in northern South Africa. There I joined in a centre meeting of the borrowers of the Small Enterprise Foundation under a large baobab tree. (The word 'banker' in this context resumed its medieval root which in French refers to the '*banc*' or bench on which bankers would sit out in the open, the community.) All the group members had gathered for miles around, and there was singing, dancing, eating, and all sorts of festivities.

I had meetings on a one-on-one basis with the borrowers, and then with the staff. I advised them that it was very risky to have mixed male and female centres because the males immediately dominate and take over the affairs of the centre.

We have only scratched the surface of the enormous need of the poor in Africa. We still have a long way to go.

Asia

In Asian countries whose socio-economic conditions are similar to Bangladesh, such as Nepal, India, Sri Lanka, Pakistan, Indonesia, there has been little difficulty in organizing Grameen-type credit programmes. Even in those south Asian societies which have formidable differences – for instance, the strong caste system in India – Grameen replications have been quite well received. This is a good thing for poverty eradication, since four-fifths of the world's poor are in Asia. I cannot name all the Grameen programmes, but a few examples will be interesting.

Malaysia

The first serious replication of Grameen was started by Professor David S. Gibbons. He first visited Bangladesh in 1986 and asked to study what we were doing in one of our branches. Several months later, he and his colleague Sukor Kasim went to evaluate our work in Rangpur, a poor district in the north-west of the country. There in Rangpur, the Grameen bug bit them both.

As a result, they started the first *bona fide* Grameen replication in the second half of 1986 in Malaysia, funded by the Selangor State government, the Science University of Malaysia and the Asia Pacific Development Center (APDC), based in Kuala Lumpur. After a few months Professor Gibbons called me to report that everything was falling apart. I sent two of my long-time colleagues from the early days, Nurjahan and Shah Alam, to investigate. They reported in blunt terms, 'We cannot find anything of Grameen here. Gibbons's replication is no good.'

The report was not couched in diplomatic language, and Gibbons was at first angered by the way they treated him and his work. But slowly, we advised him on how he could make things better, especially with regards to discipline, group unity and loans exclusively to women. The Malaysians discovered that the more they strayed from the Grameen system, the more problems their project experienced. Conversely, the more closely they copied the essential features of what they had seen in Bangladesh, the more successful they were.

Today, Amanah Ikhtiar Malaysia reaches 30,000 poor families in rural Malaysia. This replication was so successful that Gibbons undertook to help expand and replicate Grameen in other Asian countries by creating a company called CASHPOR. Grameen pilot projects have been introduced in other countries with equal success.

The Philippines

I travelled many times to the Philippines to oversee various micro-credit bank programmes there, on Negros island and other areas badly hit by floods, natural disasters and the ravages of civil war carried out by armed guerrillas. Today there are thirty-two Grameen replication programmes in the Philippines. Among the leading ones are: CARD, Project Dungannon, ASHI and TSPI.

China

There is no reason why Grameen cannot work in a Communist country as long as the authorities allow the poor to help themselves.

The Chinese government acknowledges that there are about 80 million people living under the poverty line in China. Unofficial figures put this at about 10 per cent of the population or 120 million. Whichever is the correct figure, China has the largest number of indigents in the world. It has attempted many alleviation programmes, but none of them have made a dent in the problem. The areas of greatest poverty are those that have a particularly bad climate, or hilly regions with soil erosion.

I visited two provinces which have started Grameen replications. They are working in four prefectures through the Rural Development Institute of China, which is a part of the Chinese Academy of Social Sciences: in Henan Province, the Nanzhao Project and the Yucheng Project; in Hebei Province, the Yixian Project. The RDI also has a project at Dangeng in Shaanxi Province. All four of these are under the aegis of Professor Du Xiaoshan who works at the RDI in Beijing.

In the north, I was shocked to find that the winters are so harsh that the temperatures drop to minus 25°C and the poor there live by protecting themselves from the cold in ingenious ways. They dig a hole in the ground where they make a wood fire, and they place the family bed above that hole. Smoke fills the house. The entire family stays huddled on that bed. If they have to go for food or to relieve themselves, it is always a challenging task. They rush back again, coughing and freezing, to the protective heat of the bed. Animals also suffer. Conditions are extremely harsh and adverse.

But in the summer there is forest land and grazing for the animals. The poor Chinese women I met were using their loans to raise cattle, fatten pigs, goats and cows to sell them. And I understand that in 1997, Li Peng, the then secretary general of the Communist party has officially referred to the good work done by the Grameen replicators. This is significant because it helps our efforts to gain legitimacy with a party hierarchy that might otherwise be negative towards our approach. It should also help us keep the replications away from government intervention, which, as I have said many times, is an absolute requisite if we hope to succeed and grow in any country in the world, whether capitalist or Communist.

The Americas

South America

Many micro-credit providers are working in Central and Latin America. The largest of them, Accion, has a network of twenty-five affiliated organizations working in thirteen Latin American countries (and six US cities). From 1991 to 1997, Accion disbursed $1.7 billion in loans averaging $600 to more than 1.3 million hard-working micro-entrepreneurs. One of its oldest affiliates, BancoSol, which started in 1983, has 73,432 borrowers in Bolivia, 60 per cent of whom are women.

There are other micro-credit networks, such as FINCA (Foundation for International Community Assistance) and Katalysis, doing important work in Latin America. The Grameen Foundation USA also promotes replications that target the poorest people in Latin America.

North America

Even though in absolute terms the poor in the developed world have more financial and material goods than the poor in the third world, the psychological difference is immense and makes poverty much more difficult to bear in a relatively affluent society.

In Bangladesh, the poor do not have a TV, or a car or air-conditioning, but in a village even the rich do not have these. In the third world, there are differences between rich and poor, but we all grow up together, with no segregation of the poor into ghettos. I well recall my playmates in school, and next door in my father's village were illiterate children, boys I used to dive into ponds with, and we would go seeking husked rice in the rat-holes of the fields. I remember helping these boys to fill the quotas of paddy which their parents had told them to collect from the fields by stealing from my parents' field so that the boys would have more time to play with me.

That would never happen in Chicago: a rich white boy would never go and play in a poor black ghetto.

* * *

The Calmeadow Foundation in Canada has initiated exciting micro-loan lending on Native American reservations. (In the US these have also started with the Sioux in South Dakota.) Martin Connell, the head of Calmeadow, came to visit us in Bangladesh. He has since become a valued friend and champion of micro-credit. Calmeadow has set up its own programmes whereby it lends up to $5000 to small entrepreneurs.

There are more than fifty Grameen-type micro-credit programmes in the United States. Many of them are performing very well.

Working Capital, based in Cambridge, Mass. and started by Jeffrey Ashe in 1990, targets the 'entrepreneurial poor', meaning people who are already involved in income-generating activities but who lack access to financial resources and other support services.

In just five years, Working Capital has extended $1.5 million in loans ranging from $500 to $5000 to more than 1,100 businesses. Its repayment rate is 98 per cent. They have started franchises in South Miami and Delaware. Jeffrey Ashe has big plans: he wants to help as many as 7000 small businesses by the end of 1997, and to create $60 million worth of jobs.

The following two chapters give more information on replications in the US.

Europe

Eastern Europe

Micro-credit is also working in ex-Communist countries such as Poland and most recently Bosnia. Four years ago, the World Bank underwrote an impressive Grameen replication programme in Albania which has a very high repayment level of loans. Every replication in every country has a fascinating genesis, but there is not enough space here to list them all or to do them justice.

But I must mention one replication because it may have special applications to the nascent UK micro-credit activities in places like Birmingham, Coventry, Norwich and Glasgow.

Rosalind Copisarow, a Polish graduate of Oxford and Wharton School of Business was a high-powered executive at the JP Morgan Investment Bank, and she had never made any loans smaller than $100 million when she read a *Financial Times* story on the Grameen Bank during a flight between London and Warsaw. It immediately flashed through her mind that this was what Poland needed, but she had no idea as to how she might help make it happen. She discussed Grameen with the finance minister of Poland who immediately challenged her to quit her job and devote herself to creating a Grameen programme for Poland. At Christmas 1993 she decided to accept the challenge and to engage herself in the task of introducing the Grameen concept of micro-credit to Poland. She left JP Morgan to take up this challenge.

Rosalind and her small team examined 200 different lending methodologies including goat loans where the first two female kids born are relent to others. They tested nine pilot models for about a year before deciding on the programme design. Their object was to discover what models resonated with the traditions of the country. In the end they decided to stay with the Grameen methodology.

Today, they have twenty branches lending to 4000 clients with a repayment rate of 98.5 per cent and loans of $10 million. They have created 2000 new jobs and 3000 former clients have graduated to the formal economy. By 2002, Fundusz Mikro, the organization she created, intends to be self-supporting with a full banking licence.

'When I reflect on my previous career, it seems two-dimensional,' says Rosalind today. 'It lacked soul. What I do now has put real meaning in my work – and therefore in my life.' She is just one of many social entrepreneurs who have devoted their life to helping provide micro-credit opportunities to the poor.

Western Europe

Many European charitable organizations, not to mention intellectuals, bankers and journalists are interested in our ideas, but few are willing to initiate micro-credit programmes.

I have addressed German parliamentary committees in Bonn, as well as the German Council of Bishops; I have addressed French TV audiences, received honorary degrees in England; but the process of getting real action started is very slow.

Maybe Grameen is too outlandish a concept, it upsets too many of their preconceived ideas and their old ways of doing things. In the developed world, the greatest problem is undoing the ravages of the social welfare system.

Over and over, our clones have run into the same problem: recipients of a monthly subsistence hand-out from the government feel as shy and frightened by the offer of a personal loan to start a business as the *purdah*-covered women in Bangladeshi villages. Many quickly calculate the amount of the welfare cheques and insurance coverage they would lose by becoming self-employed and conclude that there is nothing to be gained by it.

Some borrowers try to risk it in secret, hoping the government will not find out. But government inspectors are quick to call any welfare recipient found trying to help him- or herself a fraud, and they immediately remove their state benefits. In industrialized countries, 'informal businesses' are seen as illegal 'street hustles'. To be legal, the self-employed poor must file documents, petition bureaucracies, keep books and it is wholly unrealistic to expect an inexperienced person to be able to satisfy all of these requirements of government bureaucracy. So at first many borrowers from our clones in Europe were actually breaking the law.

It was a crazy situation. Our replicators in France counselled their borrowers to get paid under the table, and the micro-creditor kept its loans off the books.

(In Illinois, USA, the micro-fund avoided this situation by getting a special exemption from the governor of the state which allowed welfare recipients who took out micro-loans to be covered by welfare in the interim period until they could get their small personal businesses off the ground.)

But even when the law allows the poor to own businesses, the mind-sets of charity programme operators do not accept it. One young man, newly out of prison, wanted to start up a food-stall to sell French fries, but the Parisian charity that housed him would not accept this independence; it wanted to own the food stand itself and to hire him as a salaried employee rather than allow him to become the owner.

In order words, charity, like love, can be a prison.

But things are changing slowly. An increasing number of intellectuals and social scientists no longer look to the state to be the saviour as they did in the 1960s.

United Kingdom

In Britain there has for some time been a real awareness of the problems that micro-credit seeks to address. The Aston Reinvestment Trust, Investors in Society and many other initiatives such as the Local Investment Fund, the Industrial and Common Ownership Fund and the Community Capital Share Issue have tried different ways to help the poor. But micro-credit has never yet been tried in the UK.

The Women's Employment Enterprise & Training Unit (WEETU) is set to launch a UK pilot on the Grameen model, to be called the Full Circle Fund, starting in urban and rural Norfolk (where women are said to be the lowest paid in England). The target communities include East Norwich, North Walsham and Thetford. And the Newham Bengali Community Trust is currently setting up the Newham Micro-credit Institution which it plans to develop to be self-sufficient and sustainable in the community.

France

One of our replicators, l'Association pour le Droit à l'Initative Économique (ADIE) (which was started by Maria Nowak) discovered that it cost France about fr. 1.2 million to create a salaried job, but going through a micro-credit institution each self-employed job costs the community only fr. 50,000. ADIE's first attempts to find borrowers in France were failures. There was Leo, a Zairean ex-preacher who lived in a parking lot, and whose wife had been raped and tortured in Zairean prisons. Leo was trained as an accountant and he wanted a loan to buy himself a calculator so that he could work in his chosen profession. The loan helped him get on his feet and find a job.

There was Madame Salima, a North African woman who used the loan to open a store.

There was a young boy, Bernard, as short-sighted as a mole, who had broken his glasses and now could not see enough even to wash dishes in a restaurant. He lived in Saint Lazare train station with his girlfriend. And since he didn't have enough to pay the cost of a luggage locker, he and his girlfriend dragged their overstuffed plastic bags wherever they went.

But Madame Salima didn't care if Leo paid his loans back, nor did Leo care if Bernard paid back and vice versa. The social solidarity was not strong enough to create the effect of peer pressure and peer support which is the linchpin of Grameen's micro-credit loans.

Critics of Grameen use the early experience of our clones in France to suggest that 'peer lending' cannot work in urban settings. But all such start-ups of new programmes are extremely difficult. After its first four years of operation, Grameen barely reached five hundred people. In fact, many of our borrowers who joined in late 1976 and 1977 were in default by 1979. Yet, thanks to everything we had learned as micro-credit providers, we were able to go forward after 1979 and to progress much faster. Success comes only through a slow and difficult process of failure. I always tell anyone who wants to start up a Grameen replication that the early years of a credit programme are primarily to experiment with local conditions and to educate staff. The start-up phase is not primarily for the benefit of the borrower. It is only after the start-up, when problems are ironed out, that the organization succeeds with its borrowers in terms of out-reach and quality of service.

In spite of the difficulties encountered in urban areas, urban replications around the world prove to be successful. The Women's Self-Employment Project (WSEP) in Chicago is an excellent success story. The Shakti

Foundation in Dhaka has had extended loans to 18,000 slum dwellers in Dhaka city. TSPI in Manila is another success story.

ADIE to date has made loans to 1500 small businesses started by unemployed and/or welfare recipients. Seventy per cent of its small borrowers are still in existence eighteen months later, which in France is the average for normally financed new corporations.

Norway

In 1986, Bodil Maal came to visit her husband who was a Norwegian consultant living in Bangladesh. She became interested in Grameen activities. Bodil worked in the Norwegian fisheries ministry. One of the problems she was assigned to deal with was to encourage young girls to return and live on the Lofoten Islands where they grew up.

For some years, the Lofoten Islands off the northern coast of Norway near the town of Narvik, had been experiencing a serious depopulation problem. The boys who returned from schools and universities went back to live on the Islands and became fishermen. But the local girls did not want to return, because they did not have much to do on the Islands. While they waited for their fishermen husbands or fathers to return from sea, there was little to occupy them, and almost no social or commercial activity to speak of, so that they became extremely lonely. Since the girls were not returning, the boys started leaving too.

The same problem of depopulation was also occurring in northern Finland and in the nearby region of northern Russia. But thanks to the ceaseless efforts of Bodil Maal, the government of Norway decided to try a Grameen project through their fisheries department in order to give the women some commercial activity to help keep them on these Islands and help make their lives there less lonely and more meaningful.

Grameen had never been replicated in such harsh and Arctic conditions. It was a learning experience for us as much as for them.

I was invited to visit these projects in northern Norway, and was astonished at what I saw: another social transformation, similar in scope to what we are seeing in Bangladesh, but of a radically different nature.

Now for the first time the women of the Arctic Circle have access to credit. And thanks to the programme, they have a community support group, people who can help them and give them advice. Before, these women had no opportunity to use their talents. Now they are using their loans to make such diverse items as sweaters, paperweights in the shape of seals, fish and birds, also souvenirs, postcards, little wooden statues of trolls and paintings of the scenery. In addition to giving the women something to do, the activity is an important source of income and helps them and their families cope financially as well as making their lives more enjoyable.

What I find especially interesting about the Norwegian experience is that micro-credit was used not in order to alleviate poverty, but rather as a tool for the social integration of people who would otherwise be leaving the Islands. In other words, credit is not simply an income-generating tool, it is a powerful weapon for social change, a way to give people new meaning in their lives.

Finland

In Finland, Finnish Microcredit Ltd has started prototype operations in the Helsinki district, and the co-operative Eko-Osuusraha, a 'green' credit union, gives micro-loans to its members in ecological and social fields. Four other micro-credit initiatives in rural Finland are governed by the Ministry of Internal Affairs. All of these are based on the model (*nettverkskreditmodel*) started in Norway's Lofoten Islands.

Sweden

Even in Sweden, where in the 1960s the government pioneered a network of cradle-to-grave social benefits to eradicate the suffering caused by poverty, micro-credit is being tried to help those who are in need. In 1994 Kerstin Ericksson started a Grameen programme in the mountains of Dalarna province in central Sweden. After four years the pilot programme was closed down, but this year Ericksson hopes to start up an urban programme in the Dalarna city of Falun, with the co-operation of the labour department and the office of unemployment benefits.

* * *

Watching these experiments progress, and seeing how Grameen ideas have been reproduced in Africa, Asia, Europe and in the Americas, I have concluded that while culture, geographical and climactic conditions differ, poor people have fundamentally the same problems all over the globe. The culture of poverty, this prison into which society puts people, transcends the differences of language, race and custom.

For that reason micro-credit has near universal applications. I am convinced that credit is a universal tool that unlocks human capabilities. Our experience from the Arctic to the Andes, from Chicago to China shows that the Grameen model does not require the culture of Bangladesh to succeed.

I firmly believe that a good idea will always win through. And even if the Grameen Bank itself one day ceases to exist, for one reason or another, the concept which we have spearheaded, namely that of micro-credit, will prove itself worthy without us. Banking will never be the same again.

Sooner or later, there will be many innovators from many different fields, and the entire philosophy of grass-roots capitalism will show its genius in many practical applications, perhaps even by other organizations and groups which have no connections with us.

25

The US Urban Experience

Mary Houghton and Ronald Grzywinski are bankers from Chicago. There was no reason why I should ever know about them, but life brought us together and we soon became close friends and associates in exciting ventures.

They had bought an ailing community bank in an area of Chicago which had been abandoned by white store-owners and white-run businesses because blacks were moving into the neighbourhood. Their South Shore Bank won back the community's confidence, acquired new depositors and began lending to individuals whom traditional banks had avoided.

When the Ford Foundation needed some independent bankers to appraise my proposed guarantee fund (see pp. 146–7) Ron and Mary were asked to visit Bangladesh to evaluate the Grameen Bank. From the outset, they loved what they saw us doing, and wished to do the same in the ghettos of Chicago. It was their impetus and endless dedication that brought the Grameen experience to North America.

At the request of Ron and Mary, I visited Chicago for the first time in 1985. I was invited to talk to social activists, economists, bankers and community leaders. It was quite a novel experience for me. Almost everyone I addressed dismissed what I had to say, saying that there was no way the Bangladeshi experience could be relevant to poverty eradication in the US.

The two societies were at an astronomical distance from each other, ran their argument. Who needed a micro-loan in Chicago? People needed jobs, training, health care and protection from drugs and violence. Self-employment was a prehistoric concept lingering only in the third world and in primitive societies. 'Low-income people' in Chicago needed money for rent and to live on, not for investment; what would they invest in, anyway? They had no skills. And so on.

I advanced the same arguments I had done to bankers in Bangladesh, namely: 'the poor are very creative; they know how to earn a living, even how to change their lives. All they need is the opportunity. Credit brings that opportunity.' And I added, 'Yes our two societies are different, and thousands of miles apart, but I do not see any difference between the poor of Bangladesh and the poor of Chicago; the problems and consequences of poverty are the same.'

And so things stood. Only Ron and Mary believed in me and only they decided to try a Grameen-type credit operation in Chicago.

* * *

The Women's Self-Employment Progam (WSEP), created by Ron and Mary, was the first step in our attempt to replicate Grameen's ideas in the United States. It was a loud and clear affirmation that self-employment is relevant not only to the third world but also to help solve the problem of poverty in the most advanced and developed societies on earth.

Today the offices of the WSEP are located on the seventh floor of a building on Washington Street, in the heart of Chicago's downtown area. Twenty-five female 'enterprise agents', two-thirds of them Afro-American, with the help of interns, volunteers and support staff, track fledgling businesses, collect loans and help their borrowers map out strategy. WSEP has lent over $1 million to more than 300 businesses in Chicago and has offered business-counselling services to 5000 women. Its repayment rate is currently 93 per cent.

* * *

The WSEP programme that was the most difficult to launch and that generated the most controversy was the Full Circle Fund (FCF). Started in 1988, it encouraged economic development in depressed communities by giving women access to investment capital of $300 to $1500 if they agreed to join a group of five peers and were able to persuade them as to the soundness of their business proposal. The credit rating or access to collateral of the prospective borrowers was not taken into account as part of the loan-approval process.

Connie Evans, Executive Director of the WSEP, was new in this business but very willing to learn and make it work in Chicago. Susan Matteucci, a recent graduate from MIT, joined Connie as a staff member of the FCF, which was designed to be an exact replica of a Grameen programme in the inner city of Chicago.

I suggested that both Connie and Susan should visit Grameen to gain total exposure to our system before they launched the FCF. So they came and lived in Grameen villages to see at close range how Grameen functions. They spent long sessions with our field staff and zonal managers and when they returned to Chicago to translate their ideas into reality they were beaming with confidence and followed our Grameen handbook to the letter.

And it worked.

In organizing the FCF, I saw in practice how welfare laws in the United States created disincentives for the welfare recipients to pull themselves out of welfare. If you are on welfare, all the doors and windows are tightly locked so that you cannot find any opening even to think about getting out, and you are a virtual prisoner not only of poverty but of those who would help you: you earn a dollar, this income has to be reported to the welfare authority. They will deduct this dollar from your welfare cheque. And you are not allowed to borrow money from any institutional source.

Under the then-existing laws of Illinois, one could not operate a micro-credit programme such as the FCF with welfare recipients. The WSEP had to negotiate with the welfare authority to get a special dispensation. I was brought to the state welfare authority to testify that credit can help people get off welfare; that giving credit to welfare recipients as an experiment would be a good idea, and that they should consider giving welfare recipients who become members of the FCF a waiver from the law for an experimental period of three years. After a protracted negotiation, the State of Illinois approved a waiver for one year. Subsequently, this waiver was renewed on an annual basis. Now thanks to the success of the FCF, the law in Illinois has been amended to allow people to borrow while still on welfare.

The FCF made a bold start, defied all the conventional advice. Everybody argued that the five-woman group idea would not work because Americans are too independent. Not only did it work, it worked in one of the toughest neighbourhoods of the inner city of Chicago. One of the more difficult problems for the prospective members was finding friends with whom to form groups, so the FCF organized regular 'parties' to let people get acquainted.

I was invited to meet the borrowers, visit their homes and join them in celebrations when the FCF was well under way. What struck me most were the many similarities between Bangladesh and Chicago. I always believed these similarities existed, but seeing them so plainly in front of my eyes was quite an experience. In the poor people of Illinois I saw the same excitement as the poor of Tangail, heard the same expressions of self-discovery, same aspirations, the same warmth in their voices.

Of course, they were not raising chickens or husking rice as Bangladeshi women do. But they knew what they could do to earn an income. I could have never imagined what skills they possessed and what niche they could possibly occupy in the market. But this was not a problem for them.

One borrower told me. 'All my friends have been telling me that I make the best coffee cake in the world. They used to ask me to make coffee cakes for their guests. Now baking coffee cake has become my business. I am glad the WSEP gave me the money to turn my hobby into a business. I have a lot of customers. My coffee cake still is the best in the world. Come and try it.'

Another woman said her business was storytelling, and for the life of me I could not figure out how storytelling could be a business. She explained: 'At parties I am invited to tell stories. I get paid for that. People love my stories. With my micro-loan, I have produced cassettes of my storytelling. Now I sell them through neighbourhood stores. See my poster? Isn't this beautiful?'

It was beautiful.

Two other Chicago borrowers used their loans to go into the fashion business. They designed and sold clothes. They took me to the opening of their new store which they jointly rented. It was a great celebration, and all their fellow borrowers in the FCF showed up to participate. It was touching to see these women celebrate their economic and social freedom when for so long daily survival had depended on their standing on a welfare line to receive a cheque which degraded their dignity as human beings.

When the FCF started a programme in Englewood, they took me to visit that neighbourhood. I saw the caution they took in transporting me to Englewood. I wanted to walk in the streets to get a feel for everyday life, but I was not allowed. I met the staff inside a room, and I was taken to meet a couple of possible borrowers, but I felt tension and fear everywhere. Returning to the WSEP's office, my escorts explained to me the reasons. 'Englewood is an extremely violent place. Nobody feels safe in that neighbourhood. After sunset, even the locals do not dare walk on those streets.'

But today, the WSEP runs a very successful micro-credit programme in Englewood.

I especially remember a vivid and most moving experience I had while visiting a Hispanic neighbourhood on the west side of Chicago. The WSEP had already been working in this area for two years when I visited it. The first thing that shocked me when I arrived there was that suddenly the use of the English language disappeared. All I could hear was Spanish, a language I do not understand at all. So I became doubly a foreigner and totally dependent on the WSEP staff members who were bilingual. They took me to meet several members of their borrowing groups. I will never forget one of those members, a frightened-looking woman in her early forties who spoke only Spanish.

I told her: 'These are beautiful quilts and embroidered designs you made. When did you think of starting a business with this?'

Through an interpreter she explained her life to me in great detail: 'When Jenny (a staff member of the WSEP) came and talked to me, I was scared. I did not believe her. I thought she is going to sell me something. I avoided her. She came back another time, with another woman, a Hispanic woman from this neighbourhood. They tried to talk to me, but I was afraid to listen. They were talking about business. I had no understanding of business. My husband has a hard life. He works in a factory. He gets very angry if I ever try talking to outsiders. He does not like me going out of the apartment by myself. I didn't know anybody in Chicago. I had been living here with my husband for the last fifteen years since I came from Mexico.

'Jenny kept coming back. She told me about the Grameen Bank in Bangladesh – a faraway country. She told me how women in that country started changing their lives. I liked the stories she told me, and I wished I could be like the women in that country. But here things were so rough. I did not dare do anything by myself. My husband would kill me if I created trouble for him.

'I started talking to Jenny. She introduced me to other women in the neighbourhood. I listened to them. They told me about their hard lives, about their children, about their husbands, about their parents, about their brothers and sisters, about their childhood. I saw how much alike we were. I was no longer afraid of them. We talked about Jenny, we talked about the WSEP, we talked about the Grameen Bank. We began to imagine we might do the same things as the women of Bangladesh. We discussed what business we might engage in. We encouraged each other. We collected information for each other. We asked Jenny for more information. Finally, we formed a group. Two by two we took loans. We helped each other in business. I have paid back my first loan of $600. Now I am in the middle of my second loan. I took $1000 the second time.'

'Do you have problems in selling your products?'

'No, not at all. I am behind in filling my orders. I could sell much more, but I do everything myself by hand. I have nobody to help me. My son goes to school. He is always out. I am the only one home.'

'Are you happy with the income you make?'

She remained silent for a long time. Then in a whisper, she started talking very slowly. I thought she was probably saying in Spanish that the money was not much, but that it helped her – something like that. She stopped speaking and the interpreter said in English.

'I never expected that I would ever earn money. My husband never gives me any money to spend. We shop together. He pays. I never had money of my own. For the fifteen years that I have lived in America I have never even had a bank account. Now I have money and I have my own bank account. I have a chequebook. My husband does not know anything about it. I have not dared to tell him yet.'

I did not know what to say. To hide my emotion I asked.

'Many people tell me that if the WSEP did not insist on forming groups it would be so much easier for people to borrow. Do you agree?'

She looked at me when the interpreter translated the question and replied softly:

'In the fifteen years I have been here I never had a friend. I didn't even know anybody. I was all alone. Now I have many friends. My four friends in the group are like my own sisters. Even if the WSEP did not give us money I would not leave the group.'

Her eyes filled with tears. She covered her face with both her hands while the translation was in progress. I was stunned.

26

The US Rural Experience

In 1985, the Governor of Arkansas, Bill Clinton, was looking for ways of creating new economic opportunities for the low-income people of his state. Hillary Rodham Clinton's college roommate, Jan Piercy, had just returned from working in Bangladesh with an American NGO and was now working for the South Shore Bank. She introduced the Clintons to Ron Grzywinski and Mary Houghton who had done so much to convince the Ford Foundation to support Grameen.

Ron and Mary advised Governor Clinton on financial institutions and concluded that a Grameen-type programme was what was really needed. They therefore advised him that it would be helpful to set up a bank designed specifically for the poor in Arkansas. That is how the governor became interested in Grameen.

On my next trip to the US in February 1986, Ron and Mary arranged for me to meet Clinton. He was in Washington, DC attending the annual Governor's Conference. That made it easy. We met in the Four Seasons Hotel – Governor Clinton, his wife Hillary Rodham Clinton, Ron, Mary and myself.

At that meeting, Bill Clinton wanted to know how Grameen got started, how it worked, why nobody had tried it before. As I spoke, both the governor and his wife became immensely interested in the Grameen story. After half an hour of talk, Mrs Clinton declared, 'We want it. Can we have it in Arkansas?'

I said, 'Why not? I see no problem. If the governor wants it, how can it not happen?'

Clinton said, 'Oh yes, I sure want it.' He turned to Ron and asked: 'How long will it take to get this programme started?'

Ron explained the steps needed to start a new bank – all those legal clearances and permissions. He said: 'It will take at least six months.'

The governor was impatient and said, 'That's too long. Can't this be done faster?'

Ron gave a negative answer.

The governor looked at me as if seeking my help and asked me: 'Why must it take such a long time?'

I wanted to cheer him up, so I said, 'If you want me to do it, I can start it tomorrow morning.'

Clinton jumped up: 'What? Can you really do it? That's what I want. I want you to do it.'

I explained my plan. I said: 'Ron is thinking about setting up a bank. We don't have to set up a bank to start a Grameen programme. We can simply start a credit programme – that is, start by giving loans to people. That does not need much legal preparation. Ron and Mary are buying a bank, and this programme can be one of their bank's projects. In the meantime, we can start by organizing the borrowers.'

Mrs Clinton became very interested. She started firing a series of questions on the details of the operation. (Her support for the Grameen idea has never diminished since that day. She visited us in April 1995, and she has visited micro-credit programmes on three different continents. She also co-chaired the Micro-credit Summit of 1997.)

I promised the governor that I would visit Arkansas and present an outline of the project after meeting with state officials, potential borrowers, bankers, academics and business people.

* * *

The following week I went to Arkansas, accompanied by Ron and Mary.

My hosts were very kind. They made elaborate preparations for me to meet with poor business owners.

I was taken to a local radio-station owner, to a fast-food operator, a retail outlet, a drugstore. But at each successive stop, I became more and more withdrawn. I was not at all interested in meeting with the local small businessmen whom they scheduled for me. I thought these visits were just a waste of time. The Clintons had told me about the widespread poverty in their home state, but I was not seeing any of the poverty I was supposed to confront to try to eradicate.

Finally, I became so frustrated that I told my hosts to discontinue this. I said: 'None of these people I am meeting are really poor. I am looking for poor people.'

'But they are the owners of the smallest businesses we have in the state,' they said. 'We don't have anybody owning smaller businesses than this.'

'I am not interested in small businesses,' I said. 'I want to meet poor people.'

'These are poor business people in our community,' they explained. 'We don't have any poorer business people.'

'No, no,' I said. 'I don't want to meet poor business people. I want to meet just plain poor people.'

They looked at me puzzled, as if I had spoken to them in Bengali. They could not figure out what to do or where to take me.

Then I said: 'Do you have welfare recipients in this state?'

'A whole lot of our people are on state support,' they said.

'Is there an office which administers this programme?' I asked. 'Do they have a list of people who receive welfare benefits?'

'Yes, we do.'

'O.K.,' I said. 'Let us get the list and start visiting the people who are on the list.'

My hosts talked among themselves, made quick phone calls. Soon another person, who knew the people on state support, joined us.

Now our trip started getting more and more interesting as we went along. I began meeting welfare recipients. I asked one group: 'Suppose that your bank were to lend you money to do some business, what kind of money would you ask for?'

Everybody in that room stared at me if they could not believe that they had heard the question correctly. Finally, one person said, 'We don't have no bank account.'

'But what if you did have a bank account?' I said.

Again they stared at me.

'What if you had a bank account, and your bank were to lend you money, what would you do with it? Can anyone tell me? Have you any dreams of starting a new business? Have you some hobby which you think might help you to earn some cash if you could do it full time?'

I went around the room asking each person individually. I wanted to gauge what ideas the American poor had for self-help and self-employment. Critics had predicted that micro-credit would have trouble in America because, while Bangladesh has a long tradition of self-employment, few Americans, not even one in ten, work for themselves. They argued that Americans who wished to work for themselves typically required training, technical assistance and access to a business network.

In my gut, I believed such criticism underestimated Americans. Every day we read about white-collar and blue-collar workers being fired by their long-time employer. It seemed clear to me that in the future people would have two or three different careers in the span of one lifetime. And self-employment would become more frequent. But I had to see how Americans trapped in poverty, some for two and three generations, reacted to our offer of credit.

In that community centre in Pine Bluff, the fear, timidity and look of stark incomprehension I saw on their faces was the same as I had seen countless times in Bangladesh. So I spoke as calmly and naturally as I could.

'Look, I run a bank in Bangladesh that lends money to the poor people there. And last week, I had a meeting with your governor, and he asked me to bring my bank to your community. I am considering starting a new bank right here in Pine Bluff. And I have come today to try and find out if any of you will be interested in borrowing money from me?'

Some started to smile at my words, not really believing me. I went on:

'My bank is a special bank for the poor. It requires no collateral, no credit check on you. The only thing I need is someone on welfare or who is unemployed and who has an idea of what they would do with the money I would lend them. But you see, if there is no business here, why should I start a bank here? I could go somewhere else and give loans to the poor in some other community. So that is why I am asking if any of you have any ideas of what you might want to do with your loan?'

One woman who had been listening carefully raised her hand and afraid that I might not notice her, she shouted, 'Hey, I'd like to borrow from your bank!'

'O.K.,' I smiled, 'now we are in business. How much would you like?'

'I would like $375.'

Everyone laughed.

'What do you want this for?' I asked.

'I am a beautician, and my business is limited,' she said, 'because I don't have the right supplies. If I could get me a nail-sculpting box that costs $375, I am sure I could pay you back with the extra income I would earn.'

'Would you like to borrow more than that?' I asked.

'No, I wouldn't want to take a penny more than what the box actually costs.'

Another woman raised her hand and said, 'I've been unemployed ever since the garment factory where I worked closed and moved to Taiwan. I need a few hundred dollars so I can buy myself a used sewing machine. I want to make clothes and sell them to my neighbours.'

Another woman raised her hand and said, 'I want $600 to buy a pushcart so I can sell my hot tamales in the street. My tamales are famous in my neighbourhood, and if I had a pushcart I could sell them better.'

Every suggestion they had gave me reason to hope. I was excited. The kinds of things they were saying were so similar to what I had so often heard in Bangladesh. The aspirations of the really poor Americans that I met had a lot in common with the poor in Bangladesh, Malaysia and Togo. The day flew by without my knowing where the time went.

* * *

The Grameen pilot project in Pine Bluff, Arkansas was put in the hands of Julia Vindasius, an extremely able MIT graduate, and second-generation American of Lithuanian descent. She was working at the South Shore Bank when I met her. She was young, but extremely able, and I suggested she be put in charge. Everybody was surprised at my suggestion. She had never been to the south in her life.

They named the project, 'The Grameen Fund'. For the first two years of its operations, they wasted time having to explain the name of the Fund. After a while they discovered that the name 'Grameen Fund' was too complicated. One day in my office in Dhaka, I received a call from Mary, who was in Chicago. She said:

'It would be easier to call it the "Good Faith Fund", meaning that the bank does not rely on collateral, but rather on the good faith of its borrowers. When people hear the name "Grameen Fund", we end up having to talk about Grameen ("What is Grameen?"), we talk about Bangladesh ("Where is Bangladesh?"), we talk about Dr Yunus ("Who is he?"), only then do we start talking about collateral-free loans. Finally, after spending an hour or two, the listener usually says, "Oh, you mean good faith loans? So why not call it 'The Good Faith Fund'"?'

'Of course, that makes a lot more sense. Change the name.'

'We can save two hours by using simple words. Do you mind?'

'Of course not,' I said. 'The simpler and easier to understand, the better.'

Many of the arguments Julia heard against the possibility of adapting Grameen in Arkansas did not surprise us in the least. We had heard them all before in Bangladesh: the poor can't invest; the poor can't save; the poor need training and social services before they can start a business; the poor will never pay back their debts, etc.

During the 1992 presidential campaign, when Clinton explained to the editors of *Rolling Stone* magazine his interest in borrowing a concept from a

Bangladeshi bank, they ridiculed him for being too ready to adopt crazy ideas and being 'a policy wonk'.

This is hardly surprising, an American friend explained to me. He argued that: 'Grameen is a "Third World technology transfer" and the American elite may not yet be ready for this. Given the reluctance of the Americans to look to other countries as close to them as Canada, Germany or England when debating the reform of their national health programme, how much more difficult it would be for Clinton to convince his fellow Americans to follow a Bangladeshi model!'

But my experience is different. I felt that Americans welcomed and adopted the Grameen idea much more enthusiastically than any European nation.

As president, Bill Clinton has continued to take a personal interest in the Good Faith Fund in Arkansas, and he supported micro-credit, but unfortunately since the election of an opposing Congress in 1996 he has not deemed it feasible or wise to spend much political capital placing it on his national agenda. However, he never misses a chance to talk about Grameen and to express his support for micro-credit. He visits micro-credit borrowers on his international trips and his words and actions have helped the creation and expansion of many micro-credit programmes.

* * *

My experience in Arkansas has been repeated in many parts of the US. In the Sioux nation in South Dakota, I stayed in the house of Gerald Sherman (director of the Lakota Fund and a former alcoholic), with his wife and two children. Gerald and all the staff of the Lakota Fund are members of the Sioux nation. I saw the beautiful quilts the borrowers make and saw, too, their pride in their work. The women explained to me, 'We had nothing to do, no economic activity, now we have something to sell. Now we hold our meetings in churches in community centres, and we sell our goods ourselves.'

In Oklahoma, a most impressive tribal leader, Chief Wilma Mankiller took an active interest in the Grameen programme. When I visited the Cherokee territory, I was presented to a group of fifteen or twenty poor Cherokee women. Their faces were absolutely expressionless. I told them about Grameen, and they showed no interest whatsoever, they just sat there stony faced and uninterested. I said.

'Well, your reaction here is far more encouraging than anything I have ever encountered in Bangladesh,' I said. 'There women actively try to avoid me, they run away from us, as they tell us, "No no, we do not want or need your money." So we have to run after them, and we have to try and get a chance to talk to them, but they usually refuse to listen. You at least are seated here, and are listening to me. That is extremely encouraging to me.'

No one laughed.

'Does anyone in this room need money?' I said.

No answer, no hand was lifted, no eyes moved.

'If you don't need any money, would you happen to know of a neighbour or a friend who might need some money?'

Then after a long silence, a hand was raised: 'Yes, I have a neighbour, and I think he could use some money.'

'To do what?'

'To buy himself a little stove on wheels so he can sell tacos.'

'And is he good at that? Does he know how to make them?'

'Oh, yes, he is the best taco maker in the area. Everyone loves his tacos.'

'Well, send him around, I am certain we could give him money. Does anyone else have a neighbour or a friend who needs money?'

'Wait, do you mean to say that you would lend to our neighbour without any need for collateral, just like that?'

'Yes.'

The Cherokee in the room all thought for a while, then another hand was raised:

'I know that people in this area love puppies.'

'Yes?'

'Could I get a loan to raise and sell puppies?'

'Well, if you think you could make a go of it economically and that you could earn enough to pay back a loan, why yes, of course we could lend you the money.'

'No problem, I can raise puppies easy. You see, right now I do it for free.'

'Would you know where to sell them?'

'Oh yes, that is no problem, I already have a demand for them.'

'How much would you need?'

'Well, I don't know, to get a kennel, to advertise and get me going, with dog food and all, I suppose $500 for my first litter.'

'Well, now we are in business. I will lend you $500.'

'You agree! Just like that?'

'Just like that.'

Everyone started laughing in the room, and I could see people's eyes lighting up. Others now were raising their hands and had other ideas of what they might do.

'I have an idea, I would like to sell potted plants.'

'What makes you think you can do that?'

'I love plants, I have a green thumb. Everything I touch grows well.'

'Do you own some land?'

'That is no problem, here on the territory, there is no private ownership of the land. It is free to anyone of the tribe who wants to use it and not misuse it.'

'And do you think you could sell potted plants?'

'Oh yes, that would be easy.'

We came to an agreement for that loan, and I could see the others in the room beginning to smile and think crazy thoughts they had not thought before.

A man raised his hand in the back of the room: 'We used to raise our own corn for decades, but recently, we let the white guys come and raise corn on our land. But we could do this better than they, and we could keep the profit.'

I agreed. Soon the discussion became very concrete. And by the time I left that meeting, they were all asking:

'Yunus, when are you coming back? Bring money next time?'

* * *

Every day I am more and more convinced that the problems of modern banking that I identified in Bangladesh are worldwide problems. They are too numerous to list in detail. But in 1990, I made a speech entitled, 'Anything Wrong?' which raised the question of whether American commercial banks recognized human beings.

The system we have built refuses to recognize people. Only credit cards are recognized. Drivers' licences are recognized. But not people. People haven't any use for faces anymore, it seems. They are busy looking at your credit card, your driver's licence, your social security number. If a driver's licence is more reliable than the face I wear, then why do I have a face?

In America, I learned that cashing cheques is becoming a booming business. High rates are charged even for government-issued cheques.

Many are forced to use these cheque-cashing outlets, mainly elderly people who live on social security and the working poor who cannot establish bank accounts because they cannot keep minimum balances, cannot afford the per-cheque charges or service charges, or cannot show the bank that they have good credit. Some people also have trouble providing the required photo ID to open accounts.

I've met Americans who always take their pay-cheques to the very bank on which it was drawn and always to one of the same tellers. Every week the tellers insist on seeing a driver's licence and, as if having a state-issued driver's licence with a photograph is not enough, they demand to see a credit card too – presumably if the poor person is in debt, they must be honest!

I soon concluded that American banks treat their poor no better than Bangladeshi banks do our poor, but with assistance from micro-credit institutions, thousands of low-income minorities will be able to turn their under-capitalized 'hustles' into legitimate businesses capable of lifting them out of poverty.

One especially powerful tool in this struggle is RESULTS, a grass-roots lobbying organization headquartered in Washington, DC.

* * *

In 1987, when I was visiting the United States, I spoke before a joint session of the House Banking Subcommittee on International Development Institutions and Finance, and the House Select Committee on Hunger.

At the end of the hearing, a RESULTS volunteer took charge of me and rushed me to a tiny room where someone was busy talking on a speaker phone. I had no idea what a telephone conference call was, nobody briefed me, and I had no time to consult with anyone, but here I was, suddenly in front of another speaker phone with fifteen editorial writers from leading dailies in various cities throughout the US on the line waiting to ask me questions.

The person on the speaker phone was Sam Daley-Harris. He was an ex-Miami music high-school teacher turned social activist who had started a national network of volunteers called RESULTS. We had never met before. He had been using telephone conference calls to hold nationwide monthly meetings of all his volunteers. And what I had stepped into was an actual press conference. Sam is extremely affable and soft-spoken and he spoke in a way that briefed me and the news writers at the same time. I then took questions and explained everything relating to Grameen.

The conference call lasted for an hour. There was a short break and then it began with another twenty-three editorial writers of US dailies. That day I learned just how effective RESULTS could be.

Sam and I became instant friends from that first meeting and my admiration for him has grown ever since. He is a born fighter, and although unassuming and unimposing, he is as solid as a rock when it comes to fighting poverty and hunger.

Today, RESULTS has sister organizations in six countries – the US, Canada, the UK, Germany, Japan and Australia. They have endorsed micro-credit as a key anti-poverty strategy, working through their grass-roots network of citizen activists to ensure it is given attention by the community, the media, elected representatives and the government. Over the years, the bond between RESULTS and Grameen is ever strengthening, and each RESULTS volunteer sooner or later becomes an expert on Grameen.

* * *

The 1987 conference call accomplished something else which has remained a milestone in the history of the micro-credit movement: the articles we generated attracted the attention of the CBS's news magazine programme, *Sixty Minutes*.

In 1989, after a long process of research, two CBS TV crews, one from London and another from Rome, finally came to Dhaka. I spent long hours with the CBS correspondent Morley Safer visiting Grameen villages, inter-viewing borrowers, development experts, government officials. In all, they took over a hundred hours of film footage and boiled it down to just fourteen minutes.

In March 1990, the story was telecast and became an instant hit. I had never fully realized the power of the electronic media until then. And even today, we keep receiving letters and phone calls from around the world whenever the show is rebroadcast.

In just fourteen minutes, CBS brought out the essence of Grameen in a most inspiring way, and it moved people to action and activism more than anything else we had tried in the past.

I saw what a decisive role the media can play to bring change in the way people think and act.

PART V: PHILOSOPHY

27

Discovering Economics: The Social-Consciousness- Driven Free Market

In my youth I was a left-of-centre progressive, because I did not like the way things were, nor did I like the old conservative ways. Like many Bengalis of my generation, I was influenced by Marxist economics. But I also never liked dogmas or groups who told you what to think and what standard practices to follow.

I was never an Islamist, but neither would I ever give up my culture. I never wanted to be so radical that I could not say my prayers or show respect to the Prophet.

Most of the university friends were socialists who were of the opinion that government should take care of everything. At Vanderbilt, Professor Georgescu-Roegen, though not a Communist, admired Marxism as a logical construct. So his teaching brought a social dimension to economics. Without the human side, economics is just as hard and dry as stone.

In the United States I saw how the market liberates the individual and allows people to be free to make personal individual choices. But the biggest drawback was that the market always pushes things onto the side of the powerful. I thought the poor should take advantage of the system to improve their lot.

Grameen is a private-sector self-help bank, and as its members gain personal wealth they acquire water-pumps, latrines, housing, school, health services, and so on.

Another way to achieve this is to let a business earn profit which is then taxed by the government, and the tax can go into building schools, hospitals, etc. But in practice it never works that way. In real life, taxes only pay for a government bureaucracy that collects the tax and provides little or nothing for the poor. And since most government bureaucracy is not profit-motivated, it has no incentive to increase its efficiency.

It has a disincentive: the government cannot cut welfare without public outcry, so the behemoth just continues, blind and inefficient, year after year.

If Grameen does not make a profit, if our employees are not motivated and do not work hard, we will be out of business. Grameen could be organized as a for-profit enterprise of a non-profit organization. In any case it cannot be organized as an organization purely run on the basis of 'greed'. In Grameen we always try to run on profit, to cover all our costs, in order to protect us from future 'shocks' and to carry on expansion. Our concerns are focused on the 'welfare' of our shareholders, not on immediate cash return on their investment dollar.

* * *

No doubt the free market, as now organized, does not yet provide solutions for all social ills.

The economic opportunities for the poor, ensuring their health-care and education, well-being of the elderly and retarded people, are glaring examples of totally missed areas. Even then, I believe that 'government', as we know it today, should pull out of most things except for law enforcement and justice, national defence and foreign policy, and let the private sector, a 'Grameenized private sector', a social-consciousness-driven private sector, take over their other functions.

Almost from the start, Grameen gave rise to many controversies. Leftists said that we were a conspiracy of the Americans to plant capitalism among the poor. And that our real aim was to destroy any prospect for a revolution, by robbing the poor of their despair and their rage.

'What you are actually doing,' a Communist professor told me, 'is giving little bits of opium to the poor people, so that they won't get involved in any bigger political issues. With your micro-nothing loans, they sleep peacefully, and they don't make any noise. Their revolutionary zeal cools down. Hence, Grameen is the enemy of the revolution.'

On the right, conservative Muslim clerics said we were out to destroy our culture and our religion.

Wherever possible, I try to avoid grandiloquent philosophies and theories and 'isms'. I take a pragmatic approach grounded in social considerations. In everything I do I try to be practical, I rely on learning by doing and make sure that I am moving towards achieving a social objective.

I am not a 'capitalist' in a simplistic right/left sense. But I do believe in global free-market economy and participating in it by using capitalist tools. I believe in the power of the free market, and the power of capital in this market-place.

I deeply believe that offering unemployment benefits is not the way to redress the problem of the poor. To me, that ignores their problem and lets them rot. The able-bodied poor don't want or need charity: the dole only increases their misery; it robs them of initiative and, more importantly, of self-respect.

Poverty is not created by the poor, it is created by the structures of society, and policies pursued by society. Change the structure as we are doing in Bangladesh, and you will see the poor change their lives. Grameen's experience shows that, given the support of financial capital, however small, the poor are capable of bringing about an incredible change in their lives.

Some needed only $20, others a $100 or $500. Some wanted to husk paddy, some to make puffed rice, some to make earthenware pots and pans while others wanted to buy cows. But, and note this, development specialists around the world, not one single Grameen borrower needed any special training! They had either already received this training as part of their household chores or had acquired the necessary skills in their field of work. All they needed was financial capital.

Somehow we have persuaded ourselves that capitalist economy must be fuelled only by greed. This has become a self-fulfilling prophecy. Only the profit-maximizers get to play in the market-place and try their luck. People who are not excited about profit-making stay away from it, condemn it and keep searching for alternatives.

We can condemn the private sector for all its mistakes, but we cannot justify why we ourselves are not trying to change things, not trying to make things better by participating in it. The private sector, unlike the government, is open to everyone, even to those who are not interested in making profit.

The challenge I set before anyone who condemns private-sector business is this: if you are a socially conscious person, why don't you run your business in a way that will help achieve social objectives?

I profoundly believe, as Grameen's experience over twenty years has shown, that greed is not the only fuel for free enterprise. Social goals can replace greed as a powerful motivational force. Social-consciousness-driven enterprises can be formidable competitors for the greed-based enterprises. I believe that if we play our cards right, social-consciousness-driven enterprises can do very well in the market-place.

* * *

Economic protectionism, subsidies and doles were instituted by well-meaning people to soften capitalism's hard edges.

I believe in the central thesis of capitalism – the economic system must be competitive. Competition is the driving force for all innovations, technological changes and better management.

Another central feature of capitalism is profit maximization. Profit maximization ensures the optimal use of scarce resources. This is the feature of capitalism which led us to create the image of a greedy (almost bloodythirsty) person in the role of a profit maximizer. We have taken away all social feelings from him. We then postulated that true entrepreneurs are a rare and special breed. We are lucky to have them with us. We feel so grateful to them that we give them all the privileges we can afford – credit, social recognition, tax holidays, priority access to land, market protection, etc.

I am proposing two changes to this basic feature of capitalism. The first change relates to this overblown image of a capitalist entrepreneur. To me, an entrepreneur is not an especially gifted person. I rather take the reverse view. I believe that all human beings are potential entrepreneurs. Some of us get the opportunity to express this talent, some of us never get a chance to try it out because of the way we are made to imagine that an entrepreneur is someone enormously special and different from the rest of us.

If all of us started thinking the way I think, that is to say if we all accepted that every single human being, even one barefoot and begging in the street, is a potential entrepreneur, then we could move to build an economic system which would allow each man or woman to explore this potential. The old and intransigent wall between the entrepreneur and labour would disappear. It would become a matter of personal choice whether a person wanted to be an entrepreneur or a simple wage earner.

The individual's role in the economy need not be a foregone conclusion decided by birth or by other circumstances beyond his or her control.

* * *

The second change relates to how an entrepreneur comes to an investment decision. Economic theory depicts the entrepreneur only as a profit maximizer. (Indeed in some countries, as in the US, corporate law requires the maximization of profits and shareholders can sue an executive or a board of directors which uses corporate funds to benefit society as a whole rather than to maximize the profits of the shareholders.)

As a result, the social dimension in the thinking of the entrepreneur has been completely bypassed. For social science and society itself, this is not a good starting point. Even if social consideration has a very small role in the investment decision of an entrepreneur, we should allow it to come into play for the better interest of the overall social good. A human being's social considerations are qualities which can be inculcated through generating appropriate social values. If we leave no room for them in our theoretical framework, we will be forcing ourselves to create human beings without social values.

Indeed, the market needs rules for the efficient allocation of resources. I am proposing that we replace the narrow profit maximization principle with a generalized principle – an entrepreneur who maximizes a bundle consisting of two components: a) profit and b) social returns, subject to the condition that profit cannot be negative. (Actually, neither of these components should be negative; but I make this conceptualization in order to stay close to the existing profit-maximization principle.)

All investment decisions can be taken within a range of options. At one extreme, the capitalist will be guided purely by the profit motive. At the other extreme, an entrepreneur will continue to be in the market as long as the enterprise is financially viable. She or he will choose a particular financially viable enterprise which, in his or her perception or estimate, yields the maximum social returns.

Under this principle, an entrepreneur could run a health-care service for the poor, if it is financially viable. Other such enterprises might be: financial services for the poor, food chains for the poor, educational institutions, training centres, renewable energy ventures, old-age homes, institutions for handicapped people, recycling enterprises, marketing of products produced by the poor, and so on.

Would this type of social-consciousness-driven entrepreneurs be rare and difficult to find? I don't think so. The more we look for them, the more we'll meet them and the easier we will make it for a person to become one.

Wouldn't you like to become one? Or wish to be a partner with someone who is looking for a partner?

Think about it.

* * *

I assume that society is made up of all kinds of people. At one extreme, there are capitalists seeking personal gain who want to maximize profit alone, without any social considerations. They would not mind investing in an enterprise which creates negative social returns, as long as it yields a maximum personal profit.

At the other extreme, there exist entrepreneurs who are strongly motivated by social consciousness. They are drawn to investments that maximize social returns provided the enterprises are financially viable.

In between these two extremes, the bulk of entrepreneurs mix profit and social considerations, in a way which takes them to their highest level of self-fulfilment. Through various means of social recognition and rewards – I am thinking of prizes, honour rolls, public acknowledgement – societies can attract more and more entrepreneurs to move in the direction of social-consciousness-driven investments.

Specialized institutions can be created to help generate more and more of these investments. An individual entrepreneur can run an enterprise which pays some or no attention to social returns, but she or he can also initiate and operate one or more financially viable enterprises devoted exclusively to maximizing social returns, either as an individual or as a part of a trust or not-for-profit business organization.

This scenario I posit for our businesspeople of the future not only brings them closer to real life, but it also creates room for a socially and environmentally friendly global economy as well as within nations.

Economics must show that the economy does not necessarily have to be a playground for 'blood-thirsty' capitalists; it can be a challenging field for all good people who want to pilot the world in the right direction.

* * *

Where should one place Grameen philosophy in the spectrum of political ideologies? Right? Left? Centre?

Grameen supports less government, even advocates the least government feasible, is committed to the free market and promotes entrepreneurial institutions. So it must be on the far right.

Grameen is committed to social objectives – eliminating poverty, providing education, health-care, employment opportunities, achieving gender equality by promoting the empowerment of women, ensuring the well-being of the elderly. Grameen dreams about a poverty-free, dole-free world.

Grameen is against the existing institutional framework. It opposes greed-based enterprises. It wants to compete with and drive them out through the creation of strong social-consciousness-driven enterprises.

Grameen does not believe in *laissez-faire*. Grameen believes in social intervention without government getting involved in business or in promoting service. Social intervention should come through policy packages encouraging businesses to move in the socially desired direction, providing incentives to social-consciousness-driven enterprises encouraging competitive spirit and strength in the social-consciousness-driven sector.

All these features easily place Grameen on the political left.

* * *

Since Grameen cannot be judged on the basis of its position in relation to the public and private sectors, it is difficult to label Grameen with the familiar political labels. Grameen is opposed to both public and private sectors as they are commonly understood. Instead, it argues for the creation of a completely new sector – what I call, the social-consciousness-driven private sector.

Who will or can get involved in this? Social-consciousness-driven people. Social-consciousness can be as burning, even more burning, a desire as greed in an individual human being. Why not make room for those people to play in the market-place, to solve social problems and lead human lives to a higher and higher plane of peace, equality and creativity.

The public sector has failed. Or at least it is on the way out despite our best efforts. Bureaucratization cushioned by subsidies, economic and political protection, and lack of transparency, have killed it off. It has become an attractive playground of corruption. What started out with good intentions became a road to perdition.

With the demise of the public sector, the only thing left for the world is the personal-gain-based private sector. This is certainly not an inspiring prospect. Competition in the free market, no matter how fierce it is, cannot alone keep unchained greed in check. If nothing else, we should remember that greed and corruption are prone to lure each other into solid partnership at the slightest opportunity.

Before the world surrenders to greed and corruption, we must seriously examine the strength of social-consciousness as a contestant – Grameen, for instance.

* * *

Critics often say that micro-credit does not contribute to the economic development of a country. And even if it does contribute something, that something is insignificant.

But it all depends on what one likes to call economic development. It is per capita income? Per capita consumption? Or anything per capita?

I have always disagreed with this kind of approach when defining development. I think it misses the essence of development. To me changing the quality of life of the bottom 50 per cent of the population is the essence of development. To be more rigorous, I would define development by focusing on the quality of life of the lower 25 per cent of the population.

This is where growth and development part their ways. Those who believe growth and development are synonymous, or move at the same speed, assume that the economic layers of society are somehow linked to each other like so many railway carriages – and that all one needs is the engine to move, so that the entire train and everyone in it move at the same speed. But this is not true even as a broad approximation. Not only do the different economic layers of society not move at the same speed, they don't even move in the same direction unless extreme special care is taken all along the way.

If there is no growth, nothing moves forward – that is true. But the often-used analogy of a train and linked human socio-economic strata breaks down over one significant factor. A train is drawn by a locomotive located at the front, or pushed from behind, or both. But in the case of human society, each economic entity or group has its own engine, thus the combined power of all the engines together pushes and pulls the economy forward. If the society fails to turn on some of the engines, if it simply ignores some of those strata, the combined power of the economy with be much reduced.

Worse still, if engines of the social groups at the tail-end are not turned on – not only may they not be pulled by the engines at the front, they may start sliding backwards, independently from the rest of society, and to the detriment of everyone involved including those who are better of.

Micro-credit starts up the economic engine at the rear end of the train by starting up the engine in each passenger in that usually decaying and putrid carriage. This cannot reduce the speed of the train, it can only increase it, which most of today's so-called development projects fail to do.

Of course, investing in roads, motorways, power plants, airports turns on the engine in the forward first-class carriages, those are the fanciest and richest ones, and it enhances the train's engine capacity by many fold; but whether it can help ignite or enhance the capacity of the engines in the subsequent carriages, in all other layers and strata of society (also called 'the trickle-down effect'), remains uncertain.

Will micro-credit lead to major infrastructure building? Micro-credit ignites the tiny economic engines of the rejected underclass of society. Once a large number of tiny engines start working, the stage can be set for bigger things.

Micro-borrowers and micro-savers can be organized to own big enterprises, even infrastructure companies. Grameen has created a number of companies for speeding up the process of overcoming poverty. Some of them are large infrastructure companies:

GrameenPhone, for example, is a nationwide cellular telephone company which hopes to serve about half a million cellular phone users in both urban and rural areas of Bangladesh by the year 2003.

Grameen Check is a nationwide producer and international exporter of cotton cloth woven by the Bangladeshi poor hand-loom weavers.

Grameen Fisheries Foundation is creating a nationwide fish-farming business which the poor will manage and own as shareholders.

Grameen Cybernet provides Internet services and will bring the global job market to remote villages. Bright boys and girls from disadvantaged families will receive a world-class education through the Internet. They will not have to rush to cities to find jobs, but will find international jobs which they can perform from their villages.

Grameen Shakti (or Grameen Energy) brings solar energy into villages which have no power grids, and will power cellular phones, lights, radios, televisions and computers. Grameen Shakti will create micro-power companies owned and operated by the local poor.

In a conventional development strategy, power plants, telecommunications and other infrastructure are either owned by the richest in the country or by the multinationals, or both, and serve their interests. But Grameen and micro-credit may lead the way to think differently, and we hope act differently – in a poor-friendly way.

* * *

We should judge the quality of life in a society not by looking at the way the rich in that society live, but by the way the lowest percentile of the people live their lives.

28

Self-Employment

Unemployment is a scourge of every modern society. Even industrialized nations cannot ensure a job for everyone.

US governors and European prime ministers try to attract big business to their states by offering tax breaks and other facilities so that big industry will locate future plants on their soil, and thus create employment. But there is a limit to what industry can bring. Also, big industry often creates environmental toxic waste, air and water pollution and environmental problems which can outweigh whatever employment benefit they bring. In addition, the profits of such foreign investment is siphoned back to the parent company and foreign shareholders abroad.

Self-employment has none of these drawbacks.

The problem is that self-employment is not as obviously glamorous as a shiny new factory. But profits from self-employment remain in the country where they are produced. It is usually too small to create environmental hazards. It also puts the poor person in charge of his or her own fate.

Some of the advantages of self-employment over waged employment are:

1. The hours are flexible and can adapt to fit any family situation. It allows people to choose between running a business full-time, or part-time when they need to meet crises, or to put their business on hold and work full-time for a salary.

2. Self-employment is tailor-made for anyone who is street-smart and has many acquired and inherited traditional skills, rather than learning acquired from books and technical schools. This means the illiterate and the poor can exploit their strengths, rather than be held back by their weaknesses.

3. It allows a person to turn hobbies they enjoy into gainful employment.

4. It allows individuals who cannot work well in a rigid hierarchy to run their own show.

5. It offers a way out of welfare dependency, not just to become wage slaves, but to open a store or start a manufacturing business.

6. It can help those who have found a job and are still nonetheless poor.

7. It gives those who have just been fired from a job moral support to start a business before they become depressed and isolated.

8. It gives the victims of prejudice who would not be hired because of their colour or national origin a chance to earn a living.

9. The average cost of creating a self-employment job is ten, twenty or hundred times cheaper than creating an employment job.

10. It helps an isolated poor person gain self-confidence, step by step.

One criticism levelled at micro-credit is that in an era of mass market and mass production, self-employment is bound to remain small and cannot attain any economies of scale. But I believe that home-based production can be as mass-scale as any factory – it is simply not under one single-roof, nor wage-based.

The policy needed for the eradication of poverty must be much wider and deeper than the policy for the provision of mere employment. I believe that the real eradication of poverty begins when people are able to control their own fate. Therefore, it is not work which saves the poor, but capital linked to work; it is this which in a majority of cases eliminates poverty fast, with a minimum or no cost at all to the taxpayer, and gives the poor control over their lives.

Rather than monthly welfare payments, I would urge making seed capital available in a lump sum to those who want to start a business. In the UK, the Enterprise Allowance Scheme helped start 88,000 businesses, of which 86 per cent are still operating three years later.

Obviously self-employment has limits, but in many cases it is the only solution to help the fate of those whom our economies refuse to hire and whom taxpayers do not want to carry on their shoulders.

* * *

Take the example of Manzira Khatoon, aged thirty-nine, who was born in Outakhin Noadeeari village, in Chapainoabganj District, where she still resides.

Manzira was a diligent student and married at the age of seventeen. Then her father went bankrupt and lost all his land due to a protracted legal dispute. Her husband lost his job, and after the birth of their third child, he abandoned the family and married another woman. Manzira became so emaciated she was unable to breastfeed her youngest son, Rubel. Her father, who was very poor and had seventeen mouths to feed, would not let her bring her two older children to stay with him. She earned a little money from doing housework and trained with a tailor for no money. But her youngest son who was weak because of lack of food got an acute diarrhoea and died within twenty-four hours. Her grief was such that it took her six months to recover and arrange to work for a local tailor.

Manzira had a hand-to-mouth existence assisting the tailor and she dreamed of the day she could buy her own sewing-machine and open her own business.

In 1989, she heard about Grameen and asked her father to go out and collect information about how to join. Today, thanks to our loans, she owns a plot of land planted with twenty guava trees and has leased one planted with high-yielding rice. She owns a Grameen-financed house with brick walls and a tin roof. She uses loans to buy cloth which she turns into garments and sells from her house.

'The day I was able to start building my own house was the happiest day in my life. Grameen has provided me with the things that my parents were unable to.'

The weekly payments on all her loans amount to $4.20 which she manages to pay easily. 'For the first time in decades, I eat regularly, and now I am able to take care of my parents in their old age.'

In 1990, she was elected by her peers to represent the Rajshahi–Rangpur zone on the board of directors of Grameen. She was chosen to represent Grameen in the Royal Palace of King Baudouin of Belgium to receive the King Baudouin Award which was given to Grameen Bank in 1989. She carried herself beautifully there, like a director of a bank. Her visit is described by David Bornstein in his excellent book on Grameen, *The Price of a Dream.**

*Bornstein, D., *The Price of a Dream*, Simon & Schuster, New York, 1996.

29

What Role for Educating and Training the Poor?

We have gone against traditional methods of poverty alleviation by first handing out cash without any attempt to provide skills training.

Why give credit first?

Because I firmly believe that all human beings have an innate skill. I call it the survival skill. The fact that the poor are alive is clear proof of their ability. They do not need us to teach them how to survive, they already know this. So rather than waste our time teaching them new skills, we decided to make maximum use of their existing skills. Giving the poor access to credit allows them immediately to put into practice the skills they already know – to weave, husk rice paddy, raise cows, peddle a rickshaw. And the cash they earn is then a tool, a key that unlocks a host of other abilities, a key to explore one's own potential.

Government decision-makers, many NGOs and international consultants start the poverty alleviation work by launching a very elaborate training programme. This may be explained in three ways: first, they start with the assumption that people are poor because they lack skills. If they can acquire a skill, they will, of course, no longer remain poor. Second, they start with training because this perpetuates their own interests – more jobs with a big budget for themselves without the responsibility of having to produce any concrete results. You can show you are doing a great deal without really doing anything. Third, they don't know what else can be done.

A huge industry has evolved worldwide, thanks to aid-flow and welfare budgets, for the sole purpose of providing training. Experts on poverty alleviation keep on insisting that training is absolutely vital for the poor to move up the economic ladder. They claim this is a prerequisite.

But if you go out into the real world you cannot miss seeing that the poor are poor not because they are untrained, or illiterate, they are poor because they cannot retain the returns of their labour. The reason for this is obvious – they have no control over capital, and it is the ability to control capital which calls the tune. Profit is unashamedly biased towards capital. The poor work for the benefit of someone who controls the productive assets.

Why can't the poor control any capital? Because they do not inherit any capital or credit, nor does anybody give them access to capital, because we have been made to believe that the poor are not to be trusted with credit – they are not creditworthy. But are banks people-worthy?

* * *

Many training programmes are counter-productive. Poor persons are often offered incentives to participate in training programmes – sometimes they receive immediate financial benefits in the form of a training allowance, sometimes training is made a prerequisite to being able to obtain other important benefits, in cash or kind. This attracts the poor, even though they may not be interested in the training itself.

Training programmes start by implanting new skills, instead of building on what skills the poor already have. The new skills are delivered in a way that convinces the trainees that they are totally ignorant and stupid.

If Grameen had required a borrower to attend a training programme in business management before taking a loan to start a business, most of our borrowers would have been scared away. Learning in a formal way is a threatening experience for them. Each person has a natural learning curve of their own. If that is ignored by the imposition of a different kind of learning, their natural ability may be destroyed without being replaced with a new ability.

Rather than developing abilities, some training programmes in fact destroy people's natural capacity, or make them feel small, stupid and useless.

This is not to say that all training *per se* is bad. Training is extremely important in helping people get over their economic difficulties faster and more securely. But, what I am arguing is do not put the cart before the horse. Let people's natural abilities blossom before you cut them off with your well-researched, well-intentioned elaborate structure. Don't force training on them because you feel that they need it. Support them when they start to feel the need for it, and start to look for it; and are willing to pay in kind or cash to obtain it.

If they are willing to pay they will get what they want. If you are paying you give whatever you fancy. That's the trouble.

* * *

Grameen borrowers do look for training. Sometimes we help them find that training, sometimes we just feel overwhelmed and cannot carry out those responsibilities. Grameen borrowers want to read numbers in their pass-books. They want to figure out what amounts are written there, for example how much has been paid, how much remains to be paid back.

Grameen borrowers want to be able to read the Sixteen Decisions; they can then constantly remind themselves of the decisions they forget. They have had to learn them the hardest way – by listening to somebody repeating each one umpteen times until everyone could memorize all sixteen decisions.

Grameen members want to be able to keep accounts, read information about businesses, about health, about poultry-raising, about cattle-raising, about new ways of planting, storing, processing.

Grameen borrowers are sending their children to school. They help their parents keep accounts, read instructions, and with whatever else requires reading and writing. But that is not enough for the future.

Grameen is bringing in new technology for them: cellular telephones, solar energy, the Internet. They will start feeling the need to calculate how much they should charge for a five-minute local telephone call, how much for an international call to the US or Malaysia or Dubai.

* * *

One of the Sixteen Decisions is 'We shall educate our children'. This is a priority expressed by all borrowers. They understand that educating their children will make them better able to fight the age-old cycle of poverty which passes from generation to generation and seems to last forever. They want their children to have opportunities which neither they, their parents, nor their grandparents ever had. Grameen oversees the implementation of this decision by keeping an eye on whether all the children of Grameen families attend school.

Grameen did not plan to get involved with the education of the borrowers. As time went by we started to feel the need for it. Most of the people who join Grameen have no formal education. Nearly 80 per cent of Grameen borrowers are illiterate. This imposes a limit on the size of the venture our borrowers can undertake, even if they have the capital needed. Without the ability to read and write, our borrowers have difficulty acquiring new business ideas, or taking advantage of new business informa-tion, and of new and expanding market opportunities.

In a presentation to the director general of Unesco, Mr Frederico Mayor and his colleagues, in 1994, I threw out the following challenge:

Grameen is working to make sure all its borrowers get out of poverty. We have more than two million borrowers now. We want to make sure all of these two million families cross over the poverty line by the year 2005, and never slide back again. After the year 2005, Grameen, the bank which is known all over the world as a 'bank of the poor', should acquire a new identity; it should be known as the 'bank of the former poor'. This is our challenge. We are working hard to make our dream come true. Now I throw a challenge to Unesco. Will Unesco join hands with us to make sure all Grameen families acquire a 100 per cent literacy rate by the year 2010?

Mr Mayor immediately accepted the challenge. The following year Unesco and Grameen signed a Memorandum of Understanding at the Beijing Conference. Two years have passed, and not much progress has taken place on the ground. But neither Unesco, nor Grameen has given up on that pledge.

We made a small beginning in 1995. We started an action research. We invited an NGO, the Centre for Mass Education in Science (CMES) to organize life-oriented education in the village of Joymontop, thirty kilometers outside Dhaka. Each adult learner was required to pay 2 *taka* (5 US cents) per month. Even if the amount looks small, it is not easy to make them pay even that small amount.

After one year we reached 1600 adult learners in twenty-five centres. Each class has forty learners. They meet in a morning session or an afternoon session. The same method was repeated next year.

In the meantime we have created a new Grameen company – Grameen Shikkha (Education). This organization will gradually develop the methodology for a rapid spreading of education among Grameen families and families outside Grameen. We are exploring uses of modern technology – interactive satellite TV, radio, and the Internet – to ensure that we reach as many people as possible, as quickly as possible. Unesco and Infodev of the World Bank will be providing us with the technical assistance in these matters. Telenor of Norway and Worldview International are also joining hands with Grameen Education to bring education to the masses through the use of information technology.

The economic advancement of a poor family needs a broader enabling and sustaining environment. Micro-credit starts up the engine in the family, but that engine now needs refuelling, maintenance, expansion of capacity and a good road to make good progress. Reaching the survival point with micro-credit can be accomplished without difficulty. To go much further one needs good a health-care system, education, a pension plan, good communications, market information. If no such support system is developed the economic advancement made by the borrowers may come to a halt or even slide backwards.

30

On the Population Problem

I firmly believe that each human being is an unexplored treasure. Each person has unlimited potential.

True, each additional person born on this planet strains world resources by being a consumer. But by being a producer and contributor to the world's well-being she or he has enormous possibilities.

In 1798, Thomas Malthus predicted that population growth would overtax the world's resources, and would result in widespread poverty and starvation. But this did not happen. On the contrary, people became better off. Malthus failed to foresee the industrial revolution which led to greater urbanization and smaller families.

Bangladesh has been a very attractive country for people who study population-related issues. We were always told: you are poor because you are too many people on too small a piece of land. Bangladesh is about the size of Florida, with a population of 120 million. If half of the US population decided to live in Florida, that would equal the density we now have in Bangladesh.

This density issue can be put in another way. Take the entire world population and accommodate it in the United States, then imagine the population density this would create: the population density of Bangladesh today is slightly higher than that.

What does all this mean for Bangladesh? Should we be afraid and ban childbirth in Bangladesh? I believe there is a strong element of scare-tactics in population policies promoted by the West and by international development agencies. We in the Third World countries, often blindly echo these views and raise even more fear at home.

These scare-promoting policies almost make you believe that if you double your population you will be twice as poor.

Since Bangladesh became an independent country, our population has almost doubled. But certainly we are not twice as poor. Indeed, we are much better off today than we were twenty-seven years ago. We had greater food shortage then, than we have now. Bangladesh is close to food self-sufficiency now that it has to feed twice the population.

Population experts will say: 'Yes, but you could have been twice as better off as you are now, if your population had not grown at all since 1971.'

Maybe, maybe not; one may speculate about it and make projections about it. But the relevant issue here is that the doomsday scenario that was predicted as a result of a population explosion did not turn out to be correct.

My suspicion is that governments and international agencies choose to scare people into action in order to hide the other side of the picture. They could achieve the same result in terms of limiting population growth by enhancing the economic status of the people in general, and the people who constitute the bottom half, in particular.

All human beings have the basic intelligence to see what is good for them. If a couple finds out that having fewer children is better for them than having more, they will act on their own initiative to restrict the number of children they have (provided, of course, that supportive facilities are available close at hand).

But governments and population agencies are not putting nearly as much effort into changing the quality of life of the bottom half of the people as they put into their scare-tactics and into pressurizing poor, illiterate men and women to physically remove their ability to procreate.

I believe that the economic and social empowerment which creates income-earning opportunities for poor women, and brings them into organizational folds will have more impact on curbing population growth than the current system of trying to frighten people. 'Family' planning should be a subject left to the family. Now it seems that governments and international agencies are doing all the family-planning on behalf of families, rather than letting the families do it for themselves.

UN studies conducted in over forty developing countries show that as women gain equality, the birth rate falls. The reasons for this are numerous. Education delays marriage and children, and better-educated women are more likely to use contraceptives. They also have more options open to them in life other than child-rearing, in particular the ability to earn a livelihood.

The Grameen Bank is cited in all population discussions, because it was found that the adoption rate of family-planning practices among Grameen families is twice the national rate of Bangladesh. During the Cairo Population Conference of September 1994, Grameen was mentioned again and again because the birth rate in Grameen families was lower than in non-Grameen families.

If micro-credit can help bring family-planning awareness into families, why do governments and international agencies, which are so concerned about population growth, not enthusiastically promote micro-credit? Could it be because micro-credit runs as a profit-oriented business, and that is not of interest to them? Are there vested interests in the population programmes to run them the way they run now?

I believe that the emphasis on curbing population growth diverts attention from the more vital issue of pursuing policies that allow the population to take care of itself. The sooner we rearrange our priorities, the better it will be for all people on the planet, now and for the future.

31

Poverty: The Missing Issue in Economics

The whole world agrees on what is the best way to eliminate poverty: it is to be achieved by creating employment.

But economists recognize only one kind of employment – waged employment. In their book there is nothing called 'self-employment'. Economists have created a world for us where we are supposed to spend our childhood and part of our youth working hard to prepare ourselves to be attractive to potential employers. When our preparation is complete we present ourselves to the job market to get hired. If someone cannot find an employer, then real trouble begins. They end up either on welfare if they happen to live in an advanced industrial economy, or in poverty and misery if they live in a less developed economy.

The idea of a young human being working hard to make himself or herself useful to an employer is very repulsive to me. It reminds me of the old days when a young girl would be trained by her mother to become attractive to a young man so that she could find herself a husband. A human life is too precious to be wasted in preparing to find an employer and then devoting one's entire existence to serving that employer.

This practice is also a clear departure from our past. When our ancestors were born on this planet, they did not prepare themselves to find an employer in a job market. If they did, they would have been extinct; we wouldn't be here today. They took charge of their own destiny; they created their own jobs, became hunters, gatherers, and later, farmers. They were self-employed people.

Economics textbooks have no use for the word 'self-employment'. That is what has created trouble in real life: just because our textbooks banished this word, policy-makers banished it from their minds too.

Opening up opportunities for self-employment by creating appropriate institutions and policies is unquestionably the best strategy for eliminating unemployment and poverty.

Economics has contributed enormously to creating the kind of world we live in today. It can definitely be faulted as a social science. The elegant structures of economic theory that have built up over the years may have been useful in understanding the forces that make up our economy, but theory simply abandons the poor, and walks out on the subject of poverty alleviation.

Economics aims to inquire about the wealth of nations and the cause of that wealth. And it has always continued to explore in this same direction without ever asking the simple question, what causes poverty in a household?

Whatever attention has been given to poverty comes under so-called 'development economics', a body of literature which grew after the Second World War. But development economics remained basically an afterthought or re-interpretation of the main body of economic theory in the context of newly independent post-colonial countries.

Credit that Discredits Economics

Another area in which economic theory has played a damaging role concerns the issue of credit. Economics completely disqualifies itself as a social science when it comes to its treatment of credit.

It is very surprising that economics never understood the social power of credit. In economic theory, credit is seen as an innocent lubricant with which to lubricate the wheels of trade, commerce and industry. The fact that credit creates an entitlement to resources could have triggered the immediate thought that in the social context it would play a very significant and sensitive role. Economics failed to catch its significance.

Since credit creates economic power, and hence social power, the institution which is responsible for deciding who should and should not get credit, when one should get credit, who should get how much and on what terms, become extremely important from the social point of view. This institution can really make or break an individual, a group of individuals, or even a whole segment of society by favouring them or by rejecting them.

That is exactly what it has done.

Credit institutions and banks made rules which favoured a section of the people and rejected another section. Those whom they favoured rose in power and economic status, and those they rejected languished in poverty. Credit institutions decided they could do business only with the rich and pronounced a death sentence on the poor by announcing that they were not creditworthy. Nobody challenged them because economics tells us that the subject of credit is not socially interesting!

Why have economists remained silent when banks insisted on the ridiculous and extremely harmful generalization that the poor are not creditworthy? Nobody can provide a convincing answer. Because of this silence and indifference, financial institutions could impose financial apartheid and get away with it.

If economics were a genuine social science, economists would have discovered what a powerful socio-economic weapon credit is. They would have recognized the need to promote credit as a human right, and they would have designed a system to ensure this human right for all people. As social scientists, economists would have detected how credit gave society a particular structure, or at least how credit could have prevented society from having an undesirable structure. If we can redesign economics as a genuine social science, we will be firmly on our way to creating a poverty-free world.

The shortcomings of the core theories remained unchallenged. I think these shortcomings came from several directions. First, I feel the microeconomic theory, which plays a central role in the analytical framework of economics, is incomplete. In this theory an individual human being is introduced as a consumer in the consumer theory, and as a labourer in production theory. Production theory starts with the production function, i.e. given a technology, how can an entrepreneur mix labour and capital to produce different levels of production? This leads to the theory of a 'firm'.

These conceptualizations completely eliminated the possibility of self-employment. Entrepreneurs were considered as a specially gifted group of people, while the remaining human beings are born to serve under them. This, perhaps, appeared to the economists as an innocent piece of abstraction, but it did great damage to economics as a social science because the creativity and ingenuity of each human being was abstracted away. With that, the possibility of each human being turning into an entrepreneur disappeared. Waged employment became the only source of employment. Self-employment was explained away as a symptom of a poor economy.

To me, in order to qualify as a social science, an academic discipline must create an analytical framework which will enable and encourage human beings to explore their unlimited potential, not start with the assumption that their capacity is given and limited, and that their life-long roles are fixed.

By missing the lively world of self-employment, the 'science' of economics has moved away from the promise it once held of becoming an exciting social science. Instead, it has grown more and more, into a business science.

With self-employment out of the picture, economics has missed another very important social dimension, the family – man, woman, and children. It always amazes me how economics can get away with calling itself a social science without ever getting involved with the social dimensions of men, women, children, and their inter-relationships at the household level as well as at the macro-level.

With a theory of self-employment integrated into the micro-economic theory, economists could easily enter into issues of poverty eradication, development, family, population, gender, and build socially powerful theories in other areas (such as banking, entitlement of resources, etc.).

In many of the Third World countries, an overwhelming majority of people make a living through self-employment. Not knowing where to fit this phenomenon into their analytical framework, economists lumped it into a catch-all category called the 'informal sector'. Because they did not have the analytical tools to cope with the situation, they concluded that it was not a desirable one: as soon as these countries could eliminate this informal sector, the better off they would be.

What a shame!

Instead of supporting the creativity and energy of the people by creating enabling and empowering policies and institutions, we become eager to fit them into boxes of our own creation. But the informal sector is the brainchild of the people, not of planners or economists. It represents the people's own effort to create their own jobs.

Anyone with a minimum of understanding of people and of society as a whole would have come forward with hope and excitement to build upon what already existed, to take this informal sector to higher levels and bring more efficiency into it, rather than to undermine it and try to pull the rug out from under it.

By inventing the term 'informal sector', economists give everybody the signal that they are not quite happy with it.

PART VI: NEW HORIZONS

1990–97

Introduction

Now that the commercial side of the Grameen Bank has proved itself and is actively changing people's lives, we want to build on this success and expand into other areas so as to improve the quality of life of our borrowers, as well as that of the community in general. Specifically, we are looking at market-oriented ways of improving the social infrastructure which the government is not providing, or is providing inadequately.

For Grameen this is not an easy shift of focus.

We are now expanding to cover many functions which have little or nothing to do with banking or with our profit margin, yet it is an exciting and vital component of our work.

We have expanded the types of loans we make available to allow borrowers to finance such quality of life items as water wells, flush-toilets and housing.

We are also creating self-financing enterprises that will cover our borrowers' health, retirement and education, as well as meet the needs of the community at large.

We call this a vertical expansion, where the size of our loans is increasing to provide our borrowers with a full range of services which includes helping them to market their products or to enter into large-scale joint ventures.

I will focus only on a handful of initiatives, but their number is ever-increasing, and their role in Grameen is ever-expanding.

32

The Housing Loans:
A Great Success Story

In 1984, the Bangladesh Central Bank ran an advertisement in the newspapers announcing that it was introducing a refinancing plan for a housing loan programme for rural people.

So, referring to this advertisement, the Grameen Bank applied to the Central Bank and said it would like to introduce a housing programme for its borrowers. We explained that we were constrained by the small budgets of our borrowers and could not lend as large a sum of money as was mentioned in the Central Bank's advertisement. Our borrowers could not borrow 75,000 *taka* (about $2000), and we wanted to be able to extend 5000 *taka* ($125) housing loans.

The Central Bank rejected our application because its experts and consultants decided that whatever one builds for $125 in local currency would not qualify as a 'house', because it would not satisfy the structural definition of a house. Specifically, they said that such a house would not add to the 'housing stock of the country'.

I protested. I said, 'Who cares about the "housing stock" of the country? All we want is a leak-proof and dry space for our member to live in.'

We argued and pleaded with the Central Bank consultants to see what a major improvement even this basic minimal housing would be over how our borrowers were currently living. But it was all in vain. They rejected our application, and we were extremely disappointed.

Then we came up with another idea. We immediately sent in a second application, saying this time: 'Grameen withdraws its original application. Please treat this as a new application. We do not want to make housing loans. We want to make 'shelter loans.' We were hoping they did not have a definition or statistic for 'shelter stock' that would disqualify us.

The consultants in charge of the project had no objection in principle to us building shelters for the poor and the homeless. They even indicated their preliminary approval.

But this time, the economists said that Grameen was doing fine work with income-generating activities, with 'productive activities' as they called it; but that housing or shelter would not create income, it was 'a consumption item'. And our borrowers could not afford borrowing to consume because it would be a non-productive loan and would not generate income which would help them pay off their loans. They gave me a lot of sound theoretical reasons.

We came up with another idea to circumvent the arguments of the bureaucrats. We did not want to give up. We preferred to keep pestering them! And this time we said: 'We desire to give our borrowers "factory loans".

This perplexed the Central Bank specialists and consultants. 'Why would homeless people want a factory?'

We explained that the overwhelming majority of our borrowers were women, and our women borrowers worked in the place where they lived: 'Our borrowers look after their children, and while they do, they work and they earn money from their work, and all this activity is performed in their own houses. Since it is a place of work, we call it a "factory".'

We explained to them, 'In Bangladesh there is the monsoon for five months out of the year, and during that time our borrowers cannot work because they do not have sturdy roofs over their heads. To continue to work and generate income, they need protection from the rain.

'That is why we want to make factory loans. True, this "factory" will double as a house. It will have a direct impact on their income-generating ability as it will allow them to work round the year with some comfort.'

The consultants again rejected our application.

* * *

I met the Central Bank governor to make a personal appeal to him to override his bureaucrats.

'Are you sure the poor will repay?' the governor asked.

'Yes, they will. They do. Unlike the rich, the poor cannot risk not repaying. This is the only chance they have in life.'

The governor of the Central Bank looked at me. 'I am sorry you had difficulties with our officials.'

He said, 'OK, on an experimental basis, I will give Grameen a chance.'

And so through the personal intervention of the governor of the Central Bank, we managed to introduce our housing loan programme.

* * *

To date, thirteen years since then, we have extended a total of $151 million in loans to build nearly 450,000 houses with near perfect repayment in weekly installments. But shall I tell you what happened to the housing programmes of the conventional commercial banks? You guessed it, few of the borrowers paid back, and the programme was closed down after three years.

Our housing programme continues to this day and is expanding.

Our position was vindicated when Grameen's housing programme was chosen in 1989 by the Grand Jury, made up of top architects of the world, to receive the Aga Khan International Award for Architecture. At the Award ceremony in Cairo distinguished architects kept asking me who was the architect who designed our $300 house – it had such architectural beauty (by that time we had raised the amount of our housing loan to $300).

No professional architect designed the house built by our borrowers. They designed them and build them with love. They are the architects of their own houses – as they are the architects of their own fate.

33

Health and Retirement

In trying to create a social net and a welfare state, developed countries have created a terrible situation. The road to disaster is paved with good intentions, and nowhere is that more visible than in old-age homes. There, the aged, who are meant to be helped and looked after, are robbed of dignity and self-respect.

Why should old people just vegetate? Why keep senior citizens barely alive in that depressing environment, during their 'count-down' to death?

Even though they live off pensions, government hand-outs or what their children or grandchildren give them – there is no need for them to merely sit there doing nothing. Survival is not only financial, but also emotional and psychological. Doing nothing all day is cruel, undignified and unhealthy, not only to themselves, but also to the society at large.

What better way to achieve human dignity than by doing something creative, of your own choosing, that would make you feel useful?

Of course, many old persons are too infirm to work and would not want to do anything but watch television, but I am addressing myself to all those who are able to function, even if at a reduced level. They could do something active and worthwhile if only they were given a chance.

* * *

As with all those on whom traditional capitalism has given up, creative social-consciousness-driven care of the elderly, health-care organizations and credit programmes can play important roles in giving meaning to the lives of senior citizens. Workers and executives are now being fired at the height of their potential. At sixty or sixty-five, whenever big business turfs you out and says you are not needed anymore, you are useless, that is exactly when you can start employing yourself!

Old age should not be a reason to have your emotional and psychological rights taken away from you. On the contrary, senior citizens should enjoy inalienable human rights like anyone else. Even though they may be residing in a 'home' or a geriatric centre, senior citizens should enjoy the same opportunities to lead creative and productive lives, as long as they are willing and physically able to do so.

Traditional societies understand this much better than modern ones: on Native American reservations, I have seen senior citizens making beautiful sacred tapestries; in Africa, I have seen village elders making beautiful musical instruments.

By not admitting that even the elderly need to feel creative in order to feel alive, the West is hastening the moral and emotional decay of its old people. They are creating all the conditions for despair and for feelings of uselessness.

* * *

But even if we manage to use and harness the creativity of our aged, it is undeniable that Grameen's system of loans works efficiently only as long as the borrower and her family members are healthy and can work. If the borrower or anyone in the family is too physically or mentally sick, then something else is needed.

Independent studies of Grameen borrowers indicate that 25 per cent of our borrowers cannot bring any change in their economic situation due to ill health.

* * *

Around the world, national health programmes are in crisis. Whether it is the 'free market' system of the US, or the 'nationalized' systems of England, France or Germany, the poor are not protected. In Bangladesh, when the government spends generously, the quality of services the poor receive is appalling. That is because doctors who become government employees often neglect their duties in favour of their private practice.

So the reality of free government health care means that if you want proper treatment, you have to turn to the expensive private clinics. For the rich or even middle class that is perhaps possible. If you are destitute you are caught in a trap.

The important thing is that people be given the means to earn an income so that they can afford health care, full education and other essentials.

Until such a time as the poor can pay with money, then it seems natural that education and health should be provided in exchange for a social payment (such as community service), or at least some token social payment.

* * *

In Grameen we have noticed that as the income of our borrowers increases, an erosion of income takes place due to the higher and higher levels of expenditure made on combating malnutrition, common diseases, infant and maternal mortality and other health risks. Given the sad situation of public health services, our borrowers feel encouraged to spend their money on traditional healers, men who take a glass of water, blow on it, and then give it to you as a miracle cure. Instead of buying health, many of our borrowers thus buy themselves nothing but health hazards.

If we could persuade our borrowers to take the money they give to traditional healers and give it instead to a Grameen-sponsored health programme, we could provide them with a modern and effective health service for almost the same amount of money. That process has begun.

We are trying to make health care available to all members of the Grameen family and to all villagers who are not Grameen borrowers, on a self-financing, cost-recovery basis. We ask our borrowers to pay a fixed amount of $3 per family, per year, as a premium to a health insurance programme. (Non-Grameen borrowers pay a higher fee, the equivalent of $5 per year for health coverage for the entire family.) Then each time they have to see a doctor, they must pay a nominal amount, 2.5 US cents. Pathological services and medication are available at a discount.

After the first three years in operation, Grameen has recovered about 60 per cent of the cost of providing these medical services. In the next three years, we hope to recover about 90 per cent of our costs by persuading people to switch from wherever they get their health services to us instead. And within the next four years, we hope to recover 100 per cent of our costs.

If we can organize this as a nationwide franchise (or maybe an international one, why not?), we could turn it into a strong, competitive and sustainable pro-people enterprise.

So social infrastructure is indeed an important part of poverty alleviation. But good social infrastructure, by itself, will not create wealth. It creates a required enabling environment in our war against poverty.

* * *

The reason we are so acutely aware of health is that it can destroy even our brightest successes.

Morley Safer's *Sixty Minutes* programme of 1989 highlighted one borrower near Chittagong who, thanks to Grameen loans, had risen from being a street beggar woman, to owning seven cows, a large plot of land, a new house, a modern latrine, a three-wheeled 'baby' taxi for her husband, and she was even sending all her children to school. (This is vital to break the cycle of poverty, for destitute families usually prevent their children from attending school in order to get them to help with work around the house.)

Morley Safer called her, 'the picture of contentment and human success', yet when I met her and her husband again in 1996 I could barely recognize them. He had contracted some sort of stomach illness that was never properly diagnosed. To pay for his medical treatment they had sold off their taxi, their land and cattle. She was so frail and tired, she did not trust herself to take a new loan. All they had left to their name were four chickens.

It was one of the saddest things I have ever had to witness. They had no hope for the future and were basically just waiting for some miracle or for death to save them.

I wanted to mention this case to indicate how difficult a road we have ahead of us. Grameen is not just a series of success stories. There is immense difficulty along the way, enormous pain and suffering. And we are not always successful. Part of our ability to alleviate poverty effectively depends on our being able to know where we fail and why, and to help secure that it does not happen again.

* * *

Micro-credit cannot solve society's every problem. It has never pretended to be a cure-all, and that is why we want to extend our health plan as quickly as possible.

It is not a problem limited to Bangladesh. One Grameen replicator Abou Tall in Togo says, 'We put one finger in the dike, and there are so many social problems of nutrition, family planning, the environment, that we are called upon to do everything. That is a danger. A micro-credit bank cannot do everything. We need to create partnerships with specialists in other areas who know how to operate.'

* * *

Why should Grameen get involved in health, retirement, pensions, schools and other quality of life issues of the poor? Because nobody else is looking at the problem in a market-oriented way to provide the basic social infrastructure. We need a great many innovative initiatives, but so far they are not forthcoming.

34

Grameen Check: Weavers are Back in Fashion

Bangladesh has a long tradition of making fine hand-woven fabrics, such as muslin, that was much in demand by royalty in European courts in centuries gone by. Unfortunately, with the industrial revolution in Europe, this tradition faced stiff competition from the machine-made fabrics of the UK and elsewhere.

To gain a market share for its machine-made fabrics, our colonial masters wanted to make sure their fabrics faced no competition. In their enthusiasm to gain entry into the market, they made sure our hand-loom weavers did not weave. They even punished our weavers who violated the ban on weaving by chopping off their thumbs.

When the Indian independent movement began in the 1930s, one of its forms of expression was the boycotting of British fabric and the use only of locally made fabric. Colonial rule was seen as a power which destroyed our local economy.

Despite the wishes of the colonial power, hand-loom weavers passed on their skill from one generation to the next for their economic survival. Today in Bangladesh there are one million hand-loom weavers desperately looking for a market for their product.

Hand-loom weavers are by tradition extremely poor. They make beautiful fabrics, manufacture the most attractive *saris*, but their women cannot afford to wear them. Their children go naked.

Many of the women who joined Grameen belonged to hand-loom weavers' families. In hand-loom villages we always had repayment problems during a particular month of the Bengali calendar because it was the leanest month of the year for the hand-loom trade. This month is between two agricultural harvest seasons, and people usually run out of purchasing power.

Khalid Shams kept worrying about this repayment problem of the weaving families. He took great pride in our ancient tradition of weaving, and he wanted to see it survive and gain a rightful place in the economy of the country.

Khalid Shams joined Grameen at a late stage, in 1990. He was a greatly admired civil servant, but he did not want to go back into the civil service. When I met him in Kuala Lumpur, where he was working at the Asia Pacific Development Centre, an inter-governmental development institution, I found him worrying about his future back in Bangladesh. I invited him to join Grameen, and he readily agreed.

That is what he did when he returned. His friends and well-wishers were all shocked. This is crazy – they thought, civil service positions are the most coveted in Bangladesh. You wield so much power because of your position. How can you give up such a job when you are just about to reach the topmost position in the civil service: to become a secretary of a ministry.

Khalid changed Grameen in many ways. He took Grameen in new directions, and because of him Grameen's relationship with the government and its civil service changed completely. We moved closer, and we were much better understood.

If you can think of a person who has no enemies – you are thinking about Khalid. He is firm in his decisions, but still loved by everybody.

* * *

Khalid wanted to understand the weavers' problems by living with them and experiencing their daily struggle. He took a week off to live in a branch which had the highest density of weavers, and he spent the whole time immersed in their problems.

After this, Khalid was persuaded that the number one problem was not being able to buy yarn at a fair price. He met the civil servant in charge of the textile ministry to solve this problem. But, whereas, getting permission from the ministry to buy yarn directly from the factory is one thing, actually receiving the delivery from the factory was quite something else. We learned the hard way about how the yarn market in Bangladesh works, how textile trade union leaders and a handful of wholesalers control the price and supply of yarn – we could watch it at close range.

While going through several frustrating experiences, Khalid discovered that Bangladesh was importing Indian hand-loom fabrics called 'Madras Check' for the garment industry in Bangladesh. After much investigation, he found out that the total amount imported was in the range of $150 million a year. We were shocked. While we were trying to create a local market for our own hand-loom fabrics, we were importing $150 million worth of hand-loom fabrics from neighbouring India.

Some told us that Indian fabric was of a very high quality that our weavers could not match. Khalid wanted some samples to verify the statement.

It took a long time just to procure some samples. Nobody paid any attention to what Khalid was saying. Finally he brought some samples and showed them to me. I said: 'This fabric doesn't look at all unusual to me. I think our weavers can produce the same fabric.'

I asked Khalid to try to produce some samples from Belkuchi, the place where best lunghis (menswear) come from.

When the samples were brought in we all got excited – they looked great!

But we did not want to rely on our own judgement. We wanted the professional opinion of buyers. We circulated our samples to garment factories and buying houses, and they all agreed that the samples we produced were better than the imported Indian fabric.

But the buyers did not show any interest in buying this fabric. One explanation we received was that 'the international buyers cannot go door to door to each single weaver to buy the hundreds of thousands of yards needed. So they place a huge order with Indian suppliers, and they supply whatever is needed, right on time.'

Khalid tried to interest private businesses in organizing the production of hand-loom fabrics for the garment industry. Nobody showed any interest.

We thought that, if nobody else is interested, Grameen could move in by itself. Grameen could play the role of middleman and supplier. We could accept orders from exporters, and we could remain responsible for the quality of the cloth and the delivery date.

In 1993, we created an independent non-stock, not-for-profit company to do just that. We called it Grameen Uddog (meaning Grameen Initiatives). The objective of the company was to link up the traditional hand-loom weavers with the export-oriented garment industry. The weavers produced the cloth we asked for, and it was beautiful. They themselves took great pride in working for this export market. We gave a name to the fabric. We called it 'Grameen Check'.

It was not easy to enter an international market. We had no textile experience. Khalid worked very hard to put together a team and learned the ropes of the business quickly. Gradually it started to work. During the first year total sales came to $2.5 million. In three years the total went up to $15 million and it is expanding.

Grameen Check as a product has a great market potential. It is hand-woven, 100 per cent cotton, and very attractive. In Paris in February 1996, by courtesy of Unesco we held a fashion show of garments designed and presented by a talented Bangladesh model, Bibi Russell. Paris fashion personalities, magazines and media immediately took the designs up.

Today 8000 hand-loom weavers are engaged in the production of Grameen Check. We are selling Grameen Check to Italy, France, the UK and Germany, and trying to develop a market in the US. With all the unemployed weavers in the country we can easily raise the production level to one million metres a week. We need more buyers in Europe and North America to start asking for Grameen Check. Then our talented weavers will be delighted to produce it for them.

When we were introducing Grameen Check, we were asked by the buyers if we could supply check flannel. We had no idea what flannel was. We were taught by our buyers. We tried to produce it. But the raising machines that were available in Dhaka were of poor quality. We wanted good-quality flannel. We realized that if we wanted to enter the market we should have our own machines to convert the Grameen Check to Grameen Flannel.

We teamed up with a friend of ours, Dr Zafarullah Chowdhury, who runs a health-care NGO and a pharmaceutical company, to set up a modern textile mill. His organization was already planning to set up a textile mill and had bought land for the factory. So we had an advantage in getting started. This factory, known as Gonoshyastho Grameen Textile Mills Ltd, went into production in 1998.

Our hope is that as our fabric production becomes more diversified and the more the market expands, the more our weavers will be gainfully employed in reviving and strengthening a beautiful traditional craft.

Grameen is not doing anything fancy – all we do is promote the product, take orders, and work as a marketing agent for independent home-based weavers. We pass on the specifications of the orders to the weavers, give them the best-quality yarn so that they don't wait for working capital and ensure that they meet the quality and deadline. Weavers don't have to worry about procurement of inputs or the marketing of their products. (Some twenty years back I learned from the experiment in the Three-Share Farm how worrying an issue inputs can become for farmers.)

* * *

While we were exploring the international market for Grameen Check, we received an unexpected response from the domestic market. All of a sudden

'Grameen Check' became a household name. Every young boy and girl wanted to wear it. It became a matter of pride to wear Grameen Check and even a social statement: we are proud of our heritage, we are proud of our weavers.

To cope with this newly emerging domestic market, properly and efficiently, we created another company, Grameen Shamogree (meaning Grameen Products), which is focusing its attention on all other varieties of fabrics beside Grameen Check, and other Bangladeshi handicraft products. We are also trying to produce fabric from jute mixed with cotton. Jute is a natural fibre, grown abundantly in Bangladesh, which is losing ground to synthetic fibre as a packaging material. Grameen wants to find new uses for jute by bringing it into the production of popular fabrics.

35

Grameen Fisheries Foundation

In 1985, I received a telephone call from the permanent secretary of the fisheries ministry of Bangladesh.

'Dr Yunus, we have not met. But I know you very well through your work. I wanted to discuss a fisheries project with you. Have you ever visited Serajganj?'

'Yes, I have, but only in limited areas. We are just expanding our work in Bogra.'

'You must visit the fisheries ministry project in Nimgachi. We have nearly one thousand big ponds there which were excavated by the Pal kings [local Hindu rulers of the Pal dynasty] over one thousand years ago, to provide drinking water for the people and for the king's cattle herds. But they were all silted up. Under our project we were supposed to re-excavate them and farm fish in them.'

'What happened to the project?' I asked.

'That's the tragedy I wanted to talk to you about. I have recently visited the place, and I was stunned by the corruption and mismanagement. I wanted to find out why the British foreign aid agency, ODA, is refusing to give us more money to carry on the project. Now I have a request for you.'

'What is that?'

'My request is, please take over the project. You run it, you do whatever you want to do. We'll stay out of it.'

'What am I going to do with all these hundreds of ponds?'

'Please don't turn down my request. At least make a trip to the project area. You'll be inspired to see these beautiful ponds and the potential they hold for this country.'

'We are a bank. We don't know how to farm fish.'

'Yes, I know that. If you think you can't do it, then at least take them for safe-keeping. The way I see it, if they remain in government hands, nothing will be left of them. Our officials will make sure that everything in the ponds and everything around it go to feed their greed. If you take over, they'll at least be saved, not eaten away.'

The secretary was in a bad mood, accusing his own staff of corruption and trying to protect government property from its protectors. I did not want to get involved in something I was not familiar with, and I told him so.

He was very disappointed, but he ended the conversation by saying: 'At least think about it. Don't give the final answer now, make up your mind after visiting the project site.'

Although I was reluctant to agree with the proposal, in a way I welcomed the challenge. I discussed it with my colleagues. They also felt that if the government genuinely wanted to give it to us, we should take it.

A week later I got a telephone call again from the secretary, but I did not want to change my position yet, so I told him that my answer was still 'no'.

He said: 'I am calling you for another reason. I am convening a meeting on the future policy direction of the fisheries ministry. I want you there to help us formulate our policies.'

'If I attend you'll again bring up the subject of the Nimgachi Project and pressurize me to take it over,' I said.

'I give you my word, I'll not bring up the subject of Nimgachi at the meeting.'

I laughed and agreed. I laughed because I did not believe that he'd keep his promise. I agreed because I wanted to meet this man who had so much confidence in me, without ever having met me.

The meeting at the secretariat had about a dozen people. Half of them were top government officials from the fisheries ministry, and the other half came from universities and research institutes. The meeting went on for two hours. The secretary did not utter a word about the Nimgachi Project, and I thought he really meant what he had said.

Just before the meeting was about to conclude he whispered in my ear: 'Could you stay over for a while, so that we can have a cup of tea and a one-on-one discussion?'

When everybody had left, tea and snacks were brought in for us. He said: 'Did you see – I kept my word, I did not bring up the subject of Nimgachi during the meeting. Now that the meeting is over, I am free to bring up the subject, am I not?'

He was very happy that I was willing to give him a chance. He narrated the history of the project, corruption of his staff, his plans about handing it over to Grameen. He said he would be willing to hand over the project on our terms. He gave me a stack of reports on the project to study in order to make up my mind.

As I returned to my office I decided that we would go for it. Here was a most unusual secretary who had the good of the country at heart. He wanted to protect public property from corrupt officials. How could I not help him? How could we go wrong taking over properties from the government? We might not make any money, but we certainly would not lose any.

I wrote a long memo to the secretary when I returned to my desk, agreeing to take over the project, but giving tough conditions. We wanted a ninety-nine-year lease with low annual rent. And we wanted the government to withdraw all its staff as soon as the handing over took place. We also wanted a detailed list of everything that was being handed over.

I sent the memo the next day. The secretary immediately called me and said: 'We agree to all your conditions. I am happy that you agreed. I feel relieved.'

It was strange. In my experience with Grameen, we always met a 'Mr No' in government offices. Meeting someone at the highest level of bureaucracy who seeks you out and agrees to your conditions when handing over a government project was totally beyond my familiar world. It almost reversed the whole process of government we were used to.

The secretary could not deliver all that he had promised. At least not the ninety-nine-year lease. This was reduced to twenty-five years. Government rules were beyond his power to change. But the secretary moved with lightning speed to get everything done. His proposal had to go to the president for his approval. The land ministry also had to agree to all the provisions and sign the agreement. It was quite a bureaucratic feat, yet the whole thing was achieved within a couple of months!

When a serious official wants to get something done, it gets done!

* * *

There is a saying in southern Asia about the Bangladeshis: 'Fish and rice makes a Bengali.' Fish is an important source of protein for our people, and fishing an important income-generating activity. Land, water and people exist in a mutually supportive balance in Bangladesh. Each supports the others. Fish is a natural choice as a food item for Bangladeshis.

We saw the fisheries as an opportunity to transfer significant assets to the landless poor. We hoped that the unutilized ponds could be combined with the unutilized abilities of the poor to create a bold chemistry for improving their lives. If we succeeded in this venture, we could not only help them feed, clothe and house themselves, but also establish their claim to become major economic players, whether in agriculture, industry, trade or any other sector. So we decided to embrace the challenge. We saw the fisheries as a golden opportunity to apply our joint venture policy on a grand scale.

When the government wants to help the poor it always comes up with a policy of free distribution – free distribution of money, land, or other assets. But when the government distributes anything free, it never reaches the poor. Along the way it has to travel from the government to the poor, there are many capable people who line up to take advantage of the distribution system. A few lucky poor persons do actually receive the resources, but it is impossible for them to retain possession for very long – be it a pond, a fishery, or just a blanket.

We decided to reverse this trend once and for all.

* * *

In January 1986, we signed the agreement with the government regarding the transfer of the Nimgachi Project to the Grameen Bank. The project consisted of 783 ponds of various sizes and shapes, with a combined water-body of 1666 acres spread over four subdistricts in Pabna and Serajganj Districts.

In 1988, the government leased us more ponds, for a total of 808 ponds. We began our journey into the new world of fisheries with many dreams, but it soon turned out that we were going to have to cross some really rough seas.

Exceptionally devastating floods hit Bangladesh in 1987 and caused the farm serious losses. The following year, in 1988, we had the worst flood for a century. More losses were added. Predator fish remained in the ponds, and our efforts to eradicate them were neutralized by the floods which had brought in new predators.

We inherited so few nurseries and rearing ponds, and these were in such poor condition, that we had no alternative but to stock our excess hatchlings directly in the ponds. This led to a high mortality rate. The ponds had peaty uneven bottoms leading to turbidity, high acidity, sedimentation of harmful organic matter and other problems. While the incidents of theft greatly decreased, poaching persisted, especially in remote areas. We gave up hope for production on the scale we had initially planned.

But more difficult than the natural environment was the human sabotage of and resistance to our efforts. The old bureaucracy and local vested interests we were displacing did not accept our presence with good grace.

From the beginning our staff faced extreme hostility. The government officials who were entrusted with the operation of the project were bitter about the decision made above their heads to let Grameen run the show. Their pride was hurt. They kept on complaining that this was a biased decision to discredit them. While they worked hard to bring the project to a stage when it was about to give dividends, they were now deprived of being associated with it. And Grameen was brought in to enjoy the fruits of their labour.

Many of these officials fanned anti-Grameen feelings among the local population. The local leaders of major political parties were also antagonistic. The ones who had been in power in that area and had the most to lose became most active opponents. Leftist leaders argued that development was the job of the government, not of the private sector, and certainly not of a private bank. But the real reason for their dislike of us was that under the old set-up they had been able to exercise influence on the management which ran the fisheries, and they were now no longer able to exercise such political patronage.

In Tarash, a leading political party organized anti-Grameen demonstrations and public meetings. Leaders tried to convince villagers that we were a foreign organization intent on exploiting the locals and remitting our profits overseas. Rumours went around that Grameen was a CIA front working for the American government to destroy the revolutionary spirit among the poor in Bangladesh.

The mood of the locals ranged from scepticism to open rebellion. There were days when our staff could not step out of the project residential complex because of local hostility. But our staff had met and survived many such inimical situations and slanders elsewhere, so we were not caught totally unawares. Even in the worst, most tense stand-offs, we were confident that we could turn the situation around and win people's confidence.

We held meetings with local people, and we appealed for their support. We promised that proper management of the ponds would benefit not only the landless but the community at large. To prove our good faith, we organized some forty pre-school learning centres for poor children. Before long, the patience and sincerity of our staff began to pay off, and the initial animosity and suspicion subsided.

Ultra-left, underground armed revolutionary groups who burnt down our offices and forced our staff to leave the villages at gun-point now disappeared from the area. We could finally concentrate on the production of fish.

We had to learn the trade. As we had no background, we had enrolled our staff on crash courses on how to farm fish. We decided to acquire the technology of fish production first. Once we ourselves felt comfortable with it, we would involve the poor who lived around the ponds. Without establishing a technical, physical and managerial base for production and effective control over the ponds, we could not really help the poor. As my Grameen colleague, Khalid Shams, said: 'It would be analogous to a person crossing muddy waters carrying another person on his shoulders and drowning together.'

We sent our staff to China to learn about pond management and hatchery operations. Practical skills were developed through learning by doing. Eventually our large initial capital investment and the training of staff began to bear fruit. We organized the poor around the ponds to become our partners in the business. They gave their labour, guarded the ponds against poaching and Grameen provided all the inputs, technology and management. The harvest was divided on a 50:50 basis. Our partners received a good annual income from this, and we struggled to cover our costs.

We also adopted an incentive or bonus scheme to boost production. If fish from a pond exceeded a pre-set target, the staff was rewarded. The poor, who under the government's management stole fish (because everybody else was also stealing), now out of self-interest in a profit-share became our best farmers, protectors and owners of the fish.

As we overcome our technical, financing, and management problems we hope to create for-profit subsidiaries of our not-for-profit Fisheries Foundation. The shares in these for-profit subsidiaries will be owned by the members of fisheries groups who are now engaged in a 50:50 production partnership.

If this model of management and ownership works, we can extend it to anywhere in Bangladesh to take over the management of the idle ponds all over the country and make them productive for the benefit of the poor, as well as of the owners of the ponds.

If we can mix the micro-credit programme and the management of ponds, we will be able to utilize efficiently two hitherto unutilized resources which Bangladesh has in abundance: vast numbers of very poor people who are without land of their own; and 1.5 million idle fresh-water ponds which dot the countryside.

Grameen's experience with fisheries demonstrates that new grass-roots systems can be designed and developed from scratch so that the poor can better control sophisticated technology and share in a macro-economic project. Technology is an essential prerequisite for raising productivity, but unless we direct who it is who receives the increased production, it will end up in the hands of the rich.

With Bangladesh's resources, there is no reason why people should remain poor. Our problem is one of proper management, not lack of resources. With the proper management framework, these resources can solve our poverty problem.

36

GrameenPhone:
Technology for the Poor

Khalid came into my room one day in 1994 and introduced me to a young Bangladeshi American, a graduate of Oberlin College who said that we had met there when I went to receive an honorary degree.

Khalid said, 'Iqbal has an idea. He says we can apply for a licence to operate a cellular telephone company in Bangladesh. We can take cellular telephones into the villages.'

It looked like an exciting idea, but we had no idea how to run a cellular telephone company. How could we do it? Many people approach me with their ideas of what Bangladesh needs. I often encourage them to put those ideas to work, but people are far quicker to give you ideas than to roll up their sleeves and put those ideas into practice.

Iqbal had done his homework and briefed us fully, but I was not sure whether to take him seriously. I did not dismiss him as a bag of hot air, but I wanted to give him time to prove that he was a smart businessman.

* * *

Step by step we became more serious about cellular phones. We went through many ups and downs on our way to create a cellular telephone company. Khalid never gave up even when we reached rock-bottom, for Khalid has endless patience.

The government of Bangladesh finally issued three cellular licences in 1996, one to us. We signed the licence agreement on 11 November 1996, and I announced to the press that we would launch our service on 26 March 1997, our Independence Day, an appropriate day to launch a service which promised to bring information technology to all the people of Bangladesh, even the poorest.

We formed two independent companies – one for profit (GrameenPhone), another not for profit (Grameen Telecom). GrameenPhone is a consortium made up of four partners: Telenor of Norway (51%), Grameen Telecom

(35%), Marubeni of Japan (9.5%), and Gonophone Development Company (4.5%).

GrameenPhone was the recipient of the licence. It will serve all urban areas by building a nationwide cellular network. Grameen Telecom will buy bulk airtime from GrameenPhone and retail it through Grameen borrowers in all the villages of Bangladesh. One Grameen borrower in each of the 68,000 villages will become the 'telephone-lady' of the village. She will sell the service of the telephone to the villagers and earn money.

New information technology will become the source of her income-generating activity. Thus, the village will be connected to the world through a poor woman who uses the most modern communication system available to earn a better living for herself.

As planned, GrameenPhone launched its service on 26 March 1997. It was not easy, everybody in the company worked day and night to keep to the schedule.

The opening ceremony was organized at the prime minister's office. Using a Grameen phone, our prime minister, Sheikh Hasina, called the prime minister of Norway who was enjoying his holiday in the north of Norway.

From this end our prime minister said: 'How's the weather up there?'

'It is very cold here. It is 36°C below zero.'

'How can you enjoy your holiday in weather like that? You'd better come here for your holiday. We have nice 32°C above zero in Dhaka.'

After this international call, a domestic call came for our prime minister. A Grameen borrower, Ms Laily Begum, from the village of Patira, north of Dhaka, called the prime minister from her cellular phone. Laily Begum became Grameen's first telephone-lady, and since then she has earned money by letting others use her phone for payment.

In 1997, Bangladesh had the lowest telephone density in the region, one phone per 300 inhabitants. For a country of 120 million people we had only 400,000 telephone sets, and these were all centred in the cities, mostly in Dhaka, and many of them remained out of commission most of the time.

So you can understand why in Bangladesh, a working phone is a symbol of power and authority. People wait for years to get a telephone. But some are lucky; these fortunate people have more than one phone. The more tele-phones you have on your desk, the more important a person you are. If you have a cellular phone, everyone immediately assumes you must be earning an enormous amount of money. A cellular phone company had already been operating in Bangladesh for seven years, but it naturally aimed at the topmost end of the market by pricing its service very high.

GrameenPhone intends to add another 400,000 telephones over the next four years. We have priced it to reach the people at the bottom, and GrameenPhone now offers the cheapest cellular rate in the world, 9.0 US cents per minute in peak hours and 6.7 US cents per minute in off-peak hours, for a call.

* * *

Many villages in Bangladesh do not have access to electricity. In order to provide cellular phones to those villages we need electricity, so we considered bringing in solar energy (we have sun in abundance!). This led us to become involved with alternative sources of energy, and to enable us to do so, we created Grameen Shakti (Energy). This is a non-profit company dedicated to developing all forms of renewable energy, and supported by a financing mechanism which enables consumers to avoid large upfront payments.

Grameen Shakti is currently trying out solar (photovoltaic) home systems, battery stations, wind turbines and gasifiers. Gasifiers turn wood or agricultural waste into gas which is used to generate electricity.

* * *

We also hope to make the Internet available in rural areas through our Grameen phone network. Grameen Cybernet, an Internet service provider, will create international jobs for the children of Grameen borrowers and these boys and girls will be able to serve companies around the world in various capacities from their own village homes or community office spaces.

By bringing Internet facilities into distant rural areas, many labour-intensive enterprises can be located in those otherwise isolated rural areas, such as data entry services, data management businesses, global answering services, typing and composing services, transcription services, secretarial services, accounting services, security services for buildings and homes located thousands of miles away, and so on. Since distances will be meaningless, these services can be offered to any business anywhere in the world.

Finally, a non-profit Internet service provider, Grameen Communications, will make the Internet available to educational and research institutions in Bangladesh. Many of these institutions do not have reliable telephone lines, or the budget to afford Internet facilities. Grameen Communications will offer them packages which will solve these problems.

Coming late in the game, Grameen borrowers have the benefit of being able to use the latest technology without wasting time or money on the earlier levels of technology which have led up to the latest innovations. I am not one of those pessimists who believes technology will necessarily push the haves and the have-nots further apart. If used properly, technology can help break down structural barriers, distances and cultural differences and help the poor share in economic well-being.

In addition to creating wealth, it can affect rapid social change by linking up many rural women who now suffer abuse and social domination because they are isolated. With easy access to a telephone, they will suddenly be connected to the entire world, to other distant relatives and to friends who can help them.

Cynics and critics of our ambitious project claim that high-tech will be wasted on the stone-age existence of most of our borrowers. The truth is, we are finding out quite the opposite. Without the benefit of a telephone, our villagers were wasting a lot of time, money and effort getting messages across to dispersed family members. If they needed to tell a brother or daughter living in Dhaka to come home, that their mother was gravely ill, or that there was to be a birth or a wedding in the family, they needed to send a messenger in person! That messenger had to stop working or studying and take a bus, rickshaw or train, and the message might literally take days to reach its destination. So the cost of not having access to a phone was obviously quite high.

With solar-powered telephones, anyone who lives in a village which has no electricity grid is able to send a message instantaneously wherever they want and receive an immediate response.

Another criticism we often hear is that the rural poor do not need the luxury of a telephone, which is seen more as an accoutrement of urban and middle-class or upper-class lifestyles. But to our telephone-lady, the telephone is a very real and practical way to earn money, in the same way as owning a cow or a rickshaw.

Besides, a telephone helps Grameen borrowers improve their existing business by giving them more information and greater ability to buy and sell their products. Without the use of a phone, when a borrower needs to buy raw materials, she has to send a messenger to ask the price and the possible delivery date of her needed goods. And she may have to send her messenger to three or four different suppliers. This may take weeks and cost a prohibitive amount. With a cellular phone, she can make her calls in the space of half an hour, put in her orders and thereby immediately increase the profitability of her business.

There is no reason to suppose that in the future the Grameen telephone-lady will limit herself to renting out her telephone; as technology and energy sources evolve, we can imagine her providing her fellow villagers with the capacity to send and receive faxes, e-mail and become a sort of door-to-door communications centre, one day providing forms of communications that do not yet exist. Indeed, when telephones become as plentiful in rural Bangladesh as they are in the United States, her phone service will not be worth anything, by that time she will have graduated into other technology businesses. But that is true of every economic activity.

37

The Grameen Trust:
The People's Fund

As Grameen became better known around the world, we started receiving letters and visits from people who wanted to know more about Grameen, who wanted to do research on Grameen, or who wanted help to start a Grameen programme in their own country.

To cope with these increasing demands for information and for training and technical assistance we created the Grameen Trust in 1989.

Many replication programmes already existed and many of these needed staff training. We provided this training through the Grameen Trust and developed a methodology to identify and train other replicators which we called the International Dialogue Programme. It requires chief executives of replicating organizations to spend twelve days in Grameen, mostly in our branches, so as to immerse themselves in the day-to-day functioning of Grameen, to absorb the realities of poverty and to understand the role of credit in the individual borrower's life.

At the end of these dialogue programmes, many participants who tried to start a Grameen replication in their own country, could not get the necessary funding. Donors they approached showed no interest. In my experience, donors find it easy to handle give-away projects, such as health, education, training, etc., but the moment they are required to support a credit programme they get nervous. In order to process a Grameen replication proposal they involve their banking experts and that is then the end of the story. It becomes such a complicated exercise, they would rather not proceed with it.

We started receiving request after request: 'Please help us find funds to get started. We have tried. We have talked to the officials of familiar donors at headquarter level. We have met their officials at country level. We have offered our services to identify good projects. But nothing has worked.'

In 1991, when I was invited to visit the Women's Self-Employment Project (WSEP) in Chicago, to meet with their borrowers and attend sessions with their staff, they asked me to give a public lecture on Grameen. About fifty people showed up. I had no idea who they were, except that they were interested in Grameen. During the question and answer session, I elaborated on how difficult it was to start a replication because of the difficulty of attracting donor money. I said I was frustrated with the prevailing situation. If donors find it difficult to handle micro-credit projects because they are small, difficult and expensive to administer I would like to help them. They could give the money to us, in the Grameen Trust, and we could administer the replication for them. If they were satisfied with the use of the first tranche of money, they could give us more money to continue. If they were unhappy with our performance, they could discontinue. I wished at least one donor would try us out.

As the session continued, I received a little note from someone in the audience: 'Can I see you for a couple of minutes after your presentation?'

I passed the note to Connie Evans, executive director of WSEP, who was sitting next to me to see if she would allow us some time together.

Immediately after the lecture I was shown into a small room. A lady was also shown in, the one who wanted to see me.

'How much money do you think you'll need to start funding the replication projects,' she said.

'I guess a couple of hundred thousand dollars would be a good start,' I answered.

'Will you have difficulty in finding replication projects?'

'Oh, no. There are many who are waiting for money. Once we start funding, many more will come forward.'

'How long will you be in town?'

'Another two days. Then I go to Washington.'

'I'll try to give you a cheque for a couple of hundred thousand dollars before you leave. Can I invite you to my home this evening so that I can get a few of my colleagues to come and meet you, and I can proceed with the processing of the grant?'

I looked at Connie and asked, 'Can I?'

Connie was beaming with excitement. She said: 'How can I stop you from going to Adele Simmon's home particularly when she wants to give you a grant!'

We spent the evening at Adele Simmon's house. Connie and Mary Houghton accompanied me. Adele, the president of the MacArthur Foundation, brought three of her colleagues, and confirmed her decision to give us a grant.

I had a hectic schedule for the next two days and no time to write a project proposal. But the grant-making procedure required a project proposal. Adele was not one to slow things down. She assigned her assistant Kabita to hop into taxis with me, sit next to me in the lunches and dinners and keep asking me questions to develop the draft of a proposal.

Adele Simmon's decision to support the Grameen Trust kick-started us on our ambitious replication programme, and I will never forget meeting with her.

* * *

With funds from the MacArthur Foundation, the Grameen Trust became seriously involved in financing replication programmes around the world and developing a proper methodology.

Later, the Trust needed more money. I discussed this with Peter Goldmark, president of the Rockefeller Foundation, and he came up with another half a million dollar grant. Peter became a great friend of Grameen. Not only did he visit Grameen, but he made it a policy to bring other heads of foundations and philanthropic organizations to visit us. In one such trip he brought, among several others, Wayne Silby who founded the Calvert Group of funds. Wayne is one of the business leaders who created the concept of 'social investment' and is popularizing it in America.

After his first visit to Grameen, Peter addressed a group of Social Venture Fund managers in New York and speaking about Grameen, he said:

As I watched, I could see the smashing of ancient rules, the shattering of a traditional cannon. I could see subversion. Here is what was being subverted:

The belief that poor people are helpless people;

The belief that women are the most helpless of all;

The belief that poor landless people are terrible credit risks;

The belief that poor people cannot co-operate, cannot plan ahead, cannot decide for themselves, cannot manage or service a loan;

The belief that the best form of economic development is aid for massive, centralized projects undertaken by the state.

If the old beliefs were made of pottery, the floor of the Grameen Bank would be littered with broken shards.

* * *

From the very beginning of the Grameen Trust, we witnessed a growing interest in many countries around the world to start Grameen programmes of their own. We were extremely happy with this response to the Grameen

Trust's replication programme, but the funds at the Trust's disposal were not enough to meet the demand. More and more projects were lining up to be financed by us, and we did not have enough money to support them all. To make matters worse, outside donors were not coming forward to meet this demand.

So we made an estimate of the fund's requirements to be able to finance all the replication start-ups for a period of five years, and we concluded that we would need $100 million to meet current and emerging needs. With this fund, we wanted to provide seed money to start new micro-credit programmes anywhere they were needed in the world and to assist any already-existing programmes to scale-up their operations. This would allow us to deliver micro-credit to one million borrowers around the world, and we hoped it would introduce micro-credit to most of the third world. Once we could accomplish that goal, and with experience in the field flowing from a wide variety of countries, we hoped that donors would overcome their hesitation and come forward to assist us with their full support.

We circulated our proposal to raise $100 million over five years, but international donors did not show any interest. RESULTS groups in the US, Canada, Japan, Germany and the UK tried to draw the attention of the top aid officials in their respective countries. I had a series of meetings at the highest levels in all the aid agencies in these countries. They all admired what the Grameen Bank and the Grameen Trust were doing, but they said under their rules they could not give money to a Third World country organization to on-lend to other countries. Aid bureaucracy is organized by country desks and country field offices. Money for each country has to be processed by each respective country desk. The Grameen Trust money is not for Bangladesh, so it does not fit into any pigeon-hole because it is for all Third World countries.

I argued that if bureaucratic arrangements were the only reason for not giving money to the Grameen Trust, why not change those arrangements and clear the way.

The only positive response we finally got was from USAID which in 1994 gave the Grameen Trust $2 million, followed by the UN Capital Development Fund. We were overjoyed and expected that after this breakthrough, other donors would follow suit.

We waited and waited, but nothing happened.

PART VII: A NEW WORLD

38

A World That Will
Assist the Poorest

One evening in 1993, I received a telephone call from the World Bank. Vice-President Ismail Serageldin was on the phone. Ismail is one person in the World Bank with whom I never had problems communicating. He is a genuine admirer of Grameen, and we worked together as Steering Committee members of the Aga Khan Foundation in Geneva. Despite holding a high position in the World Bank, he has not lost the feel for the poor.

'How can we help? Is there anything we can do for you?'

'Well, I don't know. The World Bank only works with the government. You can't work with us,' I said.

'No, we very much want to work with you, but you didn't want our money.'

'We didn't need your money. We can manage our own.'

'What response are you getting on the $100 million proposal you circulated for the Grameen Trust?'

'Very frustrating experience. Nobody came forward except USAID with $2 million.'

'Did you sent a copy of the proposal to the World Bank?'

'No, we didn't. We didn't think you'd be interested.'

'Can you fax me a copy tomorrow? I'll see what we can do for you.'

The next day I faxed the proposal to Ismail. He called me back about a week later, jubilant: 'We checked your proposal. We have good news for you. We want to give you the balance of $98 million.'

'I am delighted to hear that. We thought we'd never find this money. But how are you bypassing the government? I don't think it'll be easy to get it through the Bangladesh government.'

'Don't worry, we discussed that too. We'll find a way.'

Suddenly the question came to my mind: is Ismail talking about giving the Grameen Trust a loan of $98 million? The World Bank never gives grants. How would the Trust ever pay back the loan?

'Let me get this straight, Ismail – are you talking about a loan or an outright grant?'

'A loan of $98 million,' Ismail answered.

'But Ismail, the Trust will never be able to pay back a loan.'

'This is a soft loan with a very long maturity period. It is almost like a grant,' Ismail tried to clarify.

'But I know how this works: soon your official will ask for a guarantee from the government for this loan. And why should our government guarantee a loan to the Grameen Trust which will give this money to projects in other countries? The Trust will never recover the original amount even if the loan repayment is 100 per cent. We make projects responsible only for the local currency equivalent of the loan they receive. When they pay back, they will pay back in the local currency. But the World Bank will want US dollars. Because of currency fluctuations, the Trust will receive much less in dollar terms, than what it loaned. I see no way we can take a loan, even if it is a soft loan.'

'I see your point. Exchange-rate fluctuations are really a problem,' Ismail said.

But Ismail is not the kind of person who gives up so easily. He immediately said, 'We'll give you the entire money upfront. Then you can invest it to earn enough to compensate for the losses through currency fluctuation.'

'I am not an expert on fund management in the international market. I need an expert,' I said. 'Why don't you have one look into the matter and help us draw up a business plan which will protect the Trust and the World Bank.'

Ismail promised to do that. But neither his specialists nor the ones I consulted came up with any encouraging scenario.

Ismail called again: 'My friend, we'll not give up the idea. For the time being, we'll give you a grant of $2 million. After that we'll explore ways in which we can finance your $100 million proposal.'

That certainly made it simple and straightforward. No government guarantee needed, no repayment problem.

'But I thought the World Bank cannot give grants. How do you come up with a grant?'

'My friend, our job is to come up with ways which will make it easy. This grant does not come from the World Bank's loan fund. It comes from the profit of the bank. It will actually be an allocation from the president's discretionary fund.'

This is the $2 million grant to the Grameen Trust which Louis Preston then World Bank President announced during the Hunger Conference in November 1993.

* * *

RESULTS arranges visits to Grameen for its volunteers. These visits take place within the same framework of the International Dialogue Programme organized by the Grameen Trust in Dhaka.

On the concluding day of one such programme in 1995, I was briefing twenty-three RESULTS volunteers about the future direction of the micro-credit movement, and I expressed my frustrations with the aid bureaucracies around the world for not supporting micro-credit start-up and scaling-up projects all over the world, either directly through their own agencies or through the Grameen Trust, by responding to the $100 million proposal. I then said:

'Why should we wait for governments? What about citizen power? Citizens have their own minds and their own wallets. If one million citizens decide to contribute $100 each, we can create a fund of $100 million. This $100 can go out in perpetual cycles of loans to touch so many lives.'

When I finished my briefing I saw someone raise a hand at the far end of the table. I gave him the floor.

He said: 'I like your idea about one million people giving $100 each to create a million dollar fund. All big things must start with a small step. I'll take the first small step. Here is my cheque for $100 towards that fund.'

He held up a cheque. Everybody applauded as it was passed to me. Another hand was raised. Another cheque, then several more. Some of the participants did not have their chequebooks, so they borrowed from others. Soon I had twenty-three cheques in my possession: $2300 to begin the journey to raise $100 million dollars.

I said: 'Let us call it the "People's Fund". We'll campaign to find one million people. It won't be easy, but I don't see why it can't be done.'

The idea has been slowly gaining steam. The RESULTS volunteer who wrote the first cheque was Dave Ellis from South Dakota. He is the author of a popular guidebook for first-year college students, and he has his own foundation. Dave took the idea with him and hired some professionals to prepare an attractive campaign package designed to raise $100 million for our People's Fund. However, a tax-exempt organization was needed to host the fund.

This was created by Reed Oppenheimer, a singer and one of those twenty-three RESULTS volunteers whom I had met in 1995. He went ahead and registered the Grameen Foundation as a tax-exempt organization in Oklahoma. Reed had been so moved by the struggle of one of our borrowers whom he met, that he wrote a song about her which he called 'Nurjahan' and included it on his next CD.

Finally, Alex Counts, a Fulbright scholar who learned Bangla in order better to study Grameen and who spent almost five years in Bangladesh, became executive director of the Grameen Foundation USA and set up its office in Washington, DC in April 1997.

Alex wrote a book on Grameen entitled *Give Us Credit* (Random House, 1996), which documents the lives of Grameen borrowers in one Bangladesh village and WSEP borrowers in Chicago. Interestingly, when reading this account, you soon forget whether you are reading about people in Asia or in America, they sound so much alike.

* * *

The Grameen Trust had received $2 million from the World Bank, $2 million from USAID and $500,000 from the Rockefeller Foundation, but now we still needed to find $95.5 million.

Ismail did not give up. He came up with the idea of creating a consultative group to bring together the donors who were already funding micro-credit programmes or were interested in doing so.

There was quite strong opposition to the idea. Some donors thought it was an attempt of the World Bank to play 'big brother' in their own areas of decision-making. After several rounds of meetings, Ismail managed to widen the base of his support. His immediate goal was to come up with a commitment of $100 million for micro-credit programmes.

I always insisted that whatever was being done, the focus should be on the poorest. 'Poor', I argued, was a slippery word. People interpret it so loosely that it may include even a fairly well-off person in a community. Ismail took this very seriously. When the consultative group was finally formed he persuaded others to call it the Consultative Group to Assist the Poorest (CGAP). I was very happy that the word 'poorest' appeared in the very name of the mechanism. It would help avoid unnecessary controversy – I hoped.

In selecting the location of the secretariat of CGAP, donors were divided between Paris, IFAD in Rome and the World Bank in Washington. I was very unhappy that the choice was between three cities in the First World. I argued for locating the secretariat where there was acute poverty such as

Dhaka, Katmandu, Manila or La Paz.

The donors said it would be logistically difficult to locate the secretariat in Third World countries. I was not convinced at all, but among the three cities mentioned earlier, I supported the World Bank in Washington as the location over Rome or Paris, hoping that by hosting the secretariat, the most important development finance organization in the world might have the issues of poverty rubbed into their thinking and might change their mind.

The launching ceremony of CGAP in Washington, DC in 1995 was a thrilling experience for me. I had been arguing without success for the creation of a 'third window' – a grant window in the World Bank. This was never taken seriously, but now we have CGAP as a substitute for that idea. It is my deepest hope that CGAP will lead to the creation of a permanent poverty eradication programme in the World Bank rather than being simply a tactical gesture without real consequences on the ground.

39

World Micro-Credit Summit:
To Reach 100 million
By the Year 2005

Sam Daley-Harris, executive director of RESULTS, was getting tired of lobbying for tiny sums at the US Congress. The problem of poverty was so big that you could not keep nibbling at it and hope it would disappear when in fact it was getting worse.

Something dramatic was needed. Sam had seen how effective Jim Grant, the executive director of UNICEF, was with the 1990 Children's Summit when the world's leaders came to New York City and signed unbelievably ambitious targets.

So Sam started toying with an idea of a gala event like a summit for micro-credit. He kept asking around for a reasonable target for the summit. John Hatch, of FINCA, wrote a paper for Sam in 1995 expounding his vision of reaching the 200 million poorest families – the entire population of poor people in the world – with micro-credit in ten years. I didn't think that was feasible, and nobody would take the goal seriously if it were unachievable.

I rewrote the paper setting a target of reaching the 100 million poorest families in the coming ten years, 1996–2005. Sam proposed that we organize a world summit, taking this as its goal.

At first we thought of it as a get-together, or a dream-together of about five hundred people. Gradually it was revised upwards to one thousand participants.

Preparation of a draft declaration proved to be a real hornets' nest. I never realized it would create so much tension. Everybody wanted to rewrite the declaration, and I was shocked to see how the summit preparations began opening up conflicts. Sam became extremely disappointed. I tried to cheer him up by saying that we had to confront all our academic, institutional and philosophical differences. It was easy for me to say this and disappear into safety in Dhaka, but Sam was the one who had to be in the eye of the storm. He had no place to run to.

We had to set a date for the summit. We had always planned to have it in 1996 – the initial year of our ten-year period. We needed to choose a hotel. The critical question was how many participants were we expecting. Each gave their expected number. I said 3000, which startled everybody.

'You are not serious,' they said.

'I am serious,' I said. 'Looking at the enthusiasm generated by this idea around the world, my guess is that we'd better prepare for 3000, otherwise we may end up with an overflow and total chaos.'

To play safe, Sam picked up the phone to see how many hotels there were in Washington which could accommodate a conference of 3000 participants and at least fifty seminar rooms.

There was only one. He contacted them and asked if we could reserve it for September or October 1996. But it was booked all the way through 1997. What were we to do? We were panicky. We did not want to wait until 1998 to hold the summit. That would be too late.

Then the hotel called and said there was an opening in the first week of February 1997. People don't usually want to hold conferences in Washington, DC in early February, which is why this slot was still available. We immediately decided to take it. But we needed money as a down-payment, and we left it to Sam to find money.

Summit preparations were hectic, but the widespread support for micro-credit amazed me. The Micro-credit Summit was finally held on 2–4 February 1997, and its success as a call to worldwide action fulfilled our wildest dreams. About 3000 people from 137 countries gathered in Washington, DC.

The three co-chairs of the Summit, the First Lady Hillary Rodham Clinton, Queen Sofia of Spain and Dr Tsutomu Hata, the former prime minister of Japan, made passionate and forceful speeches.

Hillary Clinton hailed the summit as 'one of the most important gatherings that we could have anywhere in our world'. She went on to explain:

It [micro-credit] is not just about giving individuals economic opportunity. It is about community. It is about responsibility. It is about seeing how we are all inter-connected and interdependent in today's world. It is recognizing that in our country, the fate of a welfare recipient in Denver or Washington is inextricably bound up with all of ours. It is understanding how lifting people out of poverty in India or Bangladesh rebounds to the benefit of the entire community and creates fertile ground for democracy to live and grow, because people have hope in the future.

Sheikh Hasina, the prime minister of Bangladesh, chaired the summit's opening plenary session. On the podium she was joined by Alpha Oumar Konare, the president of Mali, Y. K. Museveni, the president of Uganda, P. M. Mocumbi, the prime minister of Mozambique, Alberto Fujimori, the president of Peru, Queen Sofia of Spain, Dr Tsutomu Hata, Dr Siti Hasmah, the First Lady of Malaysia and myself.

It was an electrifying start to a world-first, historical event.

The summit was organized into separate sessions in so-called specialized 'Councils': the Council of Practitioners, the Council of Donor Agencies, the Council of Corporations, the Council of Religious Institutions, the Council of UN Agencies, the Council of International Financial Institutions, the Council of Advocates, the Council of NGOs, the Council of Parliamentarians.

It was indeed a macro-event for micro-credit. During those three days, the whole world came together in one place. And the energy generated by listening to other leaders, other advocates, and by meeting so many colleagues, friends and supporters, brought tears to our eyes. It was obvious to all of us there that if we could maintain this level of energy during the next nine years we could not only meet but overshoot the stated goal of the summit.

Robert Rubin, the secretary of the US treasury, Jim Wolfensohn, president of the World Bank, Gus Speth, administrator of UNDP, Carol Bellamy, executive director of UNICEF, Dr Nafis Sadik, the executive director of UNFPA, Frederico Mayor, the secretary general of Unesco, Huguette Labelle, president of the Canadian International Development Agency, Brian Atwood, administrator of the US Agency for International Development, Fawzi al-Sultan, president of IFAD, all excelled in inspiring the delegates at the plenary sessions.

Each speaker declared his or her uncompromising commitment to the alleviation and eradication of poverty through micro-credit.

Bella Abzug, the co-chair of our Council of Advocates brought the delegates to their feet when she said: 'Never, never, never underestimate the historic importance of what we do here today. And no matter how steep the pass, how discouraging the pace, I ask you to never give in and never give up.'

The delegates made their response very clear by thumping their applause, and it was easy to sense they would never give in or give up until our vision was achieved.

Micro-credit practitioners from all over the world were busy preparing themselves for the giant task ahead of us through what we called 'Meet the Challenge' sessions which were being held simultaneously at the summit.

The summit suddenly changed the status of micro-credit from being a subject dear to the heart of some practitioners, to a serious agenda for the entire world.

* * *

Life leads us in mysterious ways and calls us to achieve our greatest potential in a manner we can never predict or know in advance. Micro-borrowers, who grow up accepting that they are nobody, they are worth nothing, were placed by this summit in the global spotlight and held up as the great heroes in the fight for world development. Speaker after speaker eulogized them for their endless patience and skill in micro-managing tiny pieces of resources to craft a life with dignity. The summit underscored the fact that the trials and tribulations they go through are no less than those faced by the great heroes of history.

In teaching economics I learned about money, and now as the head of a bank I lend money, and the success of our venture lies in how many crumpled bank bills our once starving members now have in their hands. But the micro-credit movement which is built around and for and with money, ironically, is at its heart, at its deepest root, not about money at all. It is about helping each person achieve his or her fullest potential. It is not about cash capital, but about human capital. Money is merely a tool that helps unlock human dreams and helps even the poorest and most unfortunate people on this planet achieve dignity, respect and meaning in their lives.

We are a bank, that is all we are, all we pretend to be. We extend loans to help the poorest achieve human dignity, but dignity, personal happiness, self-fulfilment, meaningful lives, these are things that people create for themselves, by their own labour, their own dreams, their own desire and hard work. All we need to do is to remove structural barriers which for so long kept an underclass out of the human context. If they can achieve their full potential the world will be totally transformed not only by the lack of poverty, but by the economic and social efforts of those who until yesterday were sleeping on sidewalks, begging and loitering without knowing where their next meal was coming from.

Why is it only now at the beginning of the third millennium that anything is being done to get rid of the age-old scourge of poverty? Why does such concrete action as a world micro-credit summit have to rely on the efforts of a high-school music teacher like Sam Daley-Harris, and on his individual volunteers? Why do we not elect officials and support political parties who will put this at the top of their agenda?

* * *

When my turn came to speak at the opening plenary session of the summit, I found myself thinking of Jobra and my very first 'borrowers', and how they radically changed me from a bird's-eye-view economist who taught elegant theories in a classroom to being a worm's-eye-view practitioner helping to effect real and lasting change in people's lives.

I felt real emotion in the depths of my being, as if at last, here in this hotel ballroom in Washington, DC, we had enough political leadership on a global basis to make things begin to happen, to help all the millions of poor in the world who were waiting for things to happen, so that they could help themselves to become self-sufficient and live a life with human dignity.

I stood up and made the following statement:

As we assemble here, I ask myself, 'What is the Micro-credit Summit about? Is it another Washington gala event?'

Personally to me it is an emotional event. Like me, there are many here today for whom it is a deeply emotional experience. It is emotional, because we have been working very hard to make this day happen. Finally it has happened. I wish to take this opportunity to thank millions of micro-borrowers and thousands of staff who have been working hard to right a wrong which has caused so much avoidable human misery.

To me, this summit is a grand celebration – we are celebrating the freeing of credit from the bondage of collateral. This summit is to pronounce good-bye to the era of financial apartheid. This summit declares that credit is more than business. Just like food, credit is a human right.

This summit is about setting the stage to unleash the human creativity and endeavours of the poor. This summit is to guarantee every poor person the chance to undertake responsibility to establish his or her own human dignity.

This summit is to celebrate the success of millions of determined women who transformed their lives from extreme poverty to dignified self-sufficiency through entering into micro-credit programmes.

This summit is about creating opportunities for 100 million of the poorest families to follow in the footsteps of these successful women.

This summit is not a fund-raising event. I repeat – this summit is not a fund-raising event. This summit wants to inspire the world by putting together all the good news we have created during the past years. This summit wants to build will, wants to build capacity, wants to end poverty in the world.

Only one hundred years back, men were still struggling to find a way to fly. Many people seriously thought men would never fly. Those people who were committed to the idea of flying were looked upon as crazy people. In 1903 the Wright brothers flew their first plane. It stayed in the air for just twelve seconds. Yes, twelve seconds. It covered 120ft. At that moment the seed of a new world was planted. Only sixty-five years later, man confidently went to the moon, picked up moon rocks and returned to the world. The whole world watched every moment of it on television.

In the micro-credit field, we are just flying our Wright brothers' plane. We are covering 120ft here, 500ft there. Some find our plane unsafe, some find it clumsy, some find it not good enough for the job. We can assure you we'll soon fly our Boeings, our Concordes; we'll be ready with our booster rockets.

We believe that poverty does not belong in a civilized human society. It belongs in museums.

This summit is about creating a process which will send poverty to the museum.

Only sixty-five years after the twelve-second flight of the Wright brothers, man went to the moon. Sixty-five years after this summit, we will also go to our moon. We will create a poverty-free world.

With the energy that I feel in this room, I feel more confident than ever before that we'll make it. Ladies and gentlemen, let us make it!

Thank you.

As I finished my statement, I looked at the audience. I knew there was applause, but I did not hear it. All I heard inside of me was millions of determined voices rising from all over the world saying: 'Yes we can do it, we can make this happen, we can make this ambitious, mad, crazy, impossible dream a reality! We can have a world free of poverty!'

40

A Poverty-Free World:
How and When?

What will happen in the world in the next century?

We refer to the 'next century' as if we are talking about the next twenty-four hours. But the next century means the next one hundred years. I don't think anybody has the knowledge or wisdom to predict what will happen to the world and its inhabitants during the next one hundred years. The world is changing in unpredictable ways and will continue to become more and more unpredictable as we move along the time path. All we can say, with a fair amount of certainty, is that the speed of change will be faster and faster – it will never slow down. Take all the accumulated knowledge, discoveries, inventions up until the end of the twentieth century, and in the next fifty years alone, this will grow perhaps several times. That is the kind of incredible speed of change we are approaching.

If somehow we could come back to the world a hundred years from now, we would definitely feel as if we were visitors from some prehistoric age.

If we try to imagine what the world will be like twenty-five years from today, we would have to create a science fiction – nothing less than that.

The momentum for change is in place. The insatiable quest for knowing the unknown, the eagerness of business to put technology at the service of consumers, and the military arms race between nations, have all helped create this momentum. The real question for me is whether these changes will bring the human race closer to desired social and economic co-ordinates, or cause it to drift away from all desired locations in this multi-dimensional continuum.

The answer is obvious. If we consider ourselves as passengers in this spaceship called earth, we will find ourselves riding in a pilotless, route-mapless, destinationless journey. If we can convince ourselves that we are actually the crew of this spaceship, and we are here to take this ship to a specific socio-economic destination, then we will continue to approach this destination, even if we make mistakes along the way or are forced to take detours.

We need to know the destination – if not in a precise way, at least in a broad way. We must continue to search for the precise destination, and build up a consensus about it.

If we do a good job in identifying our precise destination, more innovations and changes will take place to help us reach it. Before we actually translate something into reality, we must be able to dream about it. Any socio-economic dream is nothing but the mapping out of our destination.

* * *

So the real question is not so much where do I think we will be in the year 2050, but where would I like the world to be in 2050?

By that time I want to see a world free from poverty. This means there will not be a single human being on this planet who may be described as a poor person. By then, the word 'poverty' will no longer have any current relevance. It should be understood only with reference to the past. The only place our progeny should be able to 'see' poverty would be in museums.

Poverty does not belong to civilized human society. Its proper place is in a museum. That's where it will be. When schoolchildren go with their teachers and tour the poverty museums, they will be horrified to see the misery and indignity of human beings. They will blame their forefathers for tolerating this inhuman condition and for allowing it to continue for such a large part of the population until the early part of the twenty-first century.

* * *

I always feel that eliminating poverty from the world is a matter of will, rather than of finding ways and means. Even today we don't pay serious attention to the issue of poverty, because we ourselves are not personally involved in it. We are not poor. We distance ourselves from the issue by saying that if the poor worked harder they wouldn't be poor.

When we want to help the poor, we usually offer them charity. Most often we use charity to avoid recognizing the problem and finding a solution for it. Charity becomes a way to shrug off our responsibility.

Charity is no solution to poverty. Charity only perpetuates poverty by taking the initiative away from the poor. Charity allows us to go ahead with our own lives without worrying about those of other people. Our conscience is adequately appeased by charity.

But the real issue is creating a level playing-field for everybody, giving every human being a fair and equal chance.

* * *

Human society has tried in many ways to ensure equal opportunities, but the poverty issue remains unresolved. The poor are left to the state to take care of. The state has created massive bureaucracies with their rules and procedures to look after the poor. Large amounts of taxpayers' money are set aside to finance these programmes.

Whatever state support has achieved, it certainly has not created equal opportunity for all people. Welfare children grow up on welfare and usually spend their lives on welfare.

Changes are products of intensive effort. The intensity of effort depends on the felt need for change, and the resources that are mobilized to bring about the changes desired. In a greed-based economy, obviously, changes will be greed driven. These changes may not always be socially desirable. Socially desired changes may not be attractive from the greed perspective.

That is where social-consciousness-driven organizations are needed. The state and civil society must provide the support of financial and other resources behind such socially-conscious organizations.

These organizations will continually devote their attention and research and development money to those areas of innovation, adaptation and development in technology which will facilitate the achievement of beneficial social goals. They will also monitor the greed-driven developments in technology to ensure that these technologies do not lead societies in undesirable directions.

* * *

As recent trends show, there is one particular technology that is going to change the world in the immediate future far more rapidly and fundamentally than any other technology so far in human history. This may be broadly described as information and communication technology. Already its speed of expansion is phenomenal.

Take the Internet, for example. It is spreading at an exponential rate. At its present speed, it is doubling its worldwide use every nine months. If this speed continues, every person on the planet will have an e-mail address by the year 2003!

The most attractive aspect of this spread of information and communication technology is that it is not under anyone's control. Neither government, nor big business, nor anyone of any authority can restrict the flow of information through the Internet. The next best aspect of it is that it is becoming cheaper every day.

Information and communication technology is raising the hope that we are approaching a world which will be free from power-brokers, and knowledge-brokers. Each individual's likes and dislikes will count. Individuals will be in command. There will be no screening authority to get to centre-stage. This is particularly exciting for all disadvantaged groups, voiceless groups, and minority groups.

Any power built on exclusive access to information will disintegrate. Any common citizen will have almost as much access to information as the head of government. Leadership will have to be based on vision and integrity, rather than on the manipulation of information.

* * *

What direction would I like to see this information and communication technology take?

I would like to see that all information is available to all people (including the poorest, the most ignorant, and the most powerless) at all times, almost cost-free, irrespective of distance.

Communication between any two persons anywhere in the world should be as easy as talking to your best friend sitting on a park bench.

All academic and social institutions should be turned into nodal points for disseminating information.

One guiding principle for future information and communication technology would be that at each step it should be creating a global environment to unleash the limitless creativity, ingenuity and productivity in each human being.

Any person anywhere would be able to enroll in any academic institution on the basis of his or her interest and ability, irrespective of his or her social upbringing, location, or financial capacity.

The entire concept of an 'academic institution' would also be vastly different from what we have known until now. In such an environment, it would not be surprising to learn that the most creative student in a very prestigious university is maybe from a poor family in a remote village in China, or Ethiopia, or Bangladesh, and that she or he has never yet visited a town!

* * *

Easy access to credit, and easy access to a global network of information for the poorest women and men anywhere in the world will eliminate poverty from our planet more surely and speedily than anything else will. But this is not to argue that all other initiatives and investments must stop while we are busy bringing credit and information to the poor. They are all complementary strategies, not substitutes for one another.

* * *

Another 'access' I would like to see is access to the market. I would like to see all barriers and protections around world markets disappear.

Protectionism is built up in each nation in the name of the poor, but its real beneficiaries are the rich and clever people who know how to manipulate the system.

The poor have a better chance in a bigger market than in a small protected market. If we can ensure the free flow of commodities, finances, and people, everybody will benefit, not just the poor.

It does not make sense to build high walls around the borders of our countries. Passports and visas did not even exist a century ago. They are a twentieth-century phenomenon. Let us leave them behind with the century which invented them. Let us take pride in our human identity above all other identities. We can wave our national flags, celebrate our regional, national, racial, local, religious, political, cultural heritage, but not by offending others, not by claiming supremacy over any other, but by glorifying in the unity of humankind, strengthened and enhanced through the friendly competition of cultures, religions and other diversities.

Needless to say, technology as well as economic necessity are bringing us closer to a borderless, and distanceless world. Let us welcome it with rapturous applause.

Today Europe is leading the way in creating a free and open market among nations. All other regional associations, groupings of countries can follow their initiative. If we start feeling comfortable we can move from regional to inter-regional, and finally to global free movement of people, finance, commodities and services from one location in the world to any other location.

With the concept of 'national government' waiting to be drastically redefined in the context of new economic and technological reality, with the importance of individual citizens and their local bodies, it would be a natural step to go beyond political borders to find friends and partners without state authority intervening in such matters.

41

What Would It Be Like?

A world without poverty.

Whenever I mention this to people who have not experienced the power of micro-credit first-hand, I see a half-smile often masking their obvious cynicism or doubts. Even supporters of micro-credit sometimes view this as an 'impossible dream' which we use to motivate ourselves and our workers.

Can anyone really conceive of a world without poverty?

What would it be like?

Would it really work?

* * *

To me, a world without poverty means that every person would have the ability to take care of his or her own basic life needs. In such a world, nobody would die of hunger or suffer from malnutrition. This is a goal world leaders have been calling for for decades, but have never set out any way of achieving it.

Today 40,000 children die each day around the world from hunger-related diseases. In a poverty-free world, no children would die of such causes.

Everybody in every part of the globe would have access to education and health-care services because he or she would be able to afford them. Unlike today, the state would not be required to provide free or subsidized health-care or schooling.

All state organizations created to provide free or subsidized services for the poor would no longer be required and could be done away with. Thus, no need for welfare, or local welfare agencies, or the national welfare department. No need for hand-outs, no soup-kitchens, no food stamps, no free schools, no free hospital care, no begging in the streets.

State-run safety-net programmes would have no rationale for existence because no one would live on charity any more. State-run social security programmes, income-support programmes would be unnecessary.

Social structures in a poverty-free world would, of course, be quite different from those that exist in a poverty-ridden world. But nobody would be at the mercy of anyone else, and that is what would make all the difference between a world without poverty and one riddled with it.

Finally, a poverty-free world would be economically much stronger and far more stable than the world today.

One-fifth of the world's inhabitants who today live a life of extreme poverty would become income earners and income spenders. They would generate extra demand in the market to make the world economy grow. They would bring their creativity and innovations into the market-place to increase the world's productive capacity.

Since nobody would ever become poor, except on a temporary and limited basis, the economy would probably not go through extreme swings. We would avoid boom-and-bust cycles and be able to surmount man-made disaster with greater ease.

* * *

But even in a poverty-free world where every man and every woman would earn enough to take care of themselves and their family, there would still be situations of temporary poverty due to a sudden catastrophe or misfortune, a bankruptcy or business downturn leading to failure, or some personal disease or disaster.

A poverty-free world might see a whole group of families, locations, or even regions devastated by some shared disaster, such as floods, fire, cyclones, riots, earthquakes or other disasters. But such temporary problems could be taken care of by the market mechanism through insurance and other self-paying programmes, assisted of course by social-consciousness-driven enterprises.

There would always remain differences in lifestyle between people at the bottom of society and those at the top income levels. Yet that difference would be the difference between the middle-class and the luxury class, just as on trains in Europe today you have only first-class and second-class carriages, whereas in the nineteenth century there were third-class and even fourth-class carriages – sometimes with no windows and just hay strewn on the floor.

* * *

Can we really create a poverty-free world? A world without third-class or fourth-class citizens, a world without a hungry, illiterate barefoot under-class?

Yes we can, in the same way as we can create 'sovereign' states, or 'demo-cratic' political systems, or 'free' market economies.

A poverty-free world would not be perfect, but it would be the best approximation of the ideal.

We have created a slavery-free world, a polio-free world, an apartheid-free world. Creating a poverty-free world would be greater than all these accomplishments while at the same time reinforcing them. This would be a world that we could all be proud to live in.

Appendix I

A Look at the Balance Sheet

Size of the Bank

In May 1998, Grameen Bank's total of loans disbursed topped $2.4 billion. We crossed the first billion dollar mark in March 1995, about eighteen years after we began our journey in 1976 by lending $27 to forty-two people. It took only twenty-seven months to lend the second billion dollars.

The total amount of loans that Grameen Bank disburses each year exceeds the total amount of rural loans disbursed by all other banks in Bangladesh put together.

As of May 1998, Grameen Bank had 1,112 branches serving 2.33 million borrowers at their doorstep in 38,551 villages. It had a workforce of nearly 13,000. On any working day, Grameen collects an average of $1.5 million in weekly instalments.

Grameen staff's daily travel to serve their clients adds up a total mileage equivalent to several times around the earth. During half this mileage they collectively carry $1.5 million on their person without fear of attack.

Right from the beginning Grameen focused on financial discipline, transparency and financial viability.

Table 1: Size of the Bank (As at 31 May 1998)

No. of villages where Grameen operates	38,551
No. of Grameen centres	65,960
No. of branches	1,112
No. of staff	12,589
No. of Grameen members	
Female:	2,210,160
Male:	124,620
Total:	2,334,780
Cumulative number of houses built with Grameen housing loans	438,764

Table 2: Savings and disbursements from Grameen Bank
(As at 31 May 1998)

Item	*Million* taka	*Million US$*
Cumulative amount disbursed	96,516.70	2,408.30
Amount disbursed during May 1998	1,560.34	33.70
Cumulative amount of housing loans disbursed	6,629.03	168.61
Housing loans disbursed during May 1998	78.27	1.69
Cumulative amount of savings in Group Fund	7,107.79	176.90
Balance of voluntary savings (i.e., excluding Group Fund)	755.38	16.31

The first external money came to Grameen in 1982. Until then Grameen carried on its business with funding from the commercial banks and the Agricultural Bank.

The first external funding came from IFAD. IFAD gave this loan to the government of Bangladesh for fifty years at 1 per cent service charge. The government of Bangladesh lent this money to Grameen for fifteen years at 3 per cent interest. Since then, Grameen has received loans and grants from NORAD (Norwegian aid agency), SIDA (Swedish aid agency), KFW and GTZ (German aid agencies), CIDA (Canadian aid agency), OECF (Japanese aid agency), IFAD (UN Development Finance agency), the Ford Foundation and the Dutch government.

Grameen has stopped negotiating for new grants or soft loans since 1995. It decided to depend fully on commercial sources of funding. It has, however, continued to receive grants and soft loans during 1996–1997 under agreements negotiated before 1996. These came to an end in June 1998.

The most thrilling experience for Grameen came in 1994–1995 when it issued bonds to raise $160.75 million from the commercial banks in Bangladesh. That helped Grameen to pay back the Central Bank loan and to create a loanable fund on a long-term basis. Tables 3 and 4 provide information on the sources of funds.

The flow of low-cost funds from the donors has declined since 1993. It came down to 39 per cent of the total available fund at the end of 1993. It declined to 34 per cent in 1997. It shows Grameen's reliance more on own funds and borrowing at the market rate. The internal resource mobilization to finance the bank's fund requirement has been one of the achievements of the bank.

Table 3: External sources of funds (In million US$)

Nature of Funds	On-lending	Non-lending	Total
Loans:			
IFAD	42.61	5.20	47.81
SIDA	6.25	1.21	7.46
NORAD	6.61	1.76	8.37
OECF	18.58	—	18.58
Dutch loan	1.39	—	1.39
Ford Foundation	—	2.07	2.07
Subtotal	**75.44**	**10.24**	**85.68**
Grants:			
SIDA	35.93	6.14	42.07
NORAD	42.26	12.25	54.51
GTZ	—	13.15	13.15
KFW	26.57	1.94	28.51
CIDA	7.51	2.47	9.98
Subtotal	**112.27**	**35.95**	**148.22**
Grand Total	**187.71**	**46.19**	**233.90**

Costs of Funds

The loan velocity of Grameen Bank has been instrumental in recycling the available funds more than six times, i.e. each *taka* has been issued as loans an average of six times. This has contributed in optimizing the use of the loan fund, ensuring loan access to a larger number of clients and generating savings from the borrowers.

The cost of funds registered sharp increases after 1993. Grameen has to pay about 5.76 per cent and 4.87 per cent interest on bonds issued by it during 1995 and 1996 respectively. The interest that Grameen paid on the bonds alone accounted for 33 per cent and 39 per cent of the total interest expenses during 1995 and 1996 respectively. The major cost of funds in 1996 was for the borrowers' deposits which alone accounted for 49 per cent of the total cost of funds. This was about 43 per cent in 1995 and only 34 per cent in 1994. Grameen offers 8.5 per cent interest to depositors. All grants are put in a revolving fund (now transferred to Grameen Kalyan, an

Table 4: Sources of funds during 1993–1997 (In million US$)

Sources	1993 Cum.	1993 Incr.	1994 Cum.	1994 Incr.	1995 Cum.	1995 Incr.	1996 Cum.	1996 Incr.	1997 Cum.	1997 Incr.
Bangladesh Bank	109.38	109.38	93.75	-15.63	41.75	-93.75	40.71	-1.04	38.95	-1.76
IFAD	42.26	2.96	42.26		41.75	-0.51	40.71	-1.04	38.95	-1.76
NORAD	8.37		8.37		8.37		8.37		8.37	
SIDA	7.46		7.46		7.46		7.46		7.46	
Ford Foundation	2.06		2.07	0.01	2.07		2.07		2.07	
Dutch loan	1.39		1.25	-0.14	1.25		1.25		1.25	
Other Banks		-0.10	0.50	0.50	3.09	2.59	10.25	7.16	5.09	-5.16
Bond & Debenture			80.75	80.75	160.75	80.00	162.50	1.75	141.00	-21.50
OECF							9.26	9.26	18.58	9.32
Grameen Kalyan							91.28	91.28	91.28	
Members' Deposits	98.44	30.44	123.01	24.57	138.87	15.86	149.53	10.66	162.56	13.03
Revolving fund	88.38	13.89	94.91	6.53	104.47	9.56	0.09	-104.38	22.30	22.21
Paid-up capital	4.69	0.01	6.35	1.66	6.61	0.26	6.72	0.11	7.02	0.30
Reserves	1.56	0.86	2.07	0.51	2.51	0.44	3.02	0.51	3.47	0.45
Other	19.65	11.09	25.17	5.52	21.20	-3.97	26.70	5.50	34.78	8.08
Grand Total	383.64	168.53	487.92	104.28	498.40	10.48	519.21	20.81	544.18	24.97

Note: There is a slight difference between the amounts shown in Table 4 and the balance sheet due to the application of conversion rates of the respective years in the incremental column of the table above.

independent organization). Grameen Bank pays variable rates of interest on this fund, the minimum interest rate being 2 per cent.

Use of Funds

Grameen Bank earns 20 per cent interest on one-year income generating loans and 8 per cent on ten-year housing loans. *Table 3* shows the external sources of the bank's funds. In 1992–1995 Grameen was on a fast-track of loan expansion. It prepared to finance this rapid expansion by raising money through issuing bonds in 1995–1996. But unforeseen circumstances nullified the plan. The year 1996 was one of severe political unrest in the country, and economic life was seriously disrupted. Disbursement in 1996 dropped below the previous year's level. These dislocations continued to cause difficulties even after the political crisis was over.

Bad Debt Provision

In spite of sincere efforts by our borrowers, natural vagaries and man-made disasters sometimes force them to seek loan re-amortization or put them in extreme circumstances when they ultimately fail to repay the bank's dues. To accommodate this reality, Grameen makes provision for loan losses in tune with actual field-level conditions. Grameen makes 100 per cent provision for income-generating loans outstanding two years from date of first disbursement and 20 per cent provision for all income-generating loans outstanding one year from date of disbursement. Grameen also makes 5 per cent provision for all housing loans disbursed.

Loans written off in the past totalled less than 1 per cent of the gross average outstanding loans of the respective accounting years. These decisions were taken on the basis of the performance record of each loan.

Profit and Loss Accounts

The bank's income shows that in spite of the increase in overall expenditure, it was possible for the bank to operate above the break-even point in past years.

Table 5: Profit and loss accounts (As at 31 December)

	1993	1994	1995	1996	1997 (*provisional*)
	Million US$				
Average Dollar Rate of Year	**39.14**	**40.00**	**40.20**	**40.86**	**45.45**
Income					
Loan Operation	26.97	41.16	49.15	42.96	30.96
Interest on Fixed Deposit	4.23	6.55	4.88	10.47	11.33
*Other Income	2.66	2.75	2.78	3.20	3.09
Total Income	**33.86**	**50.46**	**56.81**	**56.63**	**45.38**
Expenditure					
Interest Expenses	9.90	19.80	21.02	19.80	19.26
Administrative & other expenses	23.71	30.12	35.42	36.37	25.79
Total Expenditure	**33.61**	**49.92**	**56.44**	**56.17**	**45.05**
Profits	**0.25**	**0.54**	**0.37**	**0.46**	**0.33**

N.B. *Other Income = Interest on Deposit + Other Income

Borrowers

All the external research done on Grameen tells us that our borrowers keep climbing up the economic ladder. Our hopes and aspirations are to help our borrowers to keep on going up until our bank becomes known not as the 'bank of the poor' but as the 'bank of the formerly poor'.

The change is happening before our very eyes. Recently, I attended a meeting of Grameen borrowers who were mostly weavers. The meeting took place in a centre not far from Dhaka, and I began to chat with them on the issue of whether loans were improving their lives. One member immediately told me that her first loan was 1000 *taka*. She was scared when she received that loan. After eleven years with Grameen, she now pays 1,100 *taka* as her weekly instalment.

I was stunned. When I collected myself I asked:
'How many of you pay weekly instalments of more than 1000 *taka* ($25)?'
Three women raised their hands.
'How many of your pay between 850 *taka* and 1000 *taka*?'
Five more women raised their hands.

By the time I had gone down to 500 *taka* instalments, nearly twenty arms, or half the centre, were up.

'This is wonderful,' I said with pleased surprise. 'When I started out, I was giving out loans of just 500 *taka* and sometimes only 300 *taka*. Once I even gave out a loan of 30 *taka* (75 US cents). Their amounts were the maximum that a person could safely venture to borrow. And repaying these tiny sums was not easy. But I never imagined that our loans would get so high. Today I am very happy for you and for the bank.'

I started asking around in other centres, and the answers were the same.

In our head office there were two schools of thought. One argued that the increase in lending had been long overdue and was necessary if the borrowers were going to get financially strong. The other charged that it was foolhardy, that the borrowers would get overextended, and to allow them to do this was to push them to disaster.

At first I tended to fall somewhere in between these two extremes. For instance, we clearly did not want borrowers simply taking their seasonal loans and using the money to repay their general loans. A few borrowers might resort to this occasionally, but if it was too widespread, it would signal future repayment problems for us. But the more I thought about it, I concluded there was no reason to limit or stop one of our borrowers reaching a high level of loans. We should support our borrowers to grow into higher levels of businesses, so that they never slip back to poverty. If we face problems along the way we will have to learn to resolve them.

Table 6: Balance Sheet (As at 31 December)

	1993	1994	1995	1996	1997 *(provisional)*
(Average taka/dollar rate	39.14	40.00	40.20	40.86	45.45)
Property and assets (US$)					
Cash in hand	1,487	2,506	673	9,849	148,781
Balances with other banks	8,685,191	8,221,369	10,672,325	9,404,633	2,577,183
Investment-at cost	44,579,075	80,046,485	90,906,953	148,348,392	101,215,898
Loans and advances	223,903,187	276,323,642	278,014,734	268,077,806	276,987,656
Fixed assets at cost less accumulated depreciation	12,669,480	13,778,854	14,711,155	16,682,965	16,541,264
Other assets	23,789,816	35,979,674	47,174,526	36,497,499	32,120,343
Total:	313,658,236	414,352,530	441,480,366	479,021,144	429,591,125
Capital and liabilities *Share Capital:*					
Authorized	6,387,328	12,500,000	12,437,811	12,236,907	110,011,001
Paid up	3,832,397	5,412,913	5,647,077	5,676,676	5,409,835
General and other reserves	1,274,156	1,759,053	2,191,184	2,679,781	2,868,683
Revolving Funds	72,247,852	77,231,700	86,364,415	64,913	22,274,805
Deposits and other funds	80,485,719	103,314,043	118,587,183	127,572,377	127,718,165
Borrowings from banks and foreign institutions	139,753,939	205,392,534	211,506,129	320,453,435	242,938,569
Other liabilities	16,064,173	21,242,287	17,184,378	22,573,962	28,381,068
Total:	313,658,236	414,352,530	441,480,366	479,021,144	429,591,125

Appendix II

Analysis of Some of the Most Popular Grameen Loans

Table 1: General and Processing

Type of activity	No. of Loans	Amount of loans	$ conversion
Paddy husking	2,505,915	7,076,010,032	176,900,251
Bamboo works	410,391	1,401,819,667	35,045,492
Puffed rice making	169,495	582,459,084	14,561,477
Cane-works	150,876	447,620,398	11,190,510
Mat (pati) making	145,023	452,714,223	11,317,856
Fishing net making	144,451	453,054,048	11,326,351
Weaving (napkin)	67,857	300,283,917	7,507,098
Sweet meats making	63,180	221,162,453	5,529,061
Weaving (sari)	61,321	315,860,488	7,896,512
Weaving (lungi)	41,237	193,377,240	4,834,431
Garment making	39,347	165,959,449	4,148,986
Hogla making	27,922	96,709,750	2,417,744
Pottery products	25,811	104,958,362	2,623,959
Clock repairing	21,714	113,414,150	2,835,354
Earthenware container making	20,169	70,256,825	1,756,421

Table 2: Agriculture and Forestry

Type of activity	No. of Loans	Amount of loans	$ conversion
Paddy cultivation	2,102,244	6,810,388,853	170,259,721
Land lease	498,610	2,572,903,691	64,322,592
Boro-Irri cultivation	474,255	1,542,744,757	38,568,619
Rabi crop cultivation	466,405	2,056,637,660	51,415,942
Tubewells	378,826	1,283,287,632	32,082,191
Land cultivation	370,363	1,593,935,022	39,848,376
Fertilizer (for cultivation)	310,112	871,080,795	21,777,020
Potato cultivation	248,046	1,090,966,679	27,274,167
Vegetable cultivation	212,109	1,028,008,214	25,700,205
Sugarcane cultivation	205,421	760,526,179	19,013,154
Banana cultivation	156,179	631,485,937	15,787,148
Betel-leaf cultivation	149,839	714,347,592	17,858,690
Farming	70,699	340,127,859	8,503,196
Wheat Cultivation	63,297	159,862,106	3,996,553
Turmeric cultivation	46,752	144,285,795	3,607,145

Table 3: Livestock and Fisheries

Type of activity	No. of Loans	Amount of loans	$ conversion
Milch cow	2,641,224	12,544,410,100	313,610,253
Cow fattening	2,277,567	7,756,490,399	193,912,260
Goat	743,321	1,094,499,238	27,362,481
Poultry raising	725,412	1,116,319,604	27,907,990
Bullock	424,279	1,736,563,520	43,414,088
Pisciculture	288,248	869,947,097	21,748,677
Fishing net	33,478	119,958,080	2,998,952
Sheep raising	29,533	81,729,308	2,043,233
Dry fish	20,965	78,861,750	1,971,544
Duck purchase	12,481	28,045,468	701,137
Buffalo raising	10,214	49,365,125	1,234,128
Pineapple cultivation	7,585	30,483,764	762,094
Boat for fishing	5,380	19,141,390	478,535
Other domestic animals	5,307	27,244,000	681,100
Pond excavation	3,325	12,118,750	302,969

Table 4: Services

Type of activity/service	No. of Loans	Amount of loans	$ conversion
Rickshaws	94,547	437,532,340	10,938,309
Sewing machine purchases	56,835	262,690,499	6,567,262
Van purchases	41,600	170,755,840	4,268,896
Tubewell purchases	13,853	56,149,258	1,403,731
Boats for transportation	9,230	42,210,350	1,055,259
Boats for ferry service	6,439	30,936,500	773,413
Push carts	3,372	11,744,355	293,609
Barber's	2,876	11,386,702	284,668
Bicycle purchases	2,757	6,163,400	154,085
Renting irrigation pumps	2,737	14,653,700	366,343
Power tillers	2,618	57,898,013	1,447,450
Buffalo carts	2,470	10,611,684	265,292
Paddy threshing machines	2,466	13,164,600	329,115
Drain repairing	2,398	36,578,732	914,468
Baby taxis	1,563	38,585,048	964,626

Table 5: Trading

Type of activity/product	No. of Loans	Amount of loans	$ conversion
Rice/paddy	994,423	3,660,365,314	91,509,133
Cloths	213,051	1,038,593,156	25,964,829
Stationery goods	109,946	403,026,058	10,075,651
Fish	100,478	428,870,891	10,721,772
Timber	64,642	299,153,329	7,478,833
Silver	23,011	74,614,450	1,865,361
Tobacco	18,005	48,014,550	1,200,364
Chicken	16,081	68,448,450	1,711,211
Shop	12,320	57,974,850	1,449,371
Wheat	8,042	14,193,990	354,850
Hotel	7,666	29,568,100	739,203
Medicine	7,412	29,704,400	742,610
Sugarcane	6,994	23,536,300	588,408
Lead	3,453	15,642,800	391,070
Ice cream	906	3,671,400	91,785

Table 6: Peddling

Type of activity	No. of Loans	Amount of loans	$ conversion
Misc. items	54,184	167,967,303	4,199,183
Clothes	32,937	142,834,350	3,570,859
Stationery goods	22,831	78,408,546	1,960,214
Vegetables	18,619	68,895,407	1,722,385
Bamboo baskets	18,141	75,909,105	1,897,728
Dry fish	9,235	41,531,550	1,038,289
Second-hand clothes	8,381	29,499,665	737,492
Grocery goods	8,350	34,956,200	873,905
Sweetmeats	7,451	29,190,200	729,755
Oil	7,214	24,088,500	602,213
Pottery products	7,140	20,916,703	522,918
Peanuts	6,209	22,878,337	571,958
Bangles	5,708	23,889,094	597,227
Betel-leaf, biri cigarettes	5,051	15,590,400	389,760
Tobacco and betel-leaf	4,786	14,840,700	371,018

Table 7: Shopkeeping

Type of shop/product	No. of Loans	Amount of loans	$ conversion
Grocer's	617,726	2,752,860,593	68,821,515
Stationer's	275,705	1,087,705,232	27,192,631
Clothes shop	28,360	132,597,224	3,314,931
Sweetmeat	15,740	58,831,141	1,470,779
Tea stall	14,374	57,812,970	1,445,324
Medicine	10,927	43,317,642	1,082,941
Fruit	9,564	48,091,759	1,202,294
Betel-leaf biri	7,005	24,551,650	613,791
Iron	4,723	21,228,301	530,708
Seeds and plants	3,373	12,859,825	321,496
Mirror	2,339	9,450,000	236,250
Bicycle parts	2,159	12,370,260	309,257
Shoe	1,975	17,712,900	442,823
Magazine stall	1,443	5,955,690	148,892
Musical instruments	1,019	4,135,680	103,392

Appendix III

The Grameen Family of Companies

Name of Company	Year of Establishment
(For profit)	
Grameen Bank *(Credit for the poor)*	1983
Gonoshasthaya Grameen Textile *(Hand-loom fabric-processing plant)*	1995
Grameen Cybernet *(Internet service provider)*	1996
GrameenPhone *(National cellular telephone company)*	1996
(Not for profit)	
Grameen Trust *(Technical and financial support for replication of Grameen approach worldwide)*	1989
Grameen Agricultural Foundation *(To promote agricultural technology, improve yield, initiate diversification for export)*	1991
Grameen Uddog *(Production, marketing and export of handwoven fabrics, i.e. Grameen Check)*	1994
Grameen Fund *(A social venture fund for new entrepreneurs)*	1994

Grameen Fisheries Foundation   1994
*(To bring idle ponds into high-yielding
pisiculture)*

Grameen Telecom   1995
(Providing cellular phone and telecom services in rural areas)

Grameen Shamogree   1996
(Marketing of Grameen products)

Grameen Shakti   1996
*(For research and marketing of solar
and wind energy on a commercial basis)*

Grameen Kalyan   1996
*(Welfare programmes for Grameen
members and staff)*

Grameen Shikkha   1997
(Educational programmes)

Grameen Communications   1997
(Nationwide network for Internet, data-processing services)

Grameen Knitwear Ltd   1997
(Export-oriented knitwear factory)

Grameen Securities Management Ltd   1998
(A merchant banking, fund and portfolio management company)

How to contact the Grameen Bank

GRAMEEN BANK
Mirpur, Section Two
Dhaka 1216
Bangladesh

Telephone: + 880 2 9005257-68
E-mail: grameen.bank@grameen.net
Websites: http://www.grameen.com
http://www.grameen.org

Index